LESSONS FROM
THE TRIAL

LESSONS

from the

TRIAL

THE PEOPLE V. O.J. SIMPSON

GERALD F. UELMEN

ANDREWS AND McMEEL
A UNIVERSAL PRESS SYNDICATE COMPANY
KANSAS CITY

Library of Congress Cataloging-in-Publication Data

Uelmen, Gerald F.
    Lessons from the trial : the people v. O.J. Simpson / by Gerald F. Uelmen.
        p.   cm.
    ISBN 0-8362-1662-8
    1. Simpson, O.J., 1947–   —Trials, litigation, etc. 2. Trials (Murder)—
California—Los Angeles. 3. Defense (Criminal procedure) 4. Prosecution.
5. Trial practice. I. Title.
KF224.S485U34   1996
345.73'02523'0979494—dc20
[347.30525230979494]   96-926
                                                                          CIP

Attention: Schools and Businesses
Andrews and McMeel books are available at quantity discounts with bulk purchase for educational, business, or sales promotional use. For information, please write to Special Sales Department, Andrews and McMeel, 4900 Main Street, Kansas City, Missouri 64112.

To my parents, Trudy and Francis Uelmen,
Who taught me that the pursuit of justice
is just another command that we love one another.

CONTENTS

ACKNOWLEDGMENTS

Perhaps the case of *People v. O.J. Simpson* is best understood as a cultural phenomenon, rather than a lesson plan. As a law professor spending my sabbatical right in the middle of it all, however, I kept looking for lessons. After spending my entire academic career studying the strengths and weaknesses of our criminal justice system, I could not resist the opportunity to record what was done by the lawyers, explain why it was done, and question what might have been done better. Hopefully, it will contribute to some rational discussion of the trial and its aftermath, to replace the celebrity hype which has grown so tiresome. My role in the trial was that of an advocate, and I have made no effort to set aside the mantle of advocacy in these lessons. But I have made an effort to stick with the aspects of the trial I know best, and offer some thoughtful reflections on the "trial of the century" that I experienced.

I am grateful to my wife Martha, who not only put up with a year and a half of disrupted plans, but encouraged and read these reflections. My daughter Amy and my son Matt also read the manuscript. They all challenged me to enhanced clarity and, with the exception of Matt, greater charity. Matt cheered on my sardonic side. Amy had the unique perspective of never having seen any of the case on television. She was sequestered in a tiny Swiss village throughout the trial! My research assistant Daisy Altamore, a

1996 Santa Clara University law graduate, compiled the "endnotes" for those seeking sources for the cases and quotations I employ. She should be thanked for the absence of footnotes.* I also thank Barry Scheck and Peter Neufeld for their comments. Their friendship is the greatest personal dividend I derived from the trial. Finally, I thank my literary agent, Jean Naggar, for putting it all together on a very tight schedule.

*This is the only footnote in the entire book.

LESSONS FROM
THE TRIAL

LOOKING FOR

LESSONS

*A*fter overdosing on a sixteen-month binge of hype, bombast, and titillation, Americans are looking for lessons from the trial of *People v. O.J. Simpson.* And there is no shortage of prophets and pundits to tell us what we should have learned, and how we should "fix" the system. The proposals include abandoning the requirement of unanimity in criminal jury trials, lowering the standard of proof beyond a reasonable doubt, repealing the privilege against self-incrimination, eliminating the Fourth Amendment exclusionary rule, forbidding television cameras in court, imposing "gag orders" on lawyers, permitting hearsay evidence and evidence of "bad character" to be freely admitted, and abolishing peremptory challenges.

As H.L. Mencken once said, for every complex social problem there's a simple solution that is quick, easy . . . and wrong. The most serious problem our system of criminal justice faces today is not the lack of quick solutions, but the abundance of them. Never have so many offered so much so fast, with so little thought.

As one of the lawyers whose advocacy inspired the proposed immolation of our Bill of Rights, some may say I lack standing to object, or even to offer my own proposed lesson plan. But I have a great deal of confidence in the willingness of the American people to carefully assess the arguments and measure the consequences before they embark on a program of radical change. That confidence comes from an appreciation of history. When we recognize that we've ventured down this road before, the twists and turns seem less surprising. The best cure for hype is history. Reminding ourselves of where the procedural protections of our Bill of Rights came from, what values they preserve, and what sacrifices have been made to maintain them will diminish the shrill voices calling for their immediate repeal.

I will offer no apologies for the vigor of the advocacy with which O.J. Simpson was defended. Even if the conduct of his lawyers fuels the ultimate destruction of some of the constitutional protections we cherish most, there is very little we would do differently if we had it to do over again. Our purpose was not to foster greater public confidence in the "system." Our purpose was not to endear the legal profession to the American people. Our purpose was not to advance the cause of race relations. Our purpose was to employ every advantage the law permits to enhance the prospects of our client's acquittal. Our purpose was to utilize every device and strategem the law allows to weaken and discredit the prosecution's case. The vindication of our client was the beginning, the end, and the substance of our every effort. Anything less would have been a violation of our ethical responsibility to faithfully perform the duties of an attorney-at-law.

Our adversary system of justice demands that the advocates place the interests of their client above their own personal interests, or even the interests of their country. Shortly after Johnnie Cochran's closing argument to the jury, nationally syndicated columnist George Will wrote that Cochran was a "good lawyer but a bad citizen." He recognized that Cochran's arguments about the racism of Detective Mark Fuhrman would be persuasive with a jury, but he believed they would be disruptive to the racial tranquillity of the nation. He did not, however, appreciate that the duty of an advocate compelled Cochran to make the argument he did. It called to mind the position of another famous advocate, defending the Queen of England before the British Parliament. It was certainly the British "trial of the century" for 1820. King George IV had just succeeded to the throne, and he sought a bill of divorce from his wife on the grounds of her adultery. Her lawyer, Henry Lord Brougham, was criticized for threatening to defend his client by proving not only that the King himself had engaged in adultery, but had secretly married a Catholic. That was grounds to forfeit his crown. The law at that time permitted a "right of recrimination" as a defense to a divorce action. By invoking that right for his client, however, Lord Brougham threatened to bring an ignominious end to the reign of King George IV before it even began. The words with which Lord Brougham defended his advocacy are well known to the generations of lawyers who followed him:

> An advocate, in the discharge of his duty, knows but one person in all the world, and that person is his client. To save that client by all means and expedients, and at all hazards and costs to other persons, and among them, to himself, is his first and only duty. In performing this duty he must not regard the alarm, the torments, the destruction which he may bring upon others. Separating the duty of a patriot from that of an advocate, he must go on reckless of consequences, though it should be his unhappy fate to involve his country in confusion.

It seems fair to say that the successful defense of O.J. Simpson has, indeed, "involved our country in confusion." It has been credited with setting back race relations, lowering public esteem for the legal profession, diminishing respect for the police, and destroying faith that justice is equally available to all our citizens. If good race relations can be founded upon hypocrisy, if public esteem for the legal profession can be based upon the complaisance of lawyers, if respect for the police can best be accomplished by a code of silence, and if faith that justice is blind depends upon ignorance, then the credit is deserved. I believe that the parade of reformers who advocate radical changes in our system of criminal justice because they are unhappy with the verdict in *People v. O.J. Simpson* are the real sowers of public confusion.

This is not to say there are no lessons to be learned from the Simpson trial. The thesis of this book is that lessons abound. But they are not lessons about the failure of our system. They are lessons about human frailty and arrogance. They are lessons about basic human decency. They are lessons about motivation and struggle, competition and civility. They are lessons about how bizarre and distorted things appear when they are magnified and exaggerated. They are lessons about how things which appear black and white are frequently gray.

By my count, we have had thirty-two trials in the twentieth century that have been labeled a "trial of the century." We average one every three years. A "trial of the century" rarely provides a good jumping-off point for major changes or reforms in the legal system. Those who stand on the cliff and urge us to leap should be regarded with caution and skepticism. We have heard them before. In California, they are the same voices that led our system of criminal justice to the verge of bankruptcy: *intellectual bankruptcy,* by disguising the complexity of criminal justice behind simplistic labels that actually impede us in our quest for justice; *fiscal bankruptcy,* by diverting resources which are badly needed for education and social programs into a bottomless pit of prison expansion; and *moral bankruptcy,* by creating a political climate where real reform is impossible, because political leaders are obsessed with the fear that any rational consideration of alternatives will result in their being labeled "soft on crime." When have you ever heard a politician seek your vote by saying he or she is "thoughtful" about crime? "Thoughtful" is perceived as a synomym for "soft." Politicians get elected by labeling themselves as "tough."

The trial of the case of *People v. O.J. Simpson* demonstrated very little about how the criminal justice system actually operates, day in and day out. In California, 97 percent of criminal cases are disposed of without a trial ever taking place. The defendant who has the resources to hire one lawyer to defend him, much less a team of twelve, is a rarity. Despite all the procedural protections of which O.J. Simpson was able to take advantage, the system remains weighted heavily in favor of the prosecution. Nationally, fewer than

10 percent of criminal accused even invoke their right to a trial, and the prosecution prevails in 83 percent of those trials. The "mistakes" the system makes are just as likely to result in conviction of the innocent as acquittal of the guilty.

Cases are occasionally reported in which a defendant who was completely innocent has been jailed for many years, because of a mistaken identification, police perjury, or simple incompetence of his lawyer. One such case was brought to public attention within thirty days after the verdict of the jury was announced in *People v. O.J. Simpson.* Rolando Cruz of Illinois was released after eleven years on death row, after a new DNA test excluded him and matched another man who had admitted he committed the murder and rape of a ten-year-old Chicago girl. What was remarkable about the case was that the man who had admitted the crime had confessed to authorities eight years before. Police, who had fabricated evidence that Rolando Cruz described a "dream" to them which matched details of the killing, had spent eight years attempting to discredit the confession of the actual culprit, and covering up their own perjury. Rolando Cruz is not a celebrity, and the dismissal of charges against him did not make national newscasts. Even cases such as this do not suggest the system failed, and it would be foolish to advocate wholesale changes in the system to avoid them. Why is the same degree of foolishness not recognized when it shrouds an attack on a verdict of acquittal with which one disagrees? Obviously, the system does not work when those who operate it are corrupt.

The phenomenon of loud calls for dramatic "reform" of the criminal justice system in the wake of an unpopular verdict is nothing new in America. It recurs with predictable regularity, and just as predictably, the calls are put in proper perspective after public passion subsides. More than a century ago, in Cincinnati, Ohio, in 1884, a jury found that a stable boy accused of strangling his boss was guilty of manslaughter rather than murder. The newspapers editorialized that the verdict was a signal to "the criminal class" that if they could afford to hire a clever lawyer and get a jury of their "peers," they could escape the snares of justice.

A mass public meeting at the music hall was addressed by the county judge, who called for the jurors who rendered the verdict to be expelled from the city, along with the lawyer who represented the defendant. The crowd adjourned to the city jail, where an attempt to lynch the defendant was turned back. The crowd then vented its wrath on the county courthouse, burning it to the ground. Subsequent rioting left 45 dead and 125 wounded. A grand jury inquiry laid the blame for the riot not on inflammatory newspapers or irresponsible judges, but on the jury that rendered the unpopular verdict, and the wiles of criminal defense lawyers.

A witch-hunt followed, in which an eager young prosecutor sought the disbarment of the criminal defense attorney, and led a committee to urge the state legislature to reduce the number of peremptory challenges available to defense lawyers in selecting juries. Neither effort was successful, but twenty years later, that former prosecutor was still riding the crest of political prominence that would ultimately propel him to election as President of the United States and appointment as Chief Justice of the United States. His name was William Howard Taft. A law school commencement address he delivered on June 26, 1905, was recently republished by Yale Kamisar, a distinguished law professor at the University of Michigan. Professor Kamisar noted that it sounded remarkably like the political rhetoric inspired by the Simpson verdict:

> The counsel for the defense, relying on the diminished power of the court, creates, by dramatic art and by harping on the importance of unimportant details, a false atmosphere in the courtroom which the judge is powerless to dispel, and under the influence of which the counsel is able to lead the jurors to vote as jurors for a verdict which, after all the excitement of the trial has passed away, they are unable to support as men and women.
>
> [D]iscrepancy between the two sides of the case allows defense counsel to eliminate from all panels every person of force and character and standing in the community, and to assemble a collection in the jury box of nondescripts of

no character, weak and amenable to every breeze of emotion, however maudlin or irrelevant to the issue.

Then, as now, bashing criminal defense lawyers and trashing juries formed a solid foundation for a successful political career. Then, as now, unpopular verdicts led to loud invitations to burn up the Constitution, and occasionally the courthouse along with it. Then, as now, there was widespread perception of a "crisis" of criminal violence that demanded immediate attention. In Taft's time, the American people saw the value of retaining traditional safeguards. They put their faith in the common sense of juries rather than in the political rhetoric of office seekers.

One thing *is* different now, though. At the time William Howard Taft spoke in 1905, it was rare for a black person to sit on an American jury. In some states, it was rare even for a black defendant accused of murder to *have* a jury trial. There were approximately 100 lynchings of blacks in America every year. William Howard Taft never regarded that as a "crisis" of American justice. How ironic it would be if the clamor and alarm that inevitably follow an unpopular verdict in a "trial of the century," after being regularly and resoundingly ignored for 200 years of "trials of the century," finally struck a responsive chord, and led to the repeal of fundamental procedural protections that Americans have cherished since 1791. How ironic it would be if the clamor and alarm were taken seriously for the first time in American history, because the beneficiary of the unpopular verdict was a black man, and the jury which rendered the verdict included seven black women and one black man.

As the last juror filed out of the courtroom after delivering the verdict in the case of *People v. OJ Simpson*, he raised his fist in a salute. He was the only black man on the jury. It was not a gesture of defiance. He was not sticking his fist in the face of white America. He was celebrating a reality as old and as venerable as the jury itself. That reality is that no man's liberty will be taken by the state unless his guilt is proven beyond a reasonable doubt. The system worked. It hasn't always worked for black men in America. Today, at long last, reasonable doubts come in all colors.

The first lesson from the trial of *People v. O.J. Simpson* should be that "trials of the century" offer few lessons of value in undertaking major reforms of the criminal justice system. Those who seek to capitalize upon public dissatisfaction with the verdict to achieve an agenda of constitutional revision should be regarded with skepticism. But that does not mean there is nothing to learn from this ordeal. We must look beyond the hype for more elusive lessons. Rather than lessons that will change the "system," they may be lessons that change us. We may learn that our assumptions defining success or failure for the system are misguided. We may realize that we, too, wear tinted lenses, and our preconceived attitudes have much to do with our own verdict.

THE DISAPPEARING
KNIFE

I received a call from Bob Shapiro to join the defense of O.J. Simpson on June 16, 1994, three days after the bodies of Nicole Brown
Simpson and Ronald Goldman were found, and a day before the infamous slow-speed Bronco chase. Bob's timing couldn't have been
better. I was in the process of packing up to move out of the dean's
office at Santa Clara University School of Law, where I had spent
eight years juggling administrative duties with teaching and writing about my academic specialty, criminal law. Although Santa Clara
is four hundred miles north of Los Angeles, the prospect of spending a lot of time in L.A. was not unpleasant. I lived and worked in
L.A. most of my life before the move to Santa Clara. My parents
still live in the home our family moved into in 1954, when I at-
tended Mount Carmel High School in South Central Los Angeles.

With a few exceptions, the busy life of a law school dean left
little time to get involved in the trial of actual cases, and I missed
the excitement of being in court. I was looking forward to a one-
year sabbatical leave, to do some research and teaching at Stanford
Law School and resume a part-time practice consulting with other
lawyers in criminal cases. Those plans could easily be placed on
"hold."

One of the few cases on which I had been able to work during
my deanship was the defense of Christian Brando in 1991. Shapiro

called me into that case because Proposition 115, a new criminal justice initiative, had just been enacted in California. I had been doing a lot of speaking and writing about how it might be challenged. Our collaboration in the Brando case was a happy experience for both of us. I found Bob easy to work with, a sincere and honest lawyer with excellent courtroom instincts. His detractors label him a "wheeler-dealer," better at plea bargaining than cross-examination, but that label doesn't fit the reality. A lawyer does not achieve successful plea bargains by peddling snake oil to hard-nosed prosecutors. One earns them by convincing prosecutors that there are weaknesses in their case, and they are not likely to do any better than the proposed plea if the case goes to trial. That strategy worked well in the Brando case. Prosecutors started with what looked like a strong case of premeditated first-degree murder, motivated by revenge. After his pregnant sister told him her boyfriend had physically abused her, Christian stopped and picked up a gun before returning with her to the Marlon Brando home, where the shooting took place. But careful analysis of the crime scene provided persuasive corroboration of Christian's description of a struggle over the gun that led to an accidental discharge. To provide that analysis, Bob brought in the most impressive forensic experts I had ever met: Dr. Henry Lee and Dr. Michael Baden. I succeeded with a long shot motion which resulted in suppression of the statement Christian made to the police immediately after his arrest, because proper *Miranda* warnings were never given. Ultimately, the case was resolved with a manslaughter plea, and Christian was released from prison in January 1996, after serving one-half of a ten-year prison sentence.

Immediately after he was retained to defend O.J. Simpson, Bob Shapiro began assembling the same team that worked the Brando case. Dr. Lee and Dr. Baden were already on board when I told Bob I was available. One of the first things I did upon my arrival in Los Angeles was to accompany them on visits to the Bundy crime scene and Simpson's Rockingham home. At O.J. Simpson's Rockingham home on June 29, 1994, I found myself facing an ethical dilemma I had frequently presented to my students in the classroom, without ever telling them the answer. That was because I wasn't really sure of the answer.

The newspapers and television newscasts were filled with the latest development in a fast-breaking case: the discovery that just two weeks before the murders, O.J. Simpson had purchased a knife at the Ross Cutlery Store in downtown Los Angeles. The store proprietor and a salesman both remembered that Simpson had wandered into their store during a break in the filming of a television series. He asked to look at some knives on display, and purchased a large folding stiletto. The witnesses, who sold their story to the *National Enquirer* for $12,500, provided a duplicate of the knife to police detectives. Police were so convinced it was the murder weapon, they asked the coroner to match the blade with the wounds inflicted on the victims, and he eagerly complied. Police had scoured the Simpson home the day before I got there, executing a search warrant to look for it.

We questioned Simpson about the knife, and he readily confirmed that, indeed, he had purchased such a knife. He said he brought it home and tucked it away, and hadn't thought about it since. I was asked to check and see if it was still there.

When I entered the plush, second-floor master bedroom at the Rockingham mansion, I went immediately to the built-in dressing table. There were large, beveled mirrors on each side above the table, and a cursory inspection disclosed that the mirrors were hinged. I pulled the right one open, and there it was, on a wooden shelf behind the mirror. It was still in the open box in which it came, and looked brand new. Without touching it, I could see that it closely resembled the pictures of the knife I had seen on television newscasts.

I remembered the classroom exercise I had done several times when teaching legal ethics. We were exploring the issue of when defense lawyers have an obligation to turn over evidence that might assist the prosecution in building a case against their client. I walked into the classroom carrying a paper bag, and posed the following hypothetical. "Suppose a client walks into your office, and announces that he just shot his business partner. You quickly confirm that, indeed, a shooting has just taken place across the street, and the coroner is removing the body as you speak. Your client then reaches into his pocket, removes a revolver, and places it on your desk, asking, 'What should I do with this?'" To illustrate the dilemma, I would remove a toy pistol from the bag and plop it in front of a wide-eyed student in the front row.

Students invariably blurt out one of three answers. The easiest solution is to say to the client, "I'm sorry I can't represent you. Take your gun and go." That answer opens the discussion as to when a lawyer can ethically decline to represent a client. What the client said is still protected by the lawyer-client privilege, even if the lawyer declines representation. The dilemma is simply passed on to another lawyer to resolve. Professor Monroe Freedman of Hofstra University Law School tells an amusing variant of this alternative. A lawyer answers his telephone and hears a voice say, "Is this Harry Levine?" "Yes." "Mr. Levine, this is Herman Brown. I just shot my mother-in-law, and I'm standing here with the gun. What should I do with it?" The lawyer pauses, then responds, "Oh, you must want Harry Levine the lawyer. You've got the wrong number."

The students who offer the hypothetical client advice about what to do with the gun inevitably get themselves in trouble. A lawyer cannot be a party to concealing or destroying evidence. Some students fall into the ethical trap of trying to let the client know how harmful the gun might be as evidence against him, without directly telling him to get rid of it. I ask them to consider the words of advice they just rendered as evidence in a trial for obstruction of justice, and consider themselves the defendant.

The best students realize that a lawyer facing this dilemma is torn between the need to analyze the weapon to determine if it truly is incriminating evidence, and the risk that if it does turn out to be incriminating evidence, he may have to turn it over to the prosecution and strengthen the case against his own client. Thus, before making a decision, it's important to get as much information as you can about the crime and the potential evidentiary significance of the weapon. You should not assume it is incriminating, nor should you assume it is exculpatory. Like so many other decisions lawyers make, there are risks to either course, and the lawyer's job is to systematically assess the risks based on as much information as can be gathered.

As I stared at the knife behind the mirror, I realized I could simply close the mirror and walk away. If I did not disturb or alter the evidence, we would have no obligation to ever disclose it to the prosecution. But if Mr. Simpson was telling the truth, the knife would be valuable exculpatory evidence. We could refute the prosecution's theorizing about the murder weapon by producing the knife in court and demonstrating its pristine condition. If we wanted to preserve its value as exculpatory evidence, though, the worst thing I could do was take possession of it. I would then become the witness who was necessary to establish where it came from and how it was preserved. Ethically, a lawyer can't be a witness and an advocate in the same case. We needed a credible independent person to take possession and get the knife examined by an expert. And we needed to accomplish this without the prosecution finding out about it.

I closed the mirror and left the house. When I got back to Bob Shapiro's office, we did some quick research and discussed the alternatives. The plan we came up with was to go to the presiding judge of the criminal division of the superior court, and ask him to appoint a neutral person as a "Special Master" to go to Mr. Simpson's home, retrieve the knife, and return it to court in a sealed envelope. It could then be released to a defense expert for analysis. If it turned out to be incriminating, we would have to turn it over to the prosecution. If it was exculpatory, we would preserve it in its sealed condition as defense evidence for the trial.

The presiding judge of the criminal division of the superior court was Judge Lance Ito. We had previously appeared before him in challenging the grand jury. The case at this point was still in the municipal court for a preliminary hearing, long before Judge Ito was assigned to preside over the trial. On the very morning the preliminary hearing was scheduled to begin, we went to Judge Ito and asked him to clear his courtroom to hear our unusual request. Normally judges insist on both sides being represented whenever a case is discussed, but we explained that this was a matter involving the protection of privileged information. After hearing our dilemma, Judge Ito immediately agreed to the appointment of a Special Master. A highly respected superior court judge who had recently retired, Delbert Wong, was secretly appointed. Judge Wong went to the Rockingham residence and brought back the knife in a sealed envelope. It was placed in a court safe. We proceeded with the preliminary hearing, confident that the confidentiality of our secret would be preserved by the court until the forensic analysis could be performed by our expert.

In the midst of the preliminary hearing, when Judge Kathleen Kennedy Powell interrupted the proceedings to hold up the sealed envelope and suggest opening it, the most surprised people in the courtroom were Bob Shapiro and myself. Our jaws dropped. I was outraged that the confidentiality of our request had been breached by the court, setting off waves of public speculation and tipping off the prosecution to our strategy. It turned out that Judge Ito had left on a vacation, and his written order appointing the Special Master had crossed the desk of Judge Cecil Mills, the chief presiding judge. Without ascertaining any of the circumstances that required the court to maintain the confidentiality of the contents of the sealed envelope, Judge Mills delivered it to Judge Kennedy Powell with the suggestion she publicly open it! Judge Kennedy Powell was persuaded to return the envelope to the superior court unopened. We did not want to unveil our surprise at the preliminary hearing, especially before forensic tests had been completed.

After the case was assigned to Judge Ito for trial, he arranged for the Special Master to take the knife to a laboratory where Dr. Henry Lee examined it. Dr. Lee found no marks or scratches, and no traces of blood. The knife was in brand-new, pristine condition. The only fingerprints on it were those of the Special Master, Judge Wong. At that point, we thought we had blockbuster evidence of our client's innocence that we could use to blow the prosecution out of the water at trial. So we thought.

When Dr. Lee's report of his examination of the knife was returned to the court, Judge Ito immediately raised the question whether California's new reciprocal discovery law required that the knife be turned over to the prosecution even though it was not incriminating evidence. He asked the defense to submit a brief on the matter. The reach of the reciprocal discovery law was an issue that kept recurring throughout the trial. While the law was poorly drafted and ambiguous in many of its particulars, we felt confident the law was on our side with regard to the knife.

California's reciprocal discovery law was part of Proposition 115, the far-ranging initiative measure enacted in 1990. Prior to its enactment, the defense was not required to turn over any of the evidence it intended to present in advance of trial. The California courts were very protective of the defendant's privilege not to incriminate himself and reasoned that the prosecution's burden of proving guilt without the assistance of the defendant could be undercut by giving the prosecution access to the defendant's evidence before it had proven its case. The initiative measure amended California's constitution, however, so California defendants would have no greater protection of their rights than was afforded under the U.S. Constitution as interpreted by the U.S. Supreme Court. The U.S. Supreme Court had upheld reciprocal discovery in a 1970 Florida case, in which a defendant was precluded from raising an alibi defense unless he gave the prosecution advance notice of the witnesses he intended to call at trial.

Our brief to Judge Ito relied on the distinction between ordinary evidence and rebuttal evidence. The reciprocal discovery law made it clear that, while all of the witnesses one intends to call at trial must be disclosed in advance, other evidence that may only become relevant to rebut or refute evidence presented by the other side need not be disclosed. The California Supreme Court, in the first decision applying the new reciprocal discovery law, had directly addressed the issue. They declared:

> Reciprocity requires a fair trade, defense witnesses for prosecution witnesses, and nothing more. We glean nothing from the Supreme Court's interpretations of the due process clause to lead us to conclude that reciprocity requires the prosecutor to disclose other evidence gathered in response to a

compelled defense disclosure that may be used to refute the defendant's case, when the defense is not required to do the same following discovery of the prosecution's witnesses.

It seemed clear to us that the evidentiary significance of the knife would depend upon the tactical choices yet to be made by the prosecution. If the prosecutors decided to call the Ross Cutlery witnesses and contend that the knife they sold to Mr. Simpson was the murder weapon, we could *rebut* or *refute* those witnesses with the pristine condition of the actual knife. If they didn't, the knife would be irrelevant. But they weren't entitled to know what evidence we were saving for rebuttal in advance, just as we were not entitled to see their rebuttal evidence in advance.

Judge Ito's ruling surprised us. He turned over Dr. Lee's report on the examination of the knife to the prosecution. Once the prosecutors knew that we had the evidence to destroy their claim that the Ross Cutlery knife was the murder weapon, they never presented that claim at the trial. Judge Ito's ruling certainly shortened the duration of the trial, which was one of the purposes of the reciprocal discovery law. But that law did not create authority in judges to compel disclosure of any evidence that might shorten the trial. It created authority only to compel the same discovery from the defense that the prosecution is required to disclose. Later in the trial, Judge Ito followed the letter of the law in preventing discovery by the defense of any of the rebuttal evidence to be offered by the prosecution. The prosecution was not required to give advance notice of any of the evidence it presented in the rebuttal phase of its case.

At the outset of the trial, Jeffrey Toobin published an interesting analysis of Judge Ito in the *New Yorker* magazine. He described him as among a "new breed" of judges who regard a trial as a search for justice and interpret the rules first and foremost in a way that will achieve a just result. That analysis made me very nervous. It wasn't the prospect of a just result that frightened me. It was the idea that a judge would make a determination of what a "just" result was going to be before the case had even been heard, and shape his evidentiary rulings accordingly. My model of the ideal judge is one who is even-handed, applies the rules in the same way to both sides, and keeps an open mind until the case is concluded.

The ruling that required disclosure of the knife to the prosecution rendered the knife irrelevant for the remainder of the trial. Although we argued that the knife was a prime example of the "rush to judgment" that pervaded the entire prosecution case, Judge Ito would not allow the sealed envelope to be opened at any point in the trial. One of the principle reasons the prosecution did not call the coroner who performed the autopsies as a witness at the trial was to avoid the embarrassment of cross-examination about his opinion that the wounds could have been inflicted by the knife that had remained behind Mr. Simpson's bedroom mirror until it was brought to court in a sealed envelope. It was also another example of the ineptitude of the investigation conducted by the L.A.P.D. Officers had spent hours searching every nook and cranny of Mr. Simpson's home, but never noticed the hinges on the mirror that announced the presence of something behind them.

The lesson of the disappearing knife was a sobering one. The case that was presented at the preliminary hearing would not be the case that would be presented at the trial. The prosecution was still in the process of creating its case. There was a significant risk that California's reciprocal discovery law would be twisted to give the prosecution advantages the law never intended, to permit the prosecutors to strengthen their case based on evidence they obtained from the defense. The caution and reluctance of the defense to comply with the prosecution's expansive interpretation of the reciprocal discovery law led to real wrangling throughout the trial, and even to the imposition of fines and sanctions. The real reason for the defense concerns, however, was never revealed. The sealed envelope was never opened.

THREE

THE GRAND JURY

*J*ust the words "grand jury investigation" conjure up visions of a cadre of super-sleuths in black robes poring over documents and interrogating witnesses deep in the basement of a courthouse. My four years of experience directing federal grand jury investigations as a federal prosecutor in the late sixties cured me of any such illusions. Plain and simple, a grand jury investigation is a prosecutor's playpen. It permits the prosecutor to use subpoenas to summon witnesses and interrogate them at his leisure with no one looking over his shoulder. There is no judge in the grand jury room, and no lawyers except the prosecutors. No cross-examination of the witnesses is conducted, and no evidence is presented on behalf of the defense. In California, the witnesses are not even permitted to bring their lawyers with them into the grand jury room.

Normally, the prosecutors form a cozy and warm relationship with the grand jurors. A grand jury that resists the prosecutor's advice is called a "runaway" grand jury, because the normal expectation is that the prosecutor is holding the grand jurors on a tight leash. Thus, we did not greet with jubilation the news that the case of *People v. O.J. Simpson* was being presented to the Los Angeles County Grand Jury. We looked for a way to reroute the case through a preliminary hearing, where we would have the opportunity to cross-examine the witnesses and size up the strengths and weaknesses of the prosecution's case. Ironically, the way was handed to us by a blatant public relations campaign launched by the police and prosecutors.

California prosecutors get to choose between two routes to the trial of felony charges. Either way, filing charges requires only a showing of "probable cause," an easily met threshold. Prosecutors can present their evidence of probable cause to a grand jury and ask for an "indictment," or they can file a complaint in the municipal court and make their showing of probable cause at a preliminary hearing, in which case the pleading filed to bring the case to trial is called an "Information."

The choice of the route to trial has enormous consequences for the defendant. If the grand jury is utilized, the proceedings are conducted in complete secrecy. The defendant does not even see a transcript of the testimony presented against him until ten days after an indictment has been returned. If a preliminary hearing is utilized, the accused is present with his lawyer, may cross-examine the witnesses, and may present his own witnesses if he chooses. Defendants rarely put on their witnesses at the preliminary hearing, though, preferring to save them for the trial without giving the prosecutors an opportunity to probe their credibility in advance of their appearance before the jury.

The difference this prosecutorial choice makes to the defendant led the California Supreme Court to declare in 1978 that even a defendant who is indicted by a grand jury has a right to a preliminary hearing. The tremendous advantage the preliminary hearing offers for discovery of the strengths and weaknesses of the prosecution's case, the court said, should not be denied because of the prosecutor's tactical choice of the grand jury route. Letting the prosecutor create two classes of defendants, one given the procedural advantages of a preliminary hearing, the other denied those advantages, was a violation of the guarantee of equal protection of the law under the California constitution.

After this landmark decision, the use of grand juries to bring criminal charges all but disappeared in California. Since prosecutors had to subject their evidence to a preliminary hearing anyway, it made little sense to seek an indictment first. In the year before the California Supreme Court decision, California grand juries returned 689 indictments. In 1989, only 20 grand jury indictments were returned.

The 1990 criminal justice initiative measure known as Proposition 115 dramatically changed this situation. The measure not only changed reciprocal discovery rules, as already described, but also overruled the 1978 Supreme Court decision which gave all felony defendants a right to a preliminary hearing. It amended the California constitution to declare, "If a felony is prosecuted by indictment, there shall be no postindictment preliminary hearing."

The Los Angeles County Grand Jury began hearing witnesses in the Simpson case on Monday, June 20, 1994, the same day that O.J. Simpson was arraigned in municipal court. At the arraignment, the date for a preliminary hearing was routinely set for the last day within the ten-day deadline, June 30, 1994. I remember that date well, because June 30 was officially my last day as dean of the law school at Santa Clara University. My secretary, Carole Vendrick, knowing how I was looking forward to emancipation, had written on my appointment calendar for that day, "free at last!" If a grand jury indictment intervened before June 30, the scheduled preliminary hearing would be canceled, and we would proceed directly to trial.

The District Attorney hoped to conclude the grand jury investigation with an indictment for murder by week's end. Witnesses were scheduled throughout the week, and the hearing led off with testimony of the coroner and lots of grisly photographs of the bloody crime scene and the autopsies of the victims. One grand juror later described being unable to eat dinner that night, because he lost his appetite after viewing the "bloody mess."

District Attorney Gilbert Garcetti himself was not presenting the case to the grand jury, however. He was much too busy conducting a media blitz to turn public opinion against O.J. Simpson. The public sympathy for Simpson expressed during the Bronco chase led the D.A. to undertake an unprecedented public relations campaign. He explained: "public perception is important in high-profile cases," and, "like defense lawyers," he must use the media to shape popular opinion. Appearing on ABC's *Nightline*, the CBS *Evening News*, the NBC *Nightly News*, and in newspaper interviews, he expressed confidence in Mr. Simpson's guilt and made rash predictions that Simpson would acknowledge his guilt and plead "mitigating circumstances." The case was described as a "classic" example of domestic violence, and details of Simpson's 1989 prosecution for spousal battery were revealed. Garcetti roundly criticized the municipal court judge who placed Simpson on probation in the 1989 incident, provoking an unusual response. The judge produced the transcript of the 1989 hearing, demonstrating that he imposed the precise sentence the prosecutors requested in the case, and he called the District Attorney a liar. In California, where judges are elected, public criticism of a judge by a prosecutor may cost a judge his job. That may explain why so many judges appear to favor the prosecution in their rulings.

On Wednesday, June 22, two days after Simpson's arraignment, the airwaves were filled with explosive excerpts from 911 emergency telephone calls made to police by Nicole Brown Simpson in both the 1989 incident and an October 1993 incident in which Simpson broke down a door. Every television news broadcast in America led off with audio recordings of the calls, with a rolling transcript and photos and video clips of Nicole Brown Simpson. Her sobbing voice was heard saying, "he's back," "I think you know his record," and "he's crazy." The 911 tapes had the desired effect. Before they were aired, public opinion polls were reporting that more than 60 percent of the American population thought Simpson was probably innocent. After the 911 tapes, the polls showed that 60 percent thought he was probably guilty. The only problem, of course, was that the admissibility of the tapes as evidence was yet to be determined, and the only potential jurors who hadn't heard the tapes at least a half dozen times were those who lived in caves or trees.

The Los Angeles Police Department defended the release of the tapes, contending that they were released in response to a media request under the California Public Records Act, and that they had cleared the release in advance with both the L.A. County District

Attorney's office and the Los Angeles City Attorney's office. This set off a round of public finger-pointing, with both the City Attorney and the District Attorney blaming the L.A.P.D. The D.A. claimed he had no advance warning that the tapes would be released, and the City Attorney claimed his authorization was based on the assumption the D.A. had cleared it because prosecutors were not going to use the tapes in their case. L.A.P.D. sources called both of them liars, insisting police were opposed to the release, and went to the D.A. to seek backup for refusing release of the tapes. The Deputy District Attorney who handled the request was reassigned the next day and played no further role in the prosecution.

We realized that simply protesting the release of the tapes and seeking sanctions against those who released them would achieve little for the defense. The damage had been done. Without ever taking the case to court, the police and the prosecution had managed to completely reverse the high level of public willingness to reserve judgment until the evidence was presented in court. So much for the presumption of innocence.

In looking for a way to salvage some advantage from this disaster, we realized that if everyone in America had heard the 911 tapes, that "everyone" must have included some of those who were, at that very moment, sitting on the grand jury hearing the case against Mr. Simpson. The next morning, we filed an "Emergency Motion for Voir Dire of Grand Jurors and Determination of Prejudice from Improper Pretrial Publicity." The motion, which was immediately set for hearing before Judge Lance Ito on Friday morning, June 24, sought to have each member of the grand jury individually questioned to ascertain the nature and extent of their exposure to improperly released inadmissible evidence. If they had been prejudiced by such exposure, the motion sought to dismiss them from further proceedings in the case.

The chief authority I cited for this motion induced a true sense of *déjà vu*. It was the 1966 decision of *Sheppard v. Maxwell*, the landmark case which F. Lee Bailey had argued to the U.S. Supreme Court thirty years before. The trial of Dr. Samuel Sheppard for the murder of his wife had been preceded by widespread dissemination of clearly inadmissible evidence, including his refusal to take a lie detector test, and the claim there were "bombshell witnesses" who would describe his "Jekyll-Hyde" personality and fiery temper. In setting aside his conviction, the Supreme Court criticized the trial court's failure to "take strong measures" to protect the defendant's right to receive a fair trial by an impartial jury free from outside influences. At a retrial, Dr. Sheppard was acquitted.

It was not too much of a stretch to argue that the court's duty to "take strong measures" to protect the right to a fair trial also applied to protect the right to a fair grand jury hearing. Judge Ito agreed that it was appropriate to at least question the grand jurors in order to ascertain whether they had heard the 911 tapes, and recessed the hearing until after lunch.

When we returned to court Friday afternoon, we were surprised that it was not Judge Ito who assumed the bench, but Judge Cecil Mills, the chief presiding judge of the superior court. He had an amazing announcement.

Without directly referring to our motion, Judge Mills read a prepared statement announcing he had conducted a "personal inquiry" and found that grand jurors had been exposed to possibly prejudicial information "not officially presented to them by the district attorney." In order to "protect the due process rights of Mr. Simpson and the integrity of the grand jury process" he was removing the case from the grand jury and ordering grand jurors not to discuss any details of the case." The case would proceed to the preliminary hearing already scheduled for June 30.

We learned through published "leaks" that the grand jury had heard five days of testimony and was going to vote that same Friday afternoon whether to return an indictment for murder. The leaks included two grand jurors who gave press interviews on condition they remain anonymous. Both conceded they had heard the 911 tapes on television.

The order recusing the grand jury did not end all grand jury involvement in the case. A new Los Angeles County Grand Jury was impaneled on July 1, 1994, and one of the first tasks they were assigned was an investigation of any crimes that may have been committed by A.C. "Al" Cowlings, the close friend of O.J. Simpson who drove the Bronco on the slow-speed chase. We were gravely concerned that this grand jury investigation was a ruse to help the prosecution prepare their case against O.J. Simpson for trial. Once charges have been filed, a grand jury should not be used as a prosecutorial discovery tool to assist in preparations for trial. That would give the prosecution an unfair advantage not available to the defense. We, of course, would have liked nothing better than to be able to subpoena the prosecution witnesses to come to our office and be secretly interrogated in advance of trial. Since we could not do that, neither should the prosecution.

While there was little California authority on point, there was federal precedent for a court intervening to prevent prosecutorial abuse of the grand jury process to assist an ongoing prosecution. Coincidentally, this precedent was also from a historic case in which one of our defense team had participated as counsel. Back in 1973, I had served as co-counsel for Daniel Ellsberg in the Pentagon Papers prosecution in Los Angeles. My role in that case was primarily to prepare Ellsberg for cross-examination, to prepare and argue some of the pretrial motions, and to draft jury instructions. The case was dismissed on the eve of submission to the jury, because of governmental misconduct in burglarizing the office of Ellsberg's psychiatrist.

Among the issues litigated in the Ellsberg case was whether the prosecutors could run a grand jury investigation in Boston at the same time they were preparing to try Mr. Ellsberg in Los Angeles, and subpoena some of the trial witnesses to testify in the secret grand jury proceedings. In the Ellsberg case, the court ordered the Boston grand jury transcripts delivered to the Los Angeles court to determine whether "the Boston grand jury was decoyed into serving primarily as a discovery device for the government's trial preparation."

We were concerned that the same thing was going on in the O.J. Simpson case, that the Cowlings grand jury was a "decoy" to help prosecutors prepare for the Simpson trial. Our concern was certainly heightened by the public statements of District Attorney Gil

Garcetti. He told reporters that prosecutors were not seeking an indictment against Cowlings, but were using the grand jury "for investigatory purposes" to utilize the subpoena power if witnesses "thumbed their nose at us." . . . "One never knows where a grand jury investigation is going to lead one," he said, adding, "If there's other evidence that comes out that assists us in another case, you're not going to turn your back on it."

Our concern turned to alarm when grand jury subpoenas were served on our expert witnesses, including both Dr. Michael Baden and Dr. Henry Lee, as well as Robert Kardashian, a member of the defense team. A subpoena was even issued to Bob Shapiro himself, ordering him to appear before the grand jury and to produce Mr. Simpson's personal calendar. Bob's personal driver was also subpoenaed. And on August 12, 1994, a search warrant was executed at Mr. Simpson's business offices, adjoining the offices of his personal business attorney. The telephone records and other documents seized were brought back to the Cowlings grand jury.

We learned that the witnesses subpoenaed before the Cowlings grand jury were being asked to meet with the lawyers who were preparing the Simpson case for trial in conjunction with their grand jury appearances. The prosecutors handling the Cowlings grand jury and those preparing the Simpson case for trial were working hand in hand. As the deadline for reciprocal discovery approached, when we would have to turn over a complete list of all the witnesses we planned to call at trial, we were worried that our witnesses would then be summoned before the Cowlings grand jury and secretly questioned. We could not represent or advise any of our witnesses being summoned before the grand jury, because it would create a conflict of interest. The secrecy of the grand jury inquiry would also prevent or delay our access to prior statements under oath by prosecution witnesses who were scheduled to testify at the trial. Grand jury witnesses are routinely told by prosecutors not to discuss their testimony before the grand jury with anyone else.

We responded to this situation with another "emergency" motion in late August, seeking "remedies for prosecutorial abuse of the grand jury function." We also amended our pending motion to suppress evidence to include any evidence seized from Mr. Simpson's office and delivered to the Cowlings grand jury. Since the grand jury is actually a judicial body, we felt it was appropriate to ask the court to exert some supervisory authority over the way the prosecutors were using the grand jury as a trial preparation tool. In response, the court met privately with the prosecutor in charge of the grand jury investigation, who assured the court that the Cowlings grand jury was completely independent from the Simpson trial preparations. Based on this assurance, the court allowed the Cowlings grand jury investigation to continue, requiring only that advance court approval be obtained before grand jury subpoenas were issued to witnesses on the defense witness list.

The prosecution response to the amended suppression motion informed the court that the Cowlings grand jury and the Simpson trial were being kept "as separate as possible," and that no evidence from the Cowlings inquiry would be used in the Simpson trial without seeking "further guidance from the court."

The Cowlings grand jury investigation was concluded in October, and on November 7, 1994, District Attorney Gil Garcetti announced three important developments in the case:

1. There was insufficient evidence to charge Mr. Cowlings with any of the offenses being investigated by the grand jury.
2. The Deputy District Attorney in charge of the Cowlings grand jury investigation, Christopher Darden, was being assigned to the O.J. Simpson trial team, and he would play a "very active role" in the trial.
3. The wall of separation between the Cowlings grand jury investigation and the Simpson trial would be maintained. With a straight face, the D.A. pronounced: "The wall is there, believe me. That wall is inviolate. There is no conflict."

The case of *People v. O.J. Simpson* began with Detective Mark Fuhrman climbing over the wall surrounding Simpson's home. We believed that, for the second time in this case, someone was climbing over a wall. For the second time in this case, the explanation for going over the wall was transparently contrived. And for the second time in this case, the court needed to demonstrate some backbone to protect the integrity of the judicial process.

We filed a motion to recuse Christopher Darden from the case, which was heard on December 2. It was not a challenge to his integrity or competence. It simply asserted that the wall of separation between the grand jury investigation and the trial still had to be maintained, and it could not be maintained if the deputy in charge of the grand jury investigation was put on the Simpson trial team.

We had three strong arguments. First, the process of judicial supervision of the integrity of the grand jury would be subverted. There was no wall through Chris Darden's mind that would keep what he learned in the grand jury room separate from the questions he would ask at the trial. Second, the California Penal Code protected the secrecy of grand jury transcripts if no indictment is returned. A court order was necessary even for the *prosecutor* to use those transcripts in any other case. Darden, of course, had full access to those transcripts and could not purge his mind of their contents. Third, it was a violation of California's reciprocal discovery law to give a prosecutor the unfair advantage of interrogating potential trial witnesses in a secret grand jury hearing, and then have the same prosecutor cross-examine those witnesses at trial.

In a terse and superficial order issued ten days later, Judge Ito denied the motion and allowed Darden to participate as trial counsel. He concluded that, as long as the "dominant purpose" of the grand jury proceeding had been to investigate Cowlings, there was no "conflict of interest." That seemed to miss the point. Our primary contention was not Darden's "conflict of interest," but the need to protect the independence of grand jury investigations by *judicial* supervision. The ruling simply confirmed what we knew at the outset: grand juries are playpens for prosecutors, and judges like to keep out of the prosecutors' playpens.

It remained to be seen whether the prosecution gained or lost by getting Darden onto the trial team. As it turned out, the need it created to keep the Cowlings grand jury evidence separate may have contributed to the prosecution's decision not to present the evidence of the Bronco chase at the trial. Most of that evidence had been developed in the Cowlings grand jury investigation. A.C. Cowlings was never called to the witness stand at the trial of O.J. Simpson.

Irony abounds in the grand jury issues that arose in the Simpson case. Ordinarily, it is prosecutors who argue that the integrity and independence of grand juries must be respected, and their secrecy must be preserved. Defense lawyers usually argue it's all a charade, that grand juries are simply tools of the prosecution and should be treated as such. The dismissal of the grand jury in the Simpson case teaches a very practical lesson for prosecutors: They need to instruct grand jurors to avoid exposure to the publicity about cases they are investigating. The unrestrained use of the "Cowlings" grand jury also teaches a practical lesson: It's relatively easy to come up with a plausible excuse to keep the grand jury busy assisting you in preparing your case for trial. Apparently, judges have greater respect for the independence of prosecutors than they do for the independence of grand juries.

FOUR

TAKING

THE FOURTH

*T*he Fourth Amendment "exclusionary rule" has been a constitutional battleground for eighty years. The rule was first imposed on federal authorities by the U.S. Supreme Court in 1914. The
Court declared that if federal officers did not comply with the search
warrant requirements of the Fourth Amendment in seizing evidence, then the evidence could not be admitted in court. In the
words of Justice William R. Day, if illegally seized evidence is admitted, "the protection of the Fourth Amendment . . . is of no value,
and might as well be stricken from the Constitution."

The requirements of the Fourth Amendment are really quite
simple. Police and some politicians frequently refer to them as
"technicalities," but I think they are more appropriately called
"simplicities." All a police officer needs to remember are three
rules:

1. Write out the facts that show why you believe evidence
   of a crime is in the place to be searched in an "affidavit,"
   under oath.
2. Take the affidavit to a judge, who will then issue a search
   warrant if your facts are sufficient. If you don't have
   time, you can just call the judge on the telephone. She
   will swear you in by telephone, tape record your reci-

tation of the facts, and give you oral authorization to
search.

3. Execute the search warrant by going to the exact place
   it describes, then searching for and seizing the exact
   things it describes, and then report back to the court
   what you seized.

These three simple requirements all operate together to achieve
one paramount purpose: to place a neutral judge between the police officer and the citizen. Centuries of experience have taught
that police tend to be overzealous, so the warrant requirement in-
sures that a judge will be looking over their shoulders. Why police
are so resentful of these simple rules has been a source of wonder to
me during my entire legal career. Apparently, they do not like the
idea of anyone looking over their shoulders.

The exclusionary rule was extended to state and local police in
1961, in one of the most controversial rulings of the Supreme Court
on which Chief Justice Earl Warren presided. Ironically, the Court
took that step only after the supreme courts of many of the states
had themselves come to the conclusion that no other means of con-
trolling police behavior seemed to work. Those states included California, which adopted the exclusionary rule in 1955.

After eighty years, one might hope that compliance with the
warrant requirements of the Fourth Amendment would become
routine, so the exclusionary remedy would rarely have to be invoked. In some places it had. But not in Los Angeles.

In teaching the Fourth Amendment to my students at Loyola
Law School in Los Angeles, where I taught from 1970 to 1986, I liked
to point out how many of the leading Supreme Court cases inter-
preting the Fourth Amendment happened right in their backyards
in L.A. I even put together a little "guided tour" to the sites where
famous search and seizure cases took place. My favorite stop on the
tour was a public telephone in front of Carney's Restaurant on the
Sunset Strip, where a bookmaker named Charlie Katz routinely
placed daily calls to get the betting lines. An eavesdropping device
was attached to the top of the booth without a search warrant, and

the case went all the way to the U.S. Supreme Court. It established the principle that the Fourth Amendment protects "reasonable" expectations of privacy, even in a public telephone booth. I always thought a plaque should be mounted on that booth to proclaim the words Justice Potter Stewart wrote in his marvelous majority opinion in *Katz v. United States* (1967):

> No less than an individual in a business office, in a friend's apartment, or in a taxicab, a person in a telephone booth may rely upon the protection of the Fourth Amendment. One who occupies it, shuts the door behind him, and pays the toll that permits him to place a call is surely entitled to assume that the words he utters into the mouthpiece will not be broadcast to the world.

Unfortunately, there's no place to hang such a plaque. There's no way to even close the door. The booth was dismantled and replaced by one of those "open-air" telephones that lets everyone hear your telephone conversations. The telephone company has done a pretty good job of reducing our reasonable expectations of privacy. My favorite scene in the movie version of *Superman* is when Clark Kent desperately searches for a telephone booth to shed his clothes and emerge as the Man of Steel. All he can find are open-air telephones.

What happened to Charlie Katz's telephone booth is a metaphor for what has happened to the Fourth Amendment. Many of the protections recognized by earlier U.S. Supreme Court decisions of the Warren Court era have been dismantled in recent years. The expectations of privacy that are recognized as "reasonable" have been whittled down so a search warrant is rarely needed, especially for a search of an automobile. The "probable cause" needed to get a warrant was diluted to the barest minimum. A "good faith" exception was created, so even if probable cause is insufficient, if a judge issues a warrant anyway, the search can be challenged only by proving the officers lied to the judge about facts that would have made the difference between having probable cause or not. It seems only one protection remains secure: Police still need a search warrant before they can enter a person's home to search for evidence of a crime. Our homes still have doors that we can shut behind us, and we can assume that police still have to get a warrant from a judge before breaking down that door and rummaging through our personal effects. In Anglo-American jurisprudence, that is a protection we have always valued highly. It is a value that is even older than our Constitution. It goes back to the immortal words William Pitt thundered on the floor of England's Parliament: "The poorest man may, in his cottage, bid defiance to all the forces of the Crown. It may be frail; its roof may shake; the wind may blow through it; the storm may enter; the rain may enter; but the King of England may not enter; all his force dares not cross the threshold of the ruined tenement."

We reached back to the early law of England for one of the principles we asserted in *People v. O.J. Simpson*. The protection of the warrant requirement in the Fourth Amendment extends to the entire "curtilage" of a home. Curtilage is an old English term that defined the surrounding yard of one's home that was traditionally enclosed by a picket fence. O.J. Simpson's Rockingham estate was surrounded by a five-foot wall. That wall, we contended, was the "curtilage" protected by the Fourth Amendment.

Even the principle of curtilage was challenged by the prosecution. The prosecutors argued, unsuccessfully, that because Mr. Simpson let Kato Kaelin live in his guest house, that transformed the entire grounds of the estate to a "common area," that police could enter at will, like the lawn of an apartment house. Their principle argument, however, would be that a warrant was unnecessary to enter the premises because there were "exigent circumstances."

There was, however, a crucial tactical consideration to be weighed before we challenged the searches in the Simpson case. The most immediate question was *when* we should file the motion to suppress. California law permits a defendant to file a suppression motion at the preliminary hearing. While the motion can then be renewed before trial in the superior court, the superior court must accept all the factual determinations made at the preliminary hearing, unless the defendant has newly discovered evidence that was not available at the preliminary hearing. Conventional wisdom among defense lawyers is to wait until after the preliminary hearing to make the motion. By the time you get to superior court, you have more information available and can present a more complete factual showing of what took place during the search.

There were a number of reasons why I contemplated bucking conventional wisdom to challenge the search at the preliminary hearing, however. What took place during the search was not well documented. The police reports we obtained in discovery from the prosecution offered no description of what happened. Detective Fuhrman wrote no reports after he was removed from the case at 2 A.M. on June 13, three hours before the detectives all left the Bundy crime scene to go to Mr. Simpson's Rockingham estate. Although police regulations require that a "log" be kept to show the times when officers enter and leave a scene, there was no "log" started at Mr. Simpson's residence until after noon on June 13. The *only* written description we had of the search that allegedly led to discovery of a glove behind the house was contained in the affidavit for a search warrant which Detective Philip Vannatter wrote out that morning. In that affidavit, he gave a very cryptic description of the discovery of the glove: "During the securing of the residence a man's leather glove containing human blood was also observed on the south side of the residence. This glove closely resembled a brown leather glove located at the crime scene at the feet of the unidentified male white victim." Ordinarily, police don't "secure" a residence until they have seized it to exclude others and prevent them from contaminating it. The statement that they had already "secured" the residence *before* they found the glove was, I thought, a telling admission.

The search warrant affidavit also contained what appeared to be a very misleading description of what the police found, in order to make the case against O.J. Simpson appear stronger that it was at the time. Detective Vannatter asserted that a blood spot observed on the Bronco door was "later confirmed by scientific investigation personnel to be human blood," even though no such tests had been performed. He also claimed that the drops leading to the front door and the substance on the glove were human blood, although only routine presumptive tests had been done, which are not specific for blood, much less human blood. Most important was the false suggestion that O.J. Simpson had fled the state shortly after the homicides to avoid prosecution. Vannatter stated: "It was determined, by interviews of Simpson's daughter and a friend Brian Kaelin, Simpson had left on an unexpected flight to Chicago during the early morning hours of June 13, 1994, and was last seen at the residence at approximately 2300 hours, June 12, 1994." Actually, both Kaelin and Arnelle Simpson told the officers that Simpson's flight to Chicago was a prearranged business trip.

Thus, even before we filed the suppression motion, it was apparent that the oral testimony of the police officers would be the only real evidence available of precisely what happened when they got to the Rockingham estate. And it was equally apparent that these officers were ready and willing to misrepresent what happened to avoid getting evidence suppressed by the court. Under these circumstances, it was important to move quickly on our suppression motion. It offered the opportunity to confront and cross-examine the officers under oath before they had a lot of time to get together and concoct a consistent story that would meet the Fourth Amendment test of reasonableness. The only chance we had to succeed on the suppression motion was to catch them in their inconsistencies.

The motion sought to suppress all of the evidence obtained at the Rockingham residence on June 13. The glove allegedly found behind the house and the drops of suspected blood discovered on the driveway leading into the house were all located before the officers obtained a search warrant, so the burden would be on the prosecution to show the reasonableness of that search. The search of the inside of the house and the interior of the Bronco were pursuant to a search warrant, so the prosecution had the advantage of the "good faith" exception to the exclusionary rule for the later searches. We would have to show the warrant was obtained by deliberate lies or reckless misrepresentations in the affidavit, and that without those lies or misrepresentations, there was no probable cause. Since the credibility of the officers was the key issue, however, we thought the false statements in the affadavit would go a long way in persuading a court to distrust their testimony.

When the prosecution filed its response to our motion to suppress at the preliminary hearing, it announced a very shrewd tactical move. The prosecutors would not offer *any* of the evidence obtained pursuant to the search warrant at the preliminary hearing. They would save all the evidence from inside the house and inside the Bronco for the trial. Our motion could not challenge evidence that was not even being offered at the preliminary hearing. We could only challenge the glove and the drops on the driveway. The rest would have to wait until the case was sent to the superior court for trial. The prosecutors hoped to keep the false statements in the search warrant affidavit from undermining the credibility of the police officers testifying at the prelimary hearing.

The only officers who testified on the motion to suppress evidence at the preliminary hearing were Detectives Mark Fuhrman and Phil Vannatter. Even though they took the witness stand only three weeks after the events took place, they contradicted each other on many key points. Vannatter testified that he arrived at the Bundy crime scene to take charge of the investigation at 4:05 A.M., and within a half hour he decided to leave the crime scene and proceed to the home of O.J. Simpson, taking all three of the other detectives with him. He testifed that his only purpose in going to Mr. Simpson's home was to notify him of his former wife's murder and to arrange for the care of the two children who were found asleep in an upstairs bedroom. He said Simpson was not considered a suspect, nor did the detectives believe any related events had happened at Simpson's home. When asked why he brought Detective Fuhrman and his partner with him, after they had been relieved of any further responsibility for the case, he explained, "They were assisting us." He testified he had worked that division for three years, and would have no difficulty locating the Simpson residence. Fuhrman, on the other hand, testified that Vannatter and his partner "didn't know the area," and asked Detective Fuhrman to "lead us up there."

While the detectives were at the Ashford Street gate, ringing the call button and telephoning the residence, Detective Fuhrman testified that he walked over toward the Bronco and noticed it was parked "in a very haphazard manner," with the wheels to the curb and the rear end jutting out into the street. This offered confirmation of our suspicions the Bronco was entered by police and moved early that morning, because photographs taken at seven-thirty that morning from the front, rear, and both sides of the car established it was perfectly parked, parallel to the curb. Fuhrman testified he immediately inspected the Bronco with a flashlight and found the stain above the door handle on the driver's side. He also testified that he found "three or four little lines, red-stained lines" at the lower seam of the door. His discovery of the second stain was communicated to no one else, and none of the photographs taken that morning depict the three or four little lines. It was later confirmed that they were only visible when the door was open. Fuhrman testified that *after* he observed the stains, he looked through the windows into the interior and saw a package addressed to O.J. Simpson, a shovel, and what appeared to be heavy-gauge plastic.

Detective Vannatter gave a very different description of these events. He testified that both he and Fuhrman approached the Bronco and looked through the windows. After he saw the package addressed to Mr. Simpson, he said he told Fuhrman to run a Department of Motor Vehicles check, and then returned to the other detectives at the gate. He then was called *back* to the Bronco by Fuhrman, who showed him the stain above the door handle. He did not recall seeing any other stains, or being told about them by Furhman. At that point, the decision was made to "go over the wall" and enter the premises.

The justification offered by the officers to enter the premises without a search warrant was that the discovery of the tiny stain above the door handle transformed the situation into an emergency that required immediate action. There was no time to stop and call a judge for a search warrant, because there might be a bleeding victim on the premises who needed immediate assistance. While previous decisions had recognized an exception to the warrant requirement for "exigent circumstances," those circumstances had been carefully defined. They involved situations where officers were responding immediately to a scene where violence had occurred, and had a legitimate concern that immediate intervention was necessary to preserve someone's life. Even the cases that recognized the exception expressed grave concern that it could be easily manipulated by police whose real motive was to search for evidence, and simply lacked the patience to seek out a judge for a search warrant. As one California appellate court put it:

> The risk "exigent circumstances" will be used as a pretext is especially grave when officers have some suspicion, short of probable cause, that criminal activity is under way on the premises they intend to invade. This is not to say an officer's motives must be completely pure when he enters with the avowed purpose of protecting life and property. Clearly when an officer hears gunfire and screams of pain inside a house he may rush in with an investigator's curiosity as well as the savior's desire to save lives. But where mixed motives are possible the courts must be alert the savior's image is not merely pretense for an unconstitutional invasion of a suspect's private home.

We argued that Vannatter and Fuhrman were lying when they claimed Simpson was not a suspect at the time they went to his home, and that their explanation of why they entered the premises was a complete fabrication. The best evidence of their motives, however, was supplied by their own description of what they did after they went over the wall. After receiving no response to their knocks at the front door, all four detectives went to the rear of the premises to the guest rooms bordering the swimming pool. They woke up Kato Kaelin, and asked where Mr. Simpson was. None of the four officers were even interested in his answer. They expressed no concern about any injured persons on the premises. They awoke Mr. Simpson's daughter Arnelle in an adjacent guest room, and she told them she could get in touch with her father. She led them back to the front door and into the house. They did not look for injured persons anywhere in the house. A call was placed to Chicago, and Mr. Simpson was informed of his former wife's death at 5:45 A.M. Arnelle made immediate arrangements to retrieve the children from the West L.A. police station. Thus, the detectives had achieved the ostensible purposes of their visit to Mr. Simpson's home before 6 A.M., within an hour of their arrival. But the real purpose of their visit had *not* yet been accomplished: to look for evidence linking Mr. Simpson to the crime. Detective Fuhrman remained in Mr. Kaelin's room to conduct a search and interrogate Kaelin about the events of the preceding night. When Kaelin told him he heard thumps on the wall at around 10:40 the previous evening, Detective Fuhrman decided to do some follow-up investigation. He testified he then found the infamous glove in the narrow walkway behind the house at approximately 6:30 A.M.

His explanation for inspecting the area was that he was looking for a "possible victim" back there. He then led each of the other detectives back to show them his "discovery." That discovery provided the probable cause necessary to obtain a search warrant. Detective Vannatter said he decided to "secure" the premises and obtain a search warrant *after* the discovery of the glove.

We attempted to use the inconsistencies in the search warrant affidavit to challenge the credibility of Detective Vannatter. Why did he say in the affidavit that the glove was found "during the securing of the residence"? Why did he say Mr. Simpson left on an "unexpected" trip after both Kaelin and Arnelle told him it was a planned business trip? Why did he describe the Bronco stain as "human blood" when only a presumptive test had been done? In each case, our efforts were blocked by Judge Kathleen Kennedy Powell, who ruled that the affidavit could not be admitted in evidence, because the search conducted pursuant to the warrant was not in issue. The ruling was absurd. When the credibility of a witness is being challenged, a prior inconsistent statement under oath is always relevent, whether it's in a search warrant affidavit or written on a bathroom wall!

The judge's ruling upholding the search was a great disappointment. She had actually been a student in my Criminal Procedure class at Loyola Law School, but I do not know where she was when we talked about police perjury. Cops do lie, and nowhere do they lie as blatantly and boldly as on suppression motions, when the legality of a search they conducted is challenged.

We discuss the problem at length in my course in Criminal Procedure. One of the classic studies we examine was conducted in New York after the Supreme Court's 1961 ruling applying the exclusionary rule to the states. Before that ruling, police reports for narcotics arrests rarely claimed that a suspect "dropped" the contraband, making a search unnecessary. Only 14 percent of arrest reports made that claim, while 33 percent reported they simply reached into the suspect's pockets and found the drugs. After the Supreme Court decision allowed suppression of the contents of a suspect's pockets, 50 percent of police reports indicated the suspect dropped the drugs when police approached. In only 5 percent of the cases was it necessary to reach into the suspect's pockets. How remarkable that a decision of the U.S. Supreme Court in Washington, D.C., could cause an outbreak of dropsy on the sidewalks of New York! The exclusionary rule was having a strong impact on police behavior. But rather than encouraging compliance with the Fourth Amendment, it was encouraging false testimony to make it appear the police were conforming to the Fourth Amendment.

Later events, including the disclosures of Fuhrman discussing his "creative" approach to fabricating probable cause for arrests on the Fuhrman tapes, and the impeachment of Vannatter with an F.B.I. agent and a police informant, both claiming they heard him admit Simpson was a suspect before he went to the Rockingham house that morning, provided even more persuasive evidence to challenge the credibility of the detectives' testimony presented at the preliminary hearing. But one need look no further than what the detectives did after they entered Mr. Simpson's home. Admittedly, in such a high-profile case, it would have taken a good deal of judicial backbone to conclude that the police were lying, and throw out the search. But the absence of judicial backbone may be the real reason police perjury is so prevalent. They know they can get away with it. Ironically, granting the suppression motion at the preliminary hearing didn't even require a finding of police perjury. The judge could have, and should have, simply ruled that even if the testimony about "exigent circumstances" were *true*, such circumstances would permit an entry limited only to the purported emergency purpose. If that purpose was to notify Mr. Simpson of his former wife's death, to arrange for the care of his children, and to ascertain if there were any injured victims on the premises, those purposes were achieved by 6 A.M., a half hour before the alleged discovery of the glove. Even more ironically, the prosecution might have been better off if the suppression motion *had* been granted at the preliminary hearing. The circumstances surrounding Fuhrman's discovery of the glove would have been eliminated from the case, and Fuhrman's taint would not have seeped into all of their other evidence.

In the subsequent events of the trial, the importance of the glove to supply probable cause for the search warrant was often overlooked. The prosecution belittled the defense suggestion that Fuhrman may have planted the glove, because he would have had no motive to "frame" O.J. Simpson with a murder charge. I believe that the most plausible motive for planting the glove would have been to supply the probable cause needed for a search warrant, rather than any effort to "frame" Simpson. Fuhrman may well have believed Simpson was guilty, but the case needed some "extra help" to allow further searches.

After Judge Kennedy Powell denied the suppression motion, the suspense was gone. It was a foregone conclusion that O.J. Simpson would be held to answer for a trial in superior court. Despite the loss, by litigating the Fourth Amendment issues at the preliminary hearing, the defense gained some important tactical advantages. We were able to pin down both Fuhrman and Vannatter with sworn testimony that could be used to attack their credibility in front of the jury. Fuhrman made a number of "Freudian slips" in his testimony, especially in referring to seeing "them" at the foot of Ron Goldman's body when he was asked about the gloves. We could also exploit the contradictions between the testimony of Fuhrman and

Vannatter. Most important, the seed of doubt had been planted. Frankly, I was surprised at how many of those who watched the preliminary hearing on television disagreed with Judge Kennedy Powell's decision on the suppression motion. They were persuaded the police were lying to cover up what really happened in the early morning hours of June 13. It bolstered our confidence that we could persuade a jury that the prosecution's case was built on a foundation of police lies and cover-ups.

Two months later, we renewed the motion to suppress in the superior court. Those two months had been busy ones for our investigators, and we now had much more ammunition to attack the credibility of Detective Fuhrman. We discovered that he had a prior acquaintance with O.J. Simpson and Nicole Brown Simpson, having responded to a call in 1985 in which Mr. Simpson allegedly took a baseball bat to Nicole's automobile. No charges had been filed, and no police reports had been prepared, but Fuhrman described the events in vivid detail in a letter four years later, saying the events were "indelibly impressed" in his memory. It was hard to believe that Fuhrman hadn't shared his "indelible" impressions with the other detectives before they proceeded to Simpson's home on the morning of June 13. We had heard from Kathleen Bell, who recognized Fuhrman while he was testifying on television, and recalled virulent racist comments he had made about interrracial couples: that he would "make up" a reason to stop such a couple if he observed them. We learned of a pending lawsuit in which it was alleged that police moved evidence to improve the showing of reasonableness for the use of deadly force. Among the arresting officers was Detective Mark Fuhrman. We got hold of the file for his 1982 disability claim, in which his lack of candor and racist attitudes were evident. We tracked down records from Westec Security indicating that police had already gone over the wall and were at the front door before they learned that a live-in maid was supposed to be on the premises, which contradicted Detective Vannatter's testimony at the preliminary hearing. All of this "newly discovered evidence," we asserted, required the superior court judge, Judge Ito, to set aside Judge Kennedy Powell's findings as to the credibility of the detectives, and make his own findings. Judge Ito declined this invitation by applying an impossible test of diligence for lawyers litigating a suppression motion at a preliminary hearing. By holding that this newly discovered evidence could have been discovered prior to the motion at the preliminary hearing, he was able to avoid the personal embarrassment of ruling that the entry to the Rockingham premises was reasonable. He simply accepted Judge Kennedy Powell's findings, without allowing us to present additional evidence undercutting those findings. Even during the trial, when we renewed the motion to suppress based on the disclosures in the Fuhrman tapes and the impeachment of Detective Vannatter, evidence which he could not avoid finding was "newly discovered," he ruled that as long as one of the two detectives was credible, that was enough to deny the motion. The threshold was continually lowered to accommodate the diminishing evidence.

The superior court motion also challenged the search pursuant to the search warrant issued June 13, and a second search warrant issued June 28, 1994. Neither of these searches had been litigated at the preliminary hearing, so we were entitled to call witnesses and make a new factual record with respect to those searches. They raised a myriad of Fourth Amendment concerns that went beyond the "good faith" exception that normally applies to searches with warrants. We contended the June 13 search warrant was invalid because of the lies or misrepresentations contained in the affidavit. At least Judge Ito summoned the courage for some candor about police inaccuracies in search warrant affidavits. He made a factual finding that the misrepresentations in the affidavit were made with "a reckless disregard for the truth." This finding was amply supported. There was no excuse for a detective with Vannatter's experience to misrepresent the results of blood testing. He well knew the limitations of presumptive blood tests. And his description of the flight to Chicago as "unexpected" was so blatantly false that it was charitable for Judge Ito to describe it as "reckless" rather than as a deliberate lie. Nonetheless, Judge Ito concluded that even without the false representations, there was still enough probable cause to justify issuing the warrant. The discovery of the glove alone would justify a further search. I argued that the glove alone was meaningless without putting it in the context of the crime scene at Bundy. Incredibly, the search warrant affidavit contained no description of the Bundy crime scene whatsoever, other than the fact there had been a "double murder" there. For all one would know from reading the affidavit, the victims could have been poisoned or asphyxiated. When the sufficiency of a search warrant affidavit is challenged, a judge is not supposed to look beyond the four corners of the affidavit to information that was not presented to the judge who issued the warrant.

There was also a serious problem with respect to the search of the Bronco pursuant to the June 13 warrant. Instead of listing the Bronco under the places to be searched pursuant to the warrant, Detective Vannatter listed it under the property to be seized in searching the Rockingham premises. Since the Bronco was not on the Rockingham premises, but parked on the street, a literal reading of the warrant did not include the Bronco. Judge Ito ruled that the search of the Bronco would be valid even without a warrant, but the motion exposed some serious problems in the handling of the Bronco that would come back to haunt the prosecution during the trial. Two days after it was seized, the detectives released the Bronco to a storage garage without specifying that the security of the vehicle was to be maintained. Numerous unauthorized persons had access to it, including a tow-truck operator looking for souvenirs. As a result, all of the evidence taken out of the Bronco in later stages of the investigation was seriously compromised.

The execution of the second search warrant on June 28 was challenged as a "general" search. The scope of a search pursuant to warrant is supposed to be limited to the particular items of evidence listed in the warrant. A warrant is not a license for police to rummage through someone's home looking for anything that might be of interest. "Rummaging" is the only way to describe what the police did on June 28. They seized several video tapes that were not listed in the warrant, and commandeered Mr. Simpson's VCR to watch them. Twenty-nine officers of the L.A.P.D. and four representatives of the L.A. County District Attorney's office spent the entire day searching Mr. Simpson's home, primarily looking for the stiletto knife. If we hadn't come up with conclusive evidence to debunk their knife theory, they would have used the fact that they thoroughly searched for it and *didn't* find it to argue that it had to have been the murder weapon. At the hearing of the motion to suppress, we cautiously established that they never looked behind the mirror!

At times, Judge Ito seemed surprised by the level of police incompetence exposed by our motion to suppress, but he gave the police the benefit of every possible inference to support the reasonableness of the searches. After nearly two weeks of hearings spread over a month, he took the motion under submission and denied it in its entirety, with one exception. He was ready to suppress a luggage tag that had been seized at Simpson's home on June 13, even though it was not described in the search warrant. Since the tag didn't seem to prove anything anyway, the prosecutors avoided a suppression ruling by announcing they didn't intend to offer it in evidence, and would reopen the issue before they did offer it if they changed their mind.

My "victory" in winning suppression of an inconsequential luggage tag after months of research, testimony, and arguments provided some lighter moments later on. My greeting card from Bob Shapiro the following Christmas contained a hilarious note "congratulating" me for achieving the stunning triumph of suppressing the luggage tag. It accompanied a bottle of DNA aftershave lotion. Then, when the trial was into its third month, I just happened to be in court to argue a different motion. As I was sitting in the audience waiting for the motion to be called, I was stunned to watch the prosecutor pull the luggage tag out of a bag and offer it in evidence! No one even remembered that it had been tentatively suppressed! During the next recess I reminded my co-counsel of our pretrial triumph, and it led to a rather embarrassing moment for the prosecution.

The Fourth Amendment did not emerge unscathed from the case of *People v. O.J. Simpson*. The denial of the suppression motions, especially the warrantless entry to the Rockingham premises in the early morning hours of June 13, would have been one of our strongest arguments on appeal had an appeal been necessary. But the real lesson the suppression motions taught America was that cops lie. Not all cops. Not all the time. But enough to make the protections of the Fourth Amendment frequently meaningless. The Fourth Amendment does not mean much if police perjury is winked at or shrugged off by judges. It appears that American juries are much more willing than American judges to be skeptical of improbable police testimony. I would respectfully suggest that is not because judges are more gullible. It is because judges are more cynical, and frequently lack the moral courage to challenge police authority.

As a lawyer who loves the Fourth Amendment, and as a teacher who tries to inspire respect for it, the parts of the Fuhrman tapes where Detective Fuhrman explains his conception of the probable cause needed for an arrest were painful to hear. After he described the arrest of an African-American who seemed out of place in Westwood, Laura Hart McKinny asked Detective Fuhrman, "So you're allowed to just pick somebody up that you think doesn't belong in an area and arrest him?" Fuhrman replied, "I don't know. I don't know what the Supreme Court or the superior court says, and I don't really give a shit. If I was pushed into saying why I did it, I'd say suspicion of burglary. I'd be able to correlate exactly what I said into a reasonable probable cause for arrest."

The lesson that cops lie apparently hasn't reached the California legislature in Sacramento. Last year, they enacted a new law permitting criminal prosecution of any citizen who files a false complaint against a police officer. We were told that those who file truthful complaints need have no fear of retaliation. I hope someone starts counting how many California citizens are prosecuted for filing false complaints against police officers, and compares it to how many police officers are prosecuted for perjury.

There is one other lesson that I hope will be drawn from the suppression motions in the Simpson case. When the motions were filed, some pundits and commentators remarked, "If O.J. Simpson contends he's 100 percent innocent, then why is he trying to suppress the evidence against him?" If Fourth Amendment protections are viewed only as a refuge for the guilty, they will continue to shrink. The assertion of one's constitutional right to privacy should not be construed as a concession that one has something incriminating to hide. Now, the Simpson case may be offered as an example of how a spirited assertion of Fourth Amendment rights was completely consistent with a claim of innocence. In that 1961 landmark decision which imposed the exclusionary rule upon the states, Justice Tom Clark wrote that the Fourth Amendment exclusionary rule "gives to the individual no more than that which the Constitution guarantees him, to the police officer no less than that to which honest law enforcement is entitled, and, to the courts, that judicial integrity so necessary in the true administration of justice." In insisting that officers of the Los Angeles Police Department respect the constraints of the Fourth Amendment, Mr. Simpson clothed himself with the same protections available to every individual, conceded to law enforcement everything to which it was lawfully and honestly entitled, and demanded judicial integrity. And he lost.

I can add a couple more stops to my Fourth Amendment tour of Los Angeles. They can serve as monuments to a missed opportunity. Perhaps I can mount a plaque on the wall that defines the curtilage of O.J. Simpson's Rockingham home. I cannot come up with any better words to engrave on that plaque than the words of Justice Louis Brandeis, dissenting from a 1928 decision (since overruled by the Charlie Katz telephone booth decision) that permitted government wiretapping without a warrant:

> Our government is the potent, the omnipresent teacher. For good or ill, it teaches the whole people by its example. If the government becomes a lawbreaker, it breeds contempt for law; it invites every man to become a law unto himself; it invites anarchy.

THE DREAM TEAM

*D*r. David Dutton was on the witness stand. He was the prosecution's expert on the "battered women's syndrome," testifying at the pretrial hearings on whether evidence of prior incidents of spousal abuse would be admitted at the trial. Dr. Dutton was describing the prevalence of "narcissistic personality disorder" among spousal abusers. I knew the diagnostic criteria for "narcissistic personality disorder" by heart. I kept a copy of the American Psychiatric Association's Diagnostic and Statistical Manual (DSM) close at hand in the dean's office, and frequently joked that it was my "faculty manual." Narcissistic personality disorder is characterized by a grandiose sense of self-importance, a need for excessive admiration, and fantasies of unlimited power and brilliance. As Dr. Dutton paused in his testimony, I leaned over to F. Lee Bailey, who was seated next to me at the counsel table, and said, "Narcissistic personality disorder? We have a lot of those in academia." Without missing a beat, Lee replied, "Jerry, we have a lot of those on this team!"

My tenure as a law school dean frequently required some delicate massaging of overblown egos. That experience stood me in good stead as a member of the "dream team."

Actually, I never liked the term "dream team." It was a media invention, and it was rarely used to compliment the lawyers, but

more often to sneer at them. Chris Darden was the only one who
used the term in court, and he became a master at hissing the term,
even though it does not have an "s" in it. The term itself suggests
someone might "dream" of being charged with murder and assembling a crowd of highly touted, expensive lawyers to defend himself. In my book, that is among the worst nightmares one can imag-
ine. I suppose I should be grateful the media did not dub us the
"nightmare team."

There is far from universal agreement among defense lawyers
that a "team" approach is even advisable for a high-profile criminal trial. Edward Bennett Williams, one of the greatest trial lawyers
of this century, was fond of saying, "you can't try a case by committee." Two lawyers frequently team up in a death penalty case,
so one can focus on the guilt phase of the trial while the other pre-
pares for the penalty phase, but death penalty cases are the exception. Few death penalty defendants can afford retained counsel, and
many states refuse to appoint more than one lawyer as defense
counsel. Some very visible criminal defense lawyers were heard to
mutter that they did not want to participate in the Simpson defense because they didn't work well with "teams." In the case of
one highly (self-) touted lawyer, that's precisely why his overtures
to join the team were rebuffed.

Actually, few trial lawyers really work alone. In any big trial,
there will be droves of lawyers behind the scenes, doing research,
interviewing witnesses, tracking discovery, and writing motions.
But the "star" gets all the glory, and most of the money. In adopting a "team" approach, Bob Shapiro signaled he was more than willing to share the glory if it would enhance the quality of the representation.

The "team" approach was actually necessitated by the most important and far-reaching strategic decision of the entire case: the
decision to refuse to waive time limits and insist upon Mr. Simpson's right to a speedy trial. Bob Shapiro recommended that strategy very early in the case, and I fully concurred. We immediately
realized that police and prosecutors were rushing the case. There
was little risk that a person as recognizable as O.J. Simpson could

avoid arrest, so they could have taken their time to do a complete investigation before arresting him. Instead, they made the arrest four days after Mr. Simpson had voluntarily returned from Chicago and given police a complete twenty-page statement and a sample of his blood. Much of the "evidence" had not even been analyzed yet. Once an arrest is made, the clock starts ticking for the prosecutor. Unless a grand jury indictment intervenes, the preliminary hearing must be held within ten days. The trial must commence within sixty days after the preliminary hearing.

Usually, defense lawyers advise their client to "waive" these time limits, so the defense has more time to prepare the case for trial. Conventional wisdom is that delay helps the defense by allowing more time for public passions aroused by the crime to subside. If conviction is a likely outcome, more time between the offense and the sentencing usually improves the chances for leniency. We realized, however, that conventional wisdom did not apply to this situation. Our client was in custody, and likely to remain in custody until the trial was over. The prosecutors could barely keep up with the mounds of police reports, laboratory reports, and other documents. Although they easily could have made the showing necessary to justify a continuance to give them more time to adequately prepare their case for trial, we assumed that prosecutorial arrogance would win out over common sense. It usually does. Prosecutorial "machismo" is endemic. Prosecutors cannot resist playing "chicken," disdaining a motion for a continuance as a sign of weakness, like flinching in the face of the "enemy." Invariably, the defense flinches first. Superior resources ordinarily give prosecutors the advantage, and the defense waiver of time limits usually gives them all the time they need. In the Simpson case, prosecutors simply were unable to make the adjustments and accommodations they should make when the defendant has the resources to actually insist on his rights to a speedy trial. They rushed ahead, never giving themselves the time necessary for thoughtful reflection and analysis to construct a solid theory of the case.

Insisting on a speedy trial *required* a "team" approach for the defense. No single lawyer could have fully prepared the case for trial in sixty days. There were too many motions to be made, witnesses to be interviewed, experts to be briefed, and studies and reports to be read. There wasn't even time to organize much supervision or coordination. The lawyers had to be experienced and confident enough to take charge of a significant part of the case and charge ahead without much supervision. Yet they had to be wise enough to realize that frequent communication with other team members was essential, because every part of the defense had to fit together in a coherent theory of the case. Usually, lawyers of that caliber come equipped with big egos. Making the "team" approach work would take a monumental effort to keep everyone's eye on the ball. That task landed in the lap of O.J. Simpson himself.

Simpson is a keen judge of character, and a highly intelligent strategist. Undoubtedly, those are the qualities that gave him an edge on the football field. They quickly emerged as the qualities needed to keep a team of charged-up lawyers working in harness. Simpson established a warm and open personal relationship with every lawyer on the team, and insisted on being fully informed as to every step proposed to be taken on his behalf. He literally became the glue that held the "team" together.

All the lawyers on the "team" were committed to the concept of "client-centered" lawyering. Some lawyers insist that a client relinquish all control, accepting the lawyer's judgment on all questions of strategy. These lawyers pride themselves on their "client control," as though the client is a passenger in the backseat while the lawyer maneuvers his case through the system. In teaching courses in client counseling and lawyering skills, I've always recommended that lawyers spend more time explaining options to the client, and let clients make more of the decisions. The client has to live with the consequences, and in the long run will be more satisfied with the outcome if he is in greater control. The most important limitation on this concept, however, is that lawyers frequently have to deal with clients whose judgment is impaired, who are experiencing the greatest emotional trauma of their lives.

One of the many things that personally convinced me of O.J. Simpson's innocence was the lack of any impairment in his judgment. This was not a man who had set himself adrift. After he recovered from the emotional shock of his former wife's death and the trauma of being suspected and then arrested for her murder, he was clearheaded and responsive. He was never evasive or reluctant to discuss any detail of his relationship with Nicole Brown Simpson. His ability to coordinate the efforts of his lawyers was even more remarkable because he was in custody. Any client who is jailed has a significant adjustment to make. Being told when you can sleep, shower, or eat is hard for anyone, but extremely difficult for a celebrity who was used to a maid. The loss of privacy, and the indignity of being constantly chained and restrained, takes its toll on any accused person. But O.J. took it all in stride, and put everyone around him at ease, even the deputy sheriffs who guarded him. He was truly the "dream" client.

In assembling the "team," Bob Shapiro got lots of advice. I thought the most astute advice came from Charles Lindner, a gifted writer who himself has handled a dozen death penalty cases. Very early in the case, Lindner wrote in the *L.A. Times* that Bob Shapiro needed "a fighter, a writer and a rabbi."

By a "fighter," Lindner meant a scrappy bulldog who could attack the detail of the prosecution's evidence. When we saw how much of the prosecution's case would depend upon DNA testing, we called around for some recommendations of lawyers with experience challenging DNA evidence. One lawyer was at the top of everyone's list: Barry Scheck of New York. Barry combined an academic career, directing a legal clinic at Cardozo Law School of Yeshiva University, with some heavy-duty litigation experience, handling the earliest major legal challenges to the admissibility of DNA. He was a strong advocate of DNA evidence when used to exclude a suspect, but was well aware of its limitations as a means of actually identifying the perpetrator of a crime. He knew the science as well as the scientists did, and was a formidable cross-examiner.

Barry would come only as a "pair," with his good friend Peter Neufeld. They worked as a team on many cases and complemented each other's strengths and weaknesses well. When Barry gets lost in minutiae, Peter reminds him of the "big picture." Peter is a brilliant strategist, but often relies on Barry for the focused detail to back him up. For the first three months they were in the case, my wife thought Barry's name was "Barry Scheckenpeter," because whenever Barry called me at home he had Peter on the line with him, and he would say, "Is Jerry there? This is Barry Scheck and Peter."

The working relationship of Barry and Peter was a joy to behold. Consistently, Barry's harshest critic was Peter, and Peter's harshest critic was Barry. Their give and take was completely unrestrained, because their respect and admiration for each other were unassailable. When two talented lawyers can achieve such a level of cooperation, a synergism takes them far beyond what either one could achieve alone. Unfortunately, there are few lawyers who reach these heights. Their level of mutual confidence provided a sharp contrast to the distrust and dysfunction of Bob Shapiro's relationship with F. Lee Bailey.

Initially, Bob Shapiro intended F. Lee Bailey to assume the role Lindner described as the "rabbi," a trusted mentor providing astute counsel behind the scenes. Bob envisioned Lee as a consultant to help him strategize the case, rather than as co-counsel in the courtroom. They had a close relationship stretching back many years. Bob's career really took off when he became Bailey's personal choice to defend him on a drunk driving charge in San Francisco. Bob won an acquittal. Bailey became the godfather of Shapiro's eldest son, and one to whom Bob frequently looked for sage advice.

It was unrealistic, however, to expect an old warhorse like F. Lee Bailey to remain "behind the scenes" of what was touted as the "trial of the century." Some wag once quipped that the most dangerous place in a courtroom was to stand in between Alan Dershowitz and a television camera. It's probably even more dangerous to stand in between F. Lee Bailey and the podium. That is precisely where Bob Shapiro was standing.

For one who admired F. Lee Bailey and loves Bob Shapiro, the "feud" was painful to observe. Bob became reluctantly convinced that a good deal of the negative press of a highly personal nature directed at him was being planted by F. Lee Bailey. Even more treacherous was Bailey's effort to cultivate a closer relationship with O.J. Simpson and undermine his confidence in Shapiro. Simpson saw through this, and Bailey never got the starring role he sought. But Bob never should have made the dispute a public one. The feud not only hurt Bob Shapiro's reputation, and made F. Lee Bailey look ridiculous, but it hurt O.J. Simpson. Lawyers should not let their animosity for each other hurt their client. Neither Simpson nor Johnnie Cochran wanted to resolve the impasse by removing either Bailey or Shapiro from the team. It was agreed that we would proceed to trial with two lawyers who would not even speak to each other working side by side. It is a tribute to both that they managed to keep their disdain for each other in check throughout the trial. When the trial was over, they felt free to go after each other with abandon. They shouldn't have.

The role Lindner described as the "writer" fell to myself and Alan Dershowitz. Alan was already a legend for his extraordinary work representing Claus von Bülow, Mike Tyson, and other high-profile clients. He is a brilliant tactician, with a deep understanding of constitutional law. My strength was an intimate knowledge of California law and procedure.

Prior to trial, I drafted the suppression motions, while Alan focused on the motions to challenge the evidence of domestic discord. We exchanged drafts frequently, polishing up the final product. Alan's brother, Nathan Dershowitz, who has a law office in New York, also made major contributions to the motions and responses. Once the trial was underway, I did most of the motions and responses but still received a lot of input from Alan. It was enjoyable and exhilarating to work with Alan, but I must confess to some initial misgivings. When the Simpson case began, Alan had just published a newspaper column entitled "The Abuse Excuse." In it, he was highly critical of defenses based on the abuse a criminal accused suffered at the hands of his victim. He was especially harsh on the lawyers in the *Menendez* case, the trial of two Beverly Hills brothers charged with the murders of their parents. Their trial ended with hung juries after evidence was admitted of horrific abuse of the boys by their father. I was concerned by the public misunderstanding of what was really at stake in the *Menendez* case. No one was arguing the boys should be *excused*. The only issue was whether their crime was murder or manslaughter. On that issue, I thought evidence of prior abuse was highly appropriate and certainly did not warrant the jury-trashing and lawyer-bashing that Dershowitz and others were engaged in. I was incensed by what he wrote and had just published a column of my own, attacking Alan Dershowitz. It was entitled "The Afterwit of Alan Dershowitz." After remarking on the irony of a leading criminal defense lawyer warning us that the "clever ploys" and "muddled thinking" of criminal defense lawyers posed "real dangers to our safety and to the integrity of the legal system," I challenged the historical accuracy of Dershowitz's perspective:

> "It all began," he tells us, "with the so-called battered woman syndrome." No, Alan, that's not where it all began. It all began in the mists of medieval England, when a defense lawyer first convinced a judge to accept the maxim *actus non facit reum nisi mens sit rea*. An act does not make one guilty unless his or her mind is guilty. The entire history of the criminal law has been an ongoing effort to refine this concept of *mens rea*. The most important refinement came with the recognition that provocation by a victim could defeat a showing of malice and reduce the severity of a murder to manslaughter. That was about four hundred years ago, Alan.

I concluded with a sarcastic personal dig at Alan for forsaking his roots as a criminal defense lawyer to become a media hype spinner. "How sad it is," I wrote, "that one who professes pride in the label 'criminal defense lawyer' should be the source of so much of the misinformation and misunderstanding about criminal justice that recent verdicts have engendered. But that's show business. The afterwit of later days hath found out another more exquisite distinction."

Fortunately, my column was not widely circulated, and the media never picked it up. Alan laughed it off and actually responded to it when he published a collection of columns and essays under the same title, *The Abuse Excuse*. Alan and I developed a warm friendship, and I have since gained an even greater appreciation of how difficult it is to combine the roles of criminal defense lawyer and law professor as well as Alan does. My scholarship is sometimes impugned as advocacy, and my advocacy is sometimes disdained as pedantic. I would certainly argue, however, that legal education is enriched by professors who occasionally leave the classroom to serve a client. Too many law professors are refugees from the practice of law who hated every minute of it.

With all the talent that Bob Shapiro assembled for the defense team, an important element was missing. It was an all-white team. Every lawyer on the team recognized the importance of bringing an excellent African-American trial lawyer on board. It wasn't a question of symbolism or public relations; it was a question of credibility. O.J. Simpson is a highly visible African-American. The lawyers who spoke to the jury on his behalf should include an African-American.

The race of the defendant may never be regarded as irrelevant for a criminal defense lawyer. Our culture is obsessed with race. From the outset, the media emphasized the racial aspects of the case. *Time* magazine darkened the skin tones on their cover portrait of O.J. Simpson. Crime in America has been given a black face, and it was as though *Time* magazine wanted to reassure white America that the accused matched that image. *Newsweek* ran an especially ugly "hit piece," portraying O.J. Simpson as a man who "tried to be white." It was illustrated with a cropped photo of O.J. watching a white dancing girl. The photo had been taken at a family birthday party. The "demonizing" that dehumanizes an accused person was well under way, and the line that traditionally separates the legitimate press from the tabloids was already becoming blurry. The racial composition of O.J. Simpson's defense team would be closely observed and the subject of a good deal of comment and speculation. Diversity was an essential element of credibility.

O.J. Simpson was already well acquainted with Johnnie Cochran, who was just winding up his handling of the Michael Jackson child molestation investigation. Cochran was an obvious choice. He had built a solid reputation as one of the best criminal defense lawyers in Los Angeles even before he was asked to serve as chief assistant to District Attorney John Van de Kamp in the mid '70s. He knew most of the deputy D.A.'s who still worked in the prosecutor's office, and most of the judges liked and respected him. He had built a successful private practice specializing in civil rights cases as well as criminal defense, and had won some hefty judgments against L.A.P.D. for abusive police misconduct. He was a leader in the black community of Los Angeles and knew the community well.

What was not immediately obvious was what role Cochran would play. Shapiro and Cochran huddled and made a public show of unity, but there was a real undercurrent of tension in terms of who was in charge of what. Bob had agreed to a "group portrait" of the entire defense team by noted photographer Richard Avedon. We all showed up at the appointed hour on a Sunday morning, but the photo session was aborted when Cochran simply failed to show. It was as though he was delivering a message to Shapiro: "We've got a lot of work to do, and shouldn't be wasting our time primping for media attention." That is a message I thought was badly needed. Bob was doing a magnificent job of handling the "public relations" aspects of the case, but the grueling schedule of trial preparation we had set for ourselves demanded much closer supervision of the investigators and of the enormous flow of paper that accompanies pretrial discovery.

Shapiro was a solo practitioner with a single secretary when the case began. F. Lee Bailey convinced him what he needed was a high-powered computer system to stay on top of the case. He brought a computer technician on board and hired another secretary. Sara Caplan, a very capable young lawyer who assisted Bob on his civil cases, was placed in charge of monitoring and organizing all of the pretrial discovery. I began working at Bob's office researching and writing the pretrial motions. Frankly, I was surprised at how little time Bob spent in the office. Everyone seemed to be fending for themselves, with minimal leadership or direction.

The lack of supervision was a serious problem with the investigators, and we paid dearly for it. The most embarrassing moments for the defense during the trial were directly attributable to the sloppiness of attorney supervision of the investigators. The investigators were experienced and aggressive, with excellent instincts for leads which were likely to pay off. Pat McKenna and John McNally were both closely associated with F. Lee Bailey, an association that created some problems when Bailey and Shapiro began feuding. Bill Pavelic was a former L.A.P.D. officer, whose inside knowledge of L.A.P.D. procedures and manuals was especially helpful. Shapiro set up a "hot line" for the public to call in information and suggestions. It was very expensive to maintain, and 99 percent of the thousands of calls it produced were useless dead ends. The money would have been better spent on hiring more investigators to follow up on the discovery we were receiving from the prosecution.

As investigators went out to interview potential witnesses, they frequently gave oral reports to Bob Shapiro. Written reports were done on a "hit and miss" basis, and occasionally an interview was tape recorded, without preparing a transcription of the tape. Tapes ended up in a box in Shapiro's office, or in Pavelic's home, with no one maintaining a log. Little thought was given to what would have to be turned over to the prosecution under the reciprocal discovery law. When control of the case was finally shifted to Cochran's offices, some tapes apparently had disappeared.

The first time this sloppiness returned to haunt us was when Rosa Lopez was called to the witness stand. Rosa Lopez was a citizen of El Salvador who was employed as a maid at the home of O.J. Simpson's next-door neighbors. When she was interviewed by Bill Pavelic in July 1994, she said she recalled seeing the white Bronco parked at the Rockingham Avenue curb throughout the evening of June 12. Apparently Pavelic told no one he had tape recorded this interview, and the tape ended up at his home. During the prosecution's case, Rosa Lopez was called as a defense witness out of order, to preserve her testimony because she was returning to her native country and would be beyond the subpoena power of the court. Her testimony was not as strong as we hoped, largely because of language difficulties and cultural differences. Only after she had been called to the stand, however, did the lawyers learn that a prior interview had been tape recorded. As soon as they learned of the existence of the tape, it was produced and turned over to the prosecution. The delay resulted in stiff fines for the lawyers, and a devastating proposed jury instruction that the delay in disclosure could be considered for its effect on the credibility of the witness. Ultimately, we decided not to present Rosa Lopez's video testimony to the jury, so the instruction was never given. I still believe such an instruction would have been erroneous, because the witness had absolutely nothing to do with the delay, and the delay was irrelevant to her credibility. What was really at stake was the credibility of the lawyers, who had represented that *all* statements of the witness had been turned over when they hadn't been. That's not a happy situation for any lawyer. Ironically, the lawyers who were sanctioned, Johnnie Cochran and Carl Douglas, were the two lawyers who bore the least personal responsibility for the mistake.

When I appeared in court on Ash Wednesday to argue a motion for reconsideration of the sanctions, I told Judge Ito that we were all wearing "sackcloth and ashes," because we all had to share responsibility for a very embarrassing mistake. Marcia Clark retorted that she didn't care if I was wearing a dress, and Judge Ito rejected the motion for reconsideration. Just a month later, Marcia was bitterly complaining that sanctions leveled against the prosecution were demeaning, that she just wanted to try her case without the lawyers seeking sanctions against each other. None of the numerous discovery failures of the prosecution ever inspired a concession that a mistake was made, however, much less an apology. Sloppiness is a deadly vice for trial lawyers, but not half as deadly as arrogance.

I'm persuaded that the use of monetary sanctions is a fair device for enforcing discovery obligations, as long as it's understood that the sanctions are a means of providing incentives for lawyers to exercise personal responsibility over the discovery process. But jury instructions regarding the credibility of the witness, or even the credibility of the lawyers, are rarely appropriate. Litigants should not be punished for the carelessness of their lawyers.

A second tape screw-up by the defense was even more embarrassing, although it related to a witness who was never called to testify. At 7:35 P.M. on June 12, 1994, O.J. Simpson called and left a message for a friend named Gretchen Stockdale. The message was:

Uh, hey, Gretchen, sweetheart. It's Orenthal James who is finally at a place in his life where he is like totally, totally unattached with everybody. Ha ha. Ah, in any event, um, I got a Sunday evening, uh I'd love . . . I guess I'm catching a red eye at midnight or something to Chicago but I'll be back Monday night. Uh, if you leave me a message leave it on [telephone number].

It does not sound like a person distraught by jealousy who is on the verge of homicide. That may explain why the prosecutors elected not to call Gretchen Stockdale as a witness. What piqued their interest, however, was the publication of a verbatim transcript of this message which was published in the New York Daily News on May 13, 1995. They asked Ms. Stockdale for a copy of the tape and were informed she had taped over her only copy, but only after she had given another copy to defense investigator Pavelic. They then demanded we produce the tape. We insisted we had no obligation to do so, since we were not going to call Gretchen Stockdale as a witness, and our possesssion of the tape did not deny the prosecution equal access to the same evidence at the time we took possession. It was an interesting legal question, but one that Judge Ito never had to resolve because the prosecutors did not prove it. If they had, we would have ended up with more egg on our faces, because the tape had been lost. To this day, we don't know what happened to it after it was brought back to Bob Shapiro's office. I suspect that it was our copy that was leaked to the New York Daily News, which makes me shudder even more than the carelessness in its handling.

Once operations were shifted to Cochran's offices, there was much more systematic control over documents and exhibits. The difficult task of organizing and managing document control fell to Carl Douglas, one of the real "unsung heroes" of the defense team. Carl meticulously and tirelessly tracked the tons of paper that the case generated. The tedious process of sorting out all the exhibits prior to each side resting was the culmination of many hours of thankless drudgery by Carl Douglas. Shawn Chapman, also with Cochran's office, managed a lot of the preparation of evidence and witnesses going on behind the scenes. Cochran's office was a very supportive place to work. An infectious "team spirit" pervaded the entire office staff.

Johnnie Cochran assumed the role of leadership of the team with relish. His mischevious sense of humor dissipated much of the tension. Cochran works by capillary action. He is constantly assimilating and has fantastic retentive powers. He repeatedly acknowledges and reinforces those who work with him. Without being arrogant, he is completely confident, and his confidence is contagious. He infused the entire team with a real sense of mission.

For me, the most exhilarating aspect of my work on the defense team was the strategizing. Frequently, there were ten or twelve lawyers around a table, with a couple more patched in by conference telephone. Tactical options were fully discussed and explored, and everyone's input was valued. Rarely were we unanimous in the recommendations we made to our client. He was given all sides of every option before a final decision was made.

There were many other lawyers who played important roles on the defense team. When Peter Neufeld was unable to get a continuance for a previously scheduled homicide trial in New York, Robert Blasier of Sacramento was brought in to assist Barry Scheck with the scientific evidence. Bob remained even after Peter returned, and quickly assimilated every labyrinth of the case. Bob is one of the few lawyers I've met who has fully mastered the extent to which modern technology can assist the trial lawyer. Most lawyers, including myself, are intimidated by the technology, and use only a fraction of its potential. I wrote most of the motions out in longhand and faxed my handwritten drafts from home to the legal secretaries in Shapiro's or Cochran's offices. As a case goes on for months, your memory fades as to who said what to whom six months before. Bob Blasier had it all at his fingertips and could summon it forth like a magician.

Robert Kardashian's role could be described as team cheerleader, and I don't characterize it that way to demean it. Keeping a spirit of camaraderie and optimism alive is absolutely essential. There were some real low points for all of us during the trial. The pundits and commentators were engaged in ferocious Monday morning quarterbacking, and they weren't waiting until Monday morning. Defense lawyers should know that you are in no position to respond or explain anything you've done or not done until the trial is over. What I could not understand was why so many of the pundits and commentators were themselves defense lawyers, who should have known better. Kardashian maintained an optimistic good humor throughout, which was especially important for O.J. Simpson himself. Kardashian devoted months away from his regular employment and did it all simply as a loyal friend, without compensation. Being accused of a crime offers a unique opportunity to discover who your true friends are. One would hope that, at least among one's friends, judgment would be suspended and reserved until all the evidence was in. Many of O.J. Simpson's so-called "friends" only waited to see which way the public opinion polls were shifting.

Leroy "Skip" Taft handled the difficult job of financing the defense efforts. As O.J.'s personal business lawyer, he worked hard to keep costs under control. The total cost of the defense efforts was several million dollars. All of the attorneys agreed to fixed fees early in the case and ended up putting in more hours than anticipated. I estimated that the trial would take three months. I'm confident no lawyer even received what would be his or her normal hourly billing rate for the number of hours put in. Consultation fees and travel expenses for experts added considerably to the costs.

When the trial of the case of *People v. O.J. Simpson* began, Judge Ito called all the lawyers into chambers and reminded us that the world was watching and making judgments about the American system of justice based on our performance. He expressed the hope that, at the end of the trial, we could all get together for dinner as friends. I shared that hope. One ideal of the legal profession that has always inspired me is the one expressed by William Shakespeare: "Do as adversaries do in law,/strive mightily, but eat and drink as friends." I share Judge Ito's disappointment that we all fell short of this ideal. The heat of battle is no excuse for a lack of civility, and to justify incivility by a childish claim that "they started it" is beneath the dignity of our profession. I am proud of the vigor of the advocacy on both sides of the trial. But I am also ashamed that the lawyers on both sides occasionally engaged in behavior that was more appropriate for a sandbox than a courtroom. Lawyers, however, are human beings who live in the same world as everyone else. Increasingly, that world is a highly competitive one in which individuals are treated with a lack of respect. Civility is a declining commodity in our public discourse, all the way from the halls of Congress to the radio talk shows. The snarling "put-down" and the cheap shots find their way into every level of conversation. That puts an even greater burden on lawyers and judges to maintain the decorum of our courtrooms. In that respect, we should candidly admit that in the case of *People v. O.J. Simpson*, we all dropped the ball.

The lesson learned from the employment of a "dream team" may be that money makes a difference in some cases. Not all of the money spent on the defense affected the outcome. Some of it, like the "hot line," was extravagant waste. But clearly, O.J. Simpson enjoyed significant advantages that are denied to indigent defendants. An indigent defendant may make a motion to ask the judge to appoint experts, but those experts will not be available at an early stage in the investigation, when they might make the biggest difference. And normally, they will not be experts of the caliber of Dr. Henry Lee or Dr. Michael Baden.

Nor will an indigent defendant have a coterie of legal talent ready to make his defense their highest priority. A typical public defender has a caseload of 200 cases per year. Getting a "speedy trial" was the linchpin of O.J. Simpson's defense. If he were indigent, his trial would not even have commenced by the time the verdict came in.

Those who have studied the impact of the quality of counsel upon the outcome in criminal cases have concluded that the defense lawyers make an actual difference in the outcome in less than 1 percent of criminal jury trials. I would put it a little higher. Edward Bennett Williams probably had it right when he calculated that in 100 cases that are tried, the best trial lawyer in America might win 60 and lose 40, while the most incompetent will win 40 and lose 60. The suggestion that money made a difference has been the basis of much of the criticism of the Simpson defense. I find that reaction a little hypocritical. We accept without question the reality that the wealthy among us live in nicer houses, drive nicer cars, eat better food, and get better medical care. Why should it surprise us that they get better legal representation? Why should it surprise anyone that a wealthy man would use all the resources available to him to defend his liberty?

The reason for our reluctance to recognize that money can make a difference is that we must then concede that *lack* of money can make a difference too. Ninety percent of those accused of crimes in America are indigent, and they must run the gauntlet of the criminal justice system with few of the resources that were available to O.J. Simpson. In many cases, the resources would not make a difference in the outcome. But in the close case, the difference between conviction and acquittal will often ride on the quality of one's defense. In many states, a defendant on trial for his life will be limited to a total budget that wouldn't have paid the hotel bill for a week for one of Simpson's lawyers.

The challenge is to do a better job of identifying the cases where resources may make a difference, and make the necessary resources available. In one category of case, we can rest assured that resources will *always* make a difference: the death penalty cases. There are no millionaires on death row. That is not because millionaires never commit capital offenses. Yet, while commentators lamented the fact that money may have made a difference in the case of *People v. O.J. Simpson,* Congress was voting to eliminate the funding for twenty death penalty resource centers that have worked to improve the quality of representation available to indigents facing the death penalty.

Some have suggested that economic disparity should be eliminated by requiring that all defendants be represented by public defenders. It's interesting that no one has suggested that we eliminate economic disparity in housing by requiring everyone to live in public housing projects, or that we eliminate economic disparity in medical services by treating everyone at the county general hospital. One advantage of an occasional defendant with the resources of an O.J. Simpson is that it presses the entire system to a higher standard of performance. The criminal justice system is like any other bureaucracy. When it isn't challenged, it relaxes. That can lead to incompetence, corruption, or worse. We had a recent example in San Francisco, when a laboratory technician responsible for drug analysis in criminal cases noticed that she was never called to court for a challenge to her test results. She simply stopped doing the tests and certified the results without any analysis of the seized substance. Two hundred cases were processed through the system before anyone even noticed. If the result in *People v. O.J. Simpson* leads to greater competence and higher standards in the Los Angeles County Coroner's office and the L.A.P.D. crime lab, thousands of other defendants will benefit from Simpson's defense.

One of the most astute commentators writing about the Simpson trial was Erwin Chemerinsky, a law professor at U.S.C. Law Center in Los Angeles. On July 6, 1994, before the preliminary hearing was even concluded, he identified the lesson that the resources available to the Simpson defense would teach about our criminal justice system:

> Most criminal defendants receive legal representation that is like the medical care provided at a public hospital—good care, but limited by all of the constraints imposed by an underfinanced, overused system. The Simpson case likely will illustrate what has long been true: there is a double stan-

dard of justice in American society, one for the rich and one for the poor.

How ironic that those who are most critical of the Simpson defense do not seem upset by the "double standard" when it leads to unjust convictions of the poor, but complain vociferously then they perceive it as producing an unjust acquittal of the rich. These critics are the same individuals who extoll the virtues of a free market economy in every other aspect of our lives.

LEAKS AND GAGS

*T*here are two dramatically different conceptions of the appropriate role of a defense lawyer representing a high-profile client in a criminal case. The traditional view is that lawyers should restrict their advocacy to the courtroom. Under this view, press conferences on the steps of the courthouse and interviews for "profiles" are frowned upon as "unprofessional." This is the prevailing standard in the English bar, where comments to the press by barristers are unheard of. The modern view is that complete representation of all of the interests of a client includes protecting his public image and reputation as well as his liberty. This view recognizes that public opinion has a way of seeping into the courtroom, and a lawyer who ignores public opinion and disdains the opportunity to influence or shape it does so at the peril of her client.

These contrasting views are both represented on the United States Supreme Court. In 1991, the tension between them surfaced in a case from Las Vegas, Nevada. A lawyer named Dominic Gentile was retained to represent Grady Sanders, the owner of a vault used to store the drugs and money seized by narcotics officers of the Las Vegas Metropolitan Police Department. When four kilograms of cocaine and almost $300,000 in travelers' checks was reported missing from the vault, a grand jury investigation was launched which led to the indictment of Grady Sanders. There was great press interest in the case, and law enforcement officials thought it was important to maintain public confidence in the police department by allaying suspicions that police detectives who had unlimited access to the vault were responsible. During the course of the investigation, the deputy police chief announced that the two detectives who had access to the vault had been "cleared," and it was leaked to the press that they had passed lie detector tests. (It later turned out that the lie detector tests had been administered by a man who was arrested for distributing cocaine to an FBI informant.)

After his client was indicted, Dominic Gentile held a press conference. At the press conference, he charged that the accusations against his client were part of a police cover-up:

> When this case goes to trial, and as it develops, you're going to see that the evidence will prove not only that Grady Sanders is an innocent person and had nothing to do with any of the charges that are being leveled against him, but that the person that was in the most direct position to have stolen the drugs and the money, the American Express Travelers' checks, is Detective Steve Scholl. There is far more evidence that will establish that Detective Scholl took these drugs and took these American Express Travelers' checks than any other living human being. And I have to say that I feel that Grady Sanders is being used as a scapegoat to try to cover up for what has to be obvious to people at Las Vegas Metropolitan Police Department and at the District Attorney's Office.

Dominic Gentile's prediction turned out to be quite accurate. Grady Sanders was found not guilty by a jury, based on a defense that pinned the blame on police detectives. Nonetheless, Gentile was brought before the state bar of Nevada on charges that he violated a rule based on the American Bar Association's Model Rules of Professional Conduct. That rule prohibited lawyers from making any statements to the press "if the lawyer knows or reasonably should know that it will have a substantial likelihood of materially prejudicing an adjudicative proceeding." The only thing the rule permitted a lawyer to say was "the general nature of the claim or defense," without elaboration. The state bar concluded that Dominic Gentile had violated this rule, and it reprimanded him. Gentile challenged this reprimand before the United States Supreme Court, arguing that his comments at the press conference were protected by the First Amendment guaranty of free speech. Gentile's case was argued before the Supreme Court by Professor Michael Tigar of the University of Texas. Tigar more recently volunteered for the defense of those accused of the Oklahoma City bombing of the federal building. That should place him in the pantheon of heroic American lawyers, if he wasn't already there.

The Gentile case split the United States Supreme Court right down the middle. Chief Justice William Rehnquist articulated the traditional view, noting that lawyers are "officers of the court," and that status provides both an aura of greater credibility and a constitutional basis for greater regulation of their speech:

> Because lawyers have special access to information through discovery and client communications, their extrajudicial statements pose a threat to the fairness of a pending proceeding since lawyers' statements are likely to be received as especially authoritative.

The modern view was espoused by Justice Anthony Kennedy, who recognized that a defense lawyer must represent a client in the "court of public opinion" as well as in the courtroom:

> An attorney's duties do not begin inside the courtroom door. He or she cannot ignore the practical implications of a legal proceeding for the client. Just as an attorney may recommend a plea bargain or civil settlement to avoid the adverse consequences of a possible loss after trial, so too an attorney may take reasonable steps to defend a client's reputation and reduce the adverse consequences of indictment, es-

pecially in the face of a prosecution deemed unjust or commenced with improper motives.

While Chief Justice Rehnquist's views of the appropriate role of defense lawyers won five votes to Justice Kennedy's four, one of Rehnquist's votes "jumped ship" when it came to the question of upholding the reprimand the state bar dished out to Dominic Gentile. Justice Sandra Day O'Connor switched sides and gave Kennedy a majority to hold that the rule itself was unconstitutional, because it was too vague in defining what lawyers could say and couldn't say. Gentile, for example, could have reasonably believed that his press conference was well within the exception permitting a statement about "the general nature of the claim or defense."

The parallels between the Gentile case and the Simpson case are obvious. There was one important difference, however. The State Bar of California had never adopted the American Bar Association model rule governing trial publicity, or any similar rule. It was left to each individual judge to regulate the extrajudicial statements of attorneys in a pending case.

Bob Shapiro, and all of the lawyers he recruited for the defense team, including myself, are strong proponents of the "modern view" of the role of defense lawyers regarding trial publicity. Although I did not generally give press interviews or appear on television shows, it wasn't because I regard such conduct as unprofessional. It was because I think the interests of the client are better served if the lawyers speak with one voice. In the early stages of the case, that voice should have been Bob Shapiro's. The public pronouncements of other lawyers on the defense team should have been restrained, not because it was unprofessional, but because it was occasionally injurious to the best interests of our client.

I believe the public is well aware that when lawyers appear on talk shows or hold press conferences, they are still representing the interests of their clients—or at least they should be! For that very reason, I think public statements of lawyers are given *less* credibility, and again, they should be. Chief Justice Rehnquist is wrong when he asserts, without any documentation, that the public state-

ments of lawyers are likely to be received as "especially authoritative." My experience suggests that just the opposite is true.

One unfortunate consequence of a rule or court order gagging
lawyers is that it simply drives their press pronouncements under-
ground. Rather than being publicly identified as the source of information about a pending case, so that the public can intelligently
assess whether the information deserves greater or lesser credibility, lawyers subject to gag rules become confidential, anonymous
sources. You see them quoted as "a source close to the defense," or
"an authoritative source."

Bob Shapiro was very adept at handling media relations. After
the Christian Brando case, he authored an article offering other
lawyers advice about media relations. Contrary to some reports, it
was not advice about how to "manipulate" the media. Bob realizes
that the best approach to news reporters is to respect their intelligence and their integrity. If you don't respect their intelligence and
their integrity, avoid them like the bubonic plague. The press corps
covering the Simpson trial included some of the best journalists in
the world, who were sophisticated veterans with many years of experience. They were a hardworking lot, who put in long hours. They
also included a few slimeballs who would pick your pockets if they
got the chance. One advantage (or disadvantage) of a high-profile
case is that journalists may actually turn up additional evidence
your own investigators failed to uncover. A lawyer needs to know
what the media is reporting about a case, without being obsessed
by it. He also needs to know which journalists he can trust.

Journalists are generally protected by "shield laws" from having to disclose sources who have been promised anonymity. California has one of the broadest shield laws in the country, and it dates
back to the Charles Manson case. In that case, a reporter named
Bill Farr wrote a story disclosing alleged plans of the Manson family to murder other celebrities. The story was published while the
jury was temporarily unsequestered, during the penalty phase of
the trial. The trial judge held a hearing to inquire into the source
of such prejudicial publicity, and Farr admitted his source was "one
of the lawyers" in the case, but declined to identify which one. For

his refusal to identify the lawyer, Farr was held in contempt and jailed. Farr became a journalistic hero, and the California legislature enacted a shield law that generally protects journalists against being jailed for contempt when they refuse to identify their sources. The courts have carved out an exception, however, to preserve the defendant's right to a fair trial. A judge may order the disclosure of sources when it is necessary to ensure the defendant's right to a fair trial.

From the discovery of the bodies up to the final verdict, the Simpson case was a sieve, a constant source of news "leaks" that filled the columns of newspapers and magazines, as well as the airwaves of radio and television news broadcasts. The earliest press reports of the homicides included a description of a "ski mask" found at the scene. Bob Shapiro's skillful extraction of a concession from the prosecution that there was no "ski mask" was reported as a major victory for the defense! Every time a knife was turned into the L.A.P.D. (there were at least six), a flurry of news reports followed, speculating that the murder weapon had been found. As long-delayed DNA testing proceeded, the alleged results of tests were reported by the press before they were even delivered to counsel. Finally, Judge Ito ordered the testing laboratories to deliver their results directly to him, rather than to the Los Angeles Police Department. Miraculously, all further leaks stopped. Before that step had been taken, however, one such leak became a major issue that would reverberate through the entire trial.

On September 21, 1994, newscaster Tracie Savage reported on the 11 P.M. newscast for Los Angeles television station KNBC that blood samples taken from a pair of socks found in O.J. Simpson's bedroom had been tested for DNA, and produced a match to the blood of Nicole Brown Simpson. We had just been informed that DNA tests were going to be performed on the socks, so were surprised by this revelation. We immediately called it to Judge Ito's attention, and he confirmed that the tests had not been completed. He then took the unusual step of announcing from the bench that the report was inaccurate. This provoked KNBC to "reconfirm" their story with their "source," and run it again to "refute" Judge

Ito's criticism. In a subsequent letter to the court, the president and general manager of the television station wrote that the information came from "individuals knowledgeable about the investigation," and that their sources had "different avenues of information" and on previous occasions had provided "accurate information" to KNBC.

We were convinced the "source" for the KNBC story was within the L.A.P.D. Who else would even know the socks were being tested? The L.A.P.D. crime lab had performed some preliminary tests that were *not* DNA tests just the day before. The timing of the leak was also highly suspicious. It came the *same day* that Judge Ito made his finding, during the hearing of the suppression motions, that Detective Philip Vannatter's misrepresentations in the first search warrant affidavit were made with "reckless disregard for the truth." L.A.P.D. was incensed by that ruling, and the leak was probably motivated as "payback," or an attempt to upstage the negative publicity the judge's finding would generate.

We promptly made a motion for an evidentiary hearing to determine the source of this leak. We proposed putting those with knowledge within the L.A.P.D. under oath to find out who had knowledge of the results of preliminary testing and the plans for testing the socks. The concern we expressed went beyond the potential prejudice from the news stories. The jury had not yet been selected, and potential jurors were undoubtedly exposed to the news reports. But we were equally concerned that the leak could itself be proof of evidence tampering. Conceivably, an L.A.P.D. source was confident that DNA tests would produce a match with Nicole Brown Simpson's blood, because that same source had placed the blood on the socks, or knew someone else who had. Equally conceivable was the risk that the person who leaked the false information could make the information come true by splattering Nicole's blood on the socks. The motion was denied after Judge Ito received assurances that an internal investigation was being conducted by the L.A.P.D. itself to determine if the leaks came from them.

Ten months later, when the socks became a centerpiece in the defense effort to prove that evidence had been planted and manufactured, we again sought to ascertain the source of the leak. In the interim, of course, DNA testing *had* been performed on the socks and *had* produced a match to Nicole Brown Simpson's blood. And another journalist, Joseph Bosco, had published an article about the Simpson trial in the June 1995 issue of *Penthouse* magazine. Bosco wrote:

> . . . a certain police officer, whose leaks had hitherto been mostly accurate and offered with corroboration, started calling journalists with the story that blood on the socks found in O.J.'s bedroom was a DNA match with Nicole's. This time, however, the officer offered no corroboration, and became defensive and angry when asked. A number of journalists turned him down. Apparently, KNBC did not, and the rest is ugly history for both the press and the L.A.P.D.

Although it was hotly contested, the evidence we were able to muster that the blood on the socks was planted was persuasive. The seizure of the socks itself was suspicious, with an L.A.P.D. video technician confirming that the socks were not on the floor of Simpson's bedroom twenty minutes before Criminalist Dennis Fung testified he found them there. None of the L.A.P.D. criminalists or defense experts observed any blood on the socks. The first report of bloodstains on a sock didn't come until July, weeks after they were seized. A defense expert, Dr. Herbert McDonnell, testified that the presence of small, spherical blood drops dried on the interior surface opposite the stain in question led him to conclude the blood had been applied while the sock was lying flat, without a foot in it. That conclusion was later corroborated by Dr. Henry Lee. And another defense expert, Dr. Frederic Rieders, concluded that FBI tests revealed the presence of EDTA in the blood sample on the sock. EDTA is a preservative used to prevent the coagulation of blood samples in collection vials, and would not appear in the same concentration in natural blood.

We sought to corroborate the other evidence that the blood had been planted on the sock by proving that the news leak announc-

ing the results before the DNA testing had even been completed
came from within the L.A.P.D. For that purpose, we called both
KNBC newscaster Tracie Savage and *Penthouse* author Joseph Bosco
to the witness stand. We also demanded production of the internal
L.A.P.D. report of their investigation of the leak. As might be
expected, it was announced that their investigation cleared all
L.A.P.D. personnel of any responsibility, but the report itself remained confidential.

We were denied access to the L.A.P.D. report, on the ground it
was a "personnel" record protected by a statute designed to limit
defense "fishing" for adverse information about police officers accused of assaulting citizens. This is the same statute that was used
to deny us access to information about prior complaints against Detective Mark Fuhrman. Both rulings were strained. A statute that
was designed to regulate claims of police brutality was twisted and
distorted to permit the L.A.P.D. to conceal information that frus-
trated the fact-finding process.

Tracie Savage and Joseph Bosco both invoked the newsperson's
shield law, as anticipated. We argued that the limited privilege of
the shield law had to give way when it unduly infringed on the criminal defendant's right to a fair trial. A California Supreme Court
ruling declared that a defendant need only show a "reasonable possibility" that the shielded information will materially assist his defense. If the source of the leak turned out to be an officer with command authority in the L.A.P.D., or one of the laboratory personnel,
we believed a reasonable possibility existed that this would lend
strong corroboration to our claim the evidence had been tampered
with. The source of the leak himself could be summoned to the
witness stand, and closely questioned as to his or her motives and
knowledge.

Judge Ito seized on the inaccuracy of the leak to conclude that
the source was not knowledgeable or closely connected to the investigation. Therefore, he ruled, it was speculative to infer that the
source of the news leak, even if it were an L.A.P.D. officer, participated in planting evidence, or spoke with someone who did.

Judge Ito's ruling put an impossible burden on the defense. Instead of showing a "reasonable possibility," he required that the source be positively linked to the actual planting of evidence in advance. It was readily conceivable that the source had no knowledge that evidence was planted, but heard information from someone who was repeating information that could ultimately be traced to those who were handling evidence in the laboratory. The newsperson's shield law was thus transformed into an L.A.P.D. shield law. While the sources of news reports should be protected by a limited privilege, we had here an example of that privilege being abused to leak false information which prejudiced the defendant. That alone should have been relevant evidence for the defense to present to the jury, even if the name of the police source was never revealed.

Even though the law protecting leaks and shielding L.A.P.D. personnel records operated to the distinct disadvantage of O.J. Simpson, the legislative response to the case has been limited to finding more ways to muzzle defense lawyers. Citing what he described as the Simpson case "circus," State Senator Quentin L. Kopp of San Francisco sponsored a bill to require the state bar to adopt a disciplinary rule governing trial publicity by lawyers. The California State Bar reluctantly recommended a rule that would give maximum First Amendment protection for lawyer's statements, by requiring a showing of "clear and present danger" that a lawyer's statement threatened a fair trial before it could be prohibited. The California Supreme Court rejected that recommendation, and instead promulgated the American Bar Association's model rule to take effect in California on October 1, 1995. That rule is similar to the rule struck down by the Supreme Court in the Gentile case, with two differences. First, the exception for statements describing the "general nature" of the claim or defense, which the court found unconstitutionally vague, has been changed. The rule now permits only the "claim, offense or defense involved" itself to be identified. Second, a new exception permits a lawyer to respond to protect a client from the undue prejudicial effect of publicity initiated by someone else. The lawyer can release as much information as necessary to "mitigate the recent adverse publicity."

Even if this rule had been in effect during the Simpson trial, it would not have altered or changed anything that was done. The release of the 911 tapes by the L.A.P.D. would not have even been governed by the rule, since it applies only to the conduct of lawyers. And everything the defense did could be justified by the need to "mitigate" adverse publicity initiated by the L.A.P.D. The lack of guidance as to what lawyers can say or can't say also renders the mitigation exception just as vague and ambiguous as the exception struck down by the Supreme Court in the Gentile case.

The greater harm this rule will perpetrate, however, is that it will compound the problem of "leaks." Lawyers who lack clear guidance under the rule, rather than take a chance of facing bar discipline, will make their statements to the press as anonymous confidential sources protected by the newsperson's shield laws, rather than as identifiable persons speaking in public. To that extent, the public is the loser. The instant "solution" proposed by knee-jerk politicians and quickly approved by a compliant state supreme court will only make the problem worse.

Another swift legislative response to the case of *People v. O.J. Simpson* in California was the enactment of a prohibition of payments to witnesses for information. Like the lawyer's gag rule, it is poorly drafted and offers more new problems than solutions.

The checkbook journalism of the tabloid press was a source of constant anxiety for both sides during the trial of *People v. O.J. Simpson*. It was revealed during the preliminary hearing that several witnesses had received large payments from tabloid newspapers for exclusive rights to their "stories." In one instance, a grand jury witness who claimed to have seen O.J. Simpson driving his Bronco close to the alleged time of the murders was repudiated by the prosecution for selling her story. There was grave concern that the availability and the credibility of witnesses would be adversely affected by the behavior of journalists.

The California legislature responded swiftly with a law that went into effect on January 1, 1995, before the first witness was even called at the trial. The key provision is new Penal Code section 132.5, which makes it a misdemeanor for "a person who is a witness to an event or occurrence that he or she knows is a crime or who has personal knowledge of facts that he or she knows or reasonably should know may require that person to be called as a witness in a criminal prosecution" to accept or receive money or its equivalent in consideration for "providing information" obtained as a result of witnessing that event or having the personal knowledge, regardless of whether the information is provided for publication or for any other purpose.

Among those who most frequently pay for information about crimes, of course, are state and federal law enforcement officials. The rewards paid to informants with firsthand information would be encompassed by the broad language of Penal Code section 132.5, but for an exception which provides that the prohibition does not apply to "lawful compensation paid to an informant by a prosecutor or law enforcement agency." There is another limited exception for "statutorily authorized rewards offered by governmental agencies for information leading to the arrest or conviction of specified offenders."

The *informant* exception applies only to "law enforcement agencies," and the *reward* exception applies only to statutorily approved government rewards. The use of paid informants by private investigative agencies and private security companies is not unknown. That practice is now illegal in California. And the offering of private "rewards" is also quite common. It has become routine in child abduction cases, and a substantial reward was even offered on behalf of O.J. Simpson himself for information leading to the identification of the true killers. Accepting such rewards is now illegal in California. While the legislature might have been concerned about the sale of information to tabloids, they reacted with a statute so broad that it may do more harm than good.

Another curious exception to the new law might be called the "Rodney King" exception. The law provides that "information" does not include a "photograph, videotape, audiotape, or any other direct recording of an event or occurrence." Apparently, the logic of this exception is that the credibility of such evidence is not affected by its prior sale to *Hard Copy* or the *National Enquirer.*

The only punishment imposed by the new law is reserved for

the witness. The journalist who makes such payments suffers no consequences. In fact, the journalist is given a great excuse to renege on any promised payment by a provision declaring any such contract void as contrary to public policy.

A time limit of one year is imposed on Penal Code section 132.5, so a witness can sell information with impunity regarding offenses that occurred more than one year earlier, unless a prosecution has commenced. Another apparent oversight was not to provide protection if a grand jury investigation has commenced. A grand jury is not a prosecution, and the pendency of a secret grand jury investigation, even one year after a crime, makes information from witnesses a highly marketable commodity. Once a prosecution commences, sale of information by witnesses is forbidden until final judgment.

Most "legitimate" print journalists regard the payment of rewards to their sources with disdain. That disdain is not shared by reporters for tabloid newspapers and tabloid television shows. As already noted, the line between "legitimate" press and "tabloid" press became a blurry one during the Simpson case. At one point, when the *National Enquirer* ran a computer-simulated photo of a bruised and battered Nicole Brown Simpson, we asked ourselves, "Who would have ever thought that the *National Enquirer* would stoop to the level of *Time* magazine?" *Time* magazine set a sickening standard of journalistic integrity when they enhanced the booking photograph of O.J. Simpson for its cover so he would appear more black. We can anticipate that legislatures will continue to address the problems created when the behavior of journalists actually interferes with the pursuit of justice. But hopefully, other legislatures will approach the problem with greater care than the California legislature exercised.

The chief lesson from the leaks and gags of the Simpson case is that the police can engage in a public relations campaign to affect public opinion about a pending case with impunity. Gag rules cannot be enforced against them, and reporters' shield laws assure their anonymity. As long as that's the reality, defense lawyers who are worth their salt will do everything within their power to conduct their own public relations campaigns to cure the damage.

For journalists, the lesson seems to be that bad journalism drives out the good, just as economists tell us bad money drives out the good. The tabloids set the standard for press coverage of the Simpson case, and they were shameless in their pursuit of stories that would titillate and entertain. Their defense, of course, is that they are serving what the public wants. Our voracious appetite for gossip and scandal is what drives our mass media. The "legitimate" press are pushed by the instinct to survive, and for some the means of survival has become the emulation of the tabloids.

For the public, the lessons are simple ones. You are wise to give less credence to the statements of lawyers who speak on behalf of their clients. You would be wiser still to give no credence whatsoever to information coming from "a source close to the investigation." And give to the tabloid press the contempt they deserve, whenever they put on the pretensions of "journalism." They are first and foremost entertainers, and should be treated and regarded as such. Base your judgment upon the evidence that is admitted in court, and don't come to any conclusions until all of the evidence is in. If that admonition sounds familiar, it's because you've heard it before!

SEVEN

PICKING A JURY

*T*he suggestion that the defense was the first to play a "race card" at the climax of the trial of the case of *People v. O.J. Simpson* is somewhat silly. No part of a jury trial is more like a poker game than the jury selection, and during the jury selection, the prosecution played enough "race cards" to deal a round of seven card stud. What seems to be forgotten is that *both* sides had an equal opportunity to shape the jury, and *both* sides announced they were satisfied with the jury that was selected before the first witness was called. The defense was delighted with the outcome of jury selection, and the prosecution was almost immediately overcome with buyers' remorse. Ultimately, O.J. Simpson had four people to thank for the jury he got: Rodney King, District Attorney Gilbert Garcetti, Judge Lance Ito, and jury consultant Jo-Ellan Dimetrius.

O.J. Simpson never met Rodney King, but the trial of the police officers accused of beating Rodney King had a profound impact upon O.J. Simpson's trial. The King trial demonstrated the enormous impact the location of a trial can have upon the composition of the jury. The sprawling Los Angeles area is divided into a number of judicial districts. The greatest racial diversity is found in the central district, which is headquartered in the downtown criminal courts building. The least racial diversity is found in the San Fernando Valley, headquartered in Van Nuys, and on the west side, headquartered in Santa Monica. While ordinarily criminal trials end up in the district where the crime was committed, they can be freely transferred anywhere within Los Angeles County. The King trial was transferred to the Simi Valley, an area on the northern fringes of Los Angeles County that is even whiter than the San Fernando Valley. As a result, no African-American sat on the jury that acquitted the L.A.P.D. officers. When the same officers were subsequently charged with civil rights violations in federal court, the jury was selected from throughout the federal district, which produced greater racial diversity on the jury. The result, of course, was different—and that difference was widely attributed to the difference in the composition of the jury. Does that mean the second jury allowed race to influence their judgment to convict? No more so than the first jury let race influence their judgment to acquit. The reality is that the race of jurors is an important factor that affects their entire life experience, and life experience affects every judgment we make. Especially when assessing the credibility of police officers, African-Americans from South Central Los Angeles bring a different perspective to the jury room than white suburbanites from the Simi Valley.

In the wake of the riots that followed the acquittal of the L.A.P.D. officers who arrested Rodney King, there was a great deal of criticism of the Los Angeles County District Attorney for allowing the case to be assigned to the Simi Valley. The vigor with which the D.A.'s office prosecuted the police officers was questioned. Was racial gerrymandering of the jury part of a "soft ball" prosecution? At the next election, the District Attorney was defeated. His successor, Gilbert Garcetti, had strong support in the black community.

The case of *People v. O.J. Simpson* started out in the central district, because that's where the grand jury sits. The location of the crime was actually the west side, which would have put the case in Santa Monica. After the grand jury was dismissed, the preliminary hearing was already scheduled downtown. The inertia that kept it there was largely attributable to Rodney King. The District Attorney did not want to risk the criticism he would have gotten in the black community if he physically moved the case to Van Nuys or Santa Monica. After the case was over, he got criticized anyway, for *not* moving the case to Santa Monica, so there would have been fewer minorities in the jury pool. He responded to that criticism by first suggesting the earthquake-damaged Santa Monica courthouse could not have withstood the media crush, and later offering the almost laughable claim that it wouldn't have affected the composition of the jury anyway. The haunting history of the Rodney King trial was never mentioned.

Apparently, Los Angeles cannot make up its mind whether it *wants* its District Attorney to engage in racial gerrymandering when it comes to the location of a trial. The gerrymandering in Rodney King may have cost D.A. Robert Philibosian his job, and the failure to gerrymander in the Simpson trial may ultimately cost Gilbert Garcetti his job. The real message may be that Los Angeles voters want their District Attorney to win, and they don't much care how he does it, even if it takes racial gerrymandering. Why is it that efforts to get greater diversity on a jury are condemned, while efforts to limit the diversity of a jury are not? Either way, the motives include a "race card."

The diversity of the jury pool does not guarantee the diversity of the jury itself, however. Jurors are questioned about their attitudes and biases, and the attorneys for both sides have the opportunity to challenge jurors for cause, as well as to excuse a limited number of jurors without cause, or peremptorily.

The second important decision that affected the composition of Simpson's jury was the decision not to seek the death penalty. Even though the homicide included the "special circumstances" that could have qualified it for death penalty treatment (multiple victims), the prosecution's theory that the murder was motivated by the jealousy of an ex-spouse would have normally excluded it from consideration as a death case. Most Americans have little appreciation of the extent to which decisions whether to seek the death penalty or not are *political* decisions. There are 20,000 homicides in America every year, and approximately 200 defendants are sentenced to death each year. How does a homicide defendant get picked to be among the unlucky one in a hundred? Obviously, a prosecutor can't try *every* eligible homicide as a death penalty case, because the resources simply aren't available. Handling a case as a death case will typically triple the costs of the prosecution. Scarce resources require selective use of the death penalty. Prosecutors are elected officials. Thus, prosecutors tend to seek the death penalty most often against defendants who are particularly unpopular. The murder of a spouse is not ordinarily the kind of crime that arouses the passions of the community. The murder of black victims is like-wise given lower priority. Racial disparity of the perpetrator and the victim has been shown to be a significant factor in the current administration of the death penalty in America. A Texas study, for example, established it was ten times more likely that the death penalty would be sought for a black man who killed a white victim than for a white man who killed a black victim. If one took a cen-sus of the 3,000 current occupants of death rows in America, one would find very few men who were there just for killing their wives or ex-wives. One would find lots of men who were racial and eth-nic minorities. And one would look in vain for a millionaire of any color.

The most populous death rows are in states where the death penalty has greatest political popularity. Those states include Cal-ifornia, where the death row population now exceeds 300. But even within California, there is wide disparity among counties. In coun-ties where support for the death penalty is lowest, like San Fran-cisco, the death penalty is rarely sought, even though the homicide rate is comparable to counties like San Bernardino and Riverside, which are regularly among the highest contributors of death row inmates.

The Los Angeles County District Attorney's Office has been very sensitive to criticism that it was overusing or underusing the death penalty. The best way for a politician to deflect that kind of criticism is to create a committee. A committee of top line prose-cutors would make the recommendation to the District Attorney whether to seek the death penalty against O.J. Simpson. But the final call was still Gilbert Garcetti's.

Ultimately, his decision would have a significant impact upon the composition of the jury. In a death penalty case, jurors are routinely asked if they have conscientious objections to the death penalty that would prevent them from voting in favor of execution. If they do, they are excused for cause. It has been proven that, statistically, a "death qualified" jury is more likely to convict than one which includes those with objections to the death penalty. Thus, a prosecutor usually *enhances* his chances for a conviction by seeking the death penalty. This effect also impacts the likely racial composition of a jury. Polls consistently show a lower rate of support for the death penalty among minorities, so the rate of jurors excused for conscientious objections to the death penalty will be higher among minorities than among whites.

We were hardly in a position to mount a vigorous campaign against making O.J. Simpson's case a death penalty case. Usually, an attorney seeking to avoid the death penalty emphasizes "mitigating circumstances." Simpson asserted he was 100 percent innocent, and the credibility of his denial of guilt would have been undercut significantly by the suggestion he was concerned about ever facing a penalty phase trial to determine what punishment was appropriate. But many leaders in the African-American community in Los Angeles urged Garcetti *not* to seek the death penalty. The District Attorney also had to be concerned with the higher-than-normal level of public sympathy and support for O.J. Simpson. Seeking the death penalty might be perceived as overreaching and might increase sympathy for Simpson at the same time the prosecutors were mounting their media campaign to demonize him.

In response to the D.A.'s invitation, I compiled and submitted a routine letter to the death penalty committee, stressing Simpson's civic and charitable contributions to the community. The letter read like the nomination of a leading citizen for a community recognition award. It was hard to believe that its purpose was to persuade prosecutors to spare his life. My greatest fear was that the procedural advantages that would accrue to the prosecutors from the case being a capital case would be too hard to pass up. I fully anticipated the case would be a death penalty case and was pleasantly surprised by Garcetti's announcement that he would not seek the death penalty. I believe Garcetti's decision was a principled one that deserved a lot more credit than he received.

Another opportunity that lawyers have to shape the jury is by the exercise of peremptory challenges. For generations, lawyers exercised peremptory challenges based half on instinct and half on prejudice. I remember consulting all the standard manuals and textbooks the first time I had to pick a jury, in 1966, and finding the most bizarre collection of racial and ethnic stereotypes I had ever encountered. One manual I consulted for guidance in presenting an insanity defense advised:

> Least desirable [as a juror] would be the Roman Catholic with his emphasis on free will, moral responsibility and payment for sins. In addition, all fundamentalist faiths would be generally non-receptive to the defense. . . . For once the sentimental Irish and sympathetic Italian are to be avoided because of their affinity for Catholicism. More receptive strains may be found among the Scandinavian backgrounds. . . . Negroes are generally ill equipped to evaluate psychiatric testimony.

The older manuals didn't say a lot about black jurors. In many states, blacks were systematically excluded from the jury pool. As the law changed and more of them made it into the jury pools, many prosecutors then used their peremptory challenges to routinely excuse black jurors who were called into the jury box, especially if the defendant was black.

The problem was addressed by the California Supreme Court in a trend-setting decision in 1978, authored by Justice Stanley Mosk. The court ruled that peremptory challenges could not be used to systematically discriminate against a cognizable racial or ethnic group, or on the basis of gender. The United States Supreme Court finally adopted a similar rule in 1986, requiring all states to follow it. If a pattern of discrimination appears in the exercise of peremptory challenges, a lawyer for either side bears the burden of establishing that there is an explanation other than group bias for the challenges. If only one or two black jurors are excused, and others aren't, the necessary pattern would not appear. But if a prosecutor uses peremptories to ding every black juror in the pool, or uses all peremptories against blacks and none against other groups, the requisite pattern would be readily apparent.

Most cases fall between these two extremes, and it is not difficult for a prosecutor to come up with a plausible nonracial explanation for a peremptory challenge. In one recent Virginia case, the prosecutor explained that he used a peremptory challenge to excuse an African-American man not because he was black, but because he was wearing a crucifix, which he thought was evidence of an undesirable "sympathetic disposition." The Supreme Court of Virginia accepted that as a "race neutral" explanation.

The jury pool called for the Simpson case included substantial numbers of minorities. Each side had the same number of peremptory challenges, twenty. Although we had made a motion seeking extra peremptory challenges for the defense to compensate for the impact of the police and prosecutorial media campaign to prejudice the defendant, Judge Ito wisely declined to rule on that motion until we had exhausted the twenty challenges already allotted to us. We never did. The jury was selected after the prosecution exercised only ten of their twenty challenges, and the defense exercised nine of theirs. I believe the reason both sides accepted the jury when they did is because neither saw any prospects of doing any better than they already had, and there was a substantial risk the prosecution's exercise of peremptories would cross the line as a deliberate pattern of racial discrimination.

The ten peremptory challenges by the prosecution excused eight jurors who were African-Americans. The nine challenges by the defense excused five white jurors, one African-American, one Hispanic, and two Native Americans. The two sides alternated in exercising their peremptory challenges, and as each challenge was announced, the other side would ask to approach the bench. The bench conferences were to make objections that a pattern of racial discrimination had emerged. The lawyers offered race-neutral reasons for the challenges, but after using 80 percent of their peremptories to excuse blacks, the explanations offered by the prosecution were wearing thin. Even though the objections were being made at the bench out of the hearing of the jurors, the prosecution also faced the risk of a backlash from the remaining black jurors, because the discriminatory pattern of their challenges was so readily apparent. The representation of African-Americans in the jury pool was substantial enough that frequently another black juror was called to replace the one the prosecution had just excused. Thus, the "race cards" being played by the prosecution had been trumped by a Supreme Court decision, and by the numerical strength of minorities in the jury pool.

The defense was not as vulnerable in terms of the pattern of our challenges, although the number of whites we excused was higher than the number of minority jurors. Once the prosecution accepted the jury, we quickly accepted it too. If we had continued to exercise more of our peremptory challenges, the prosecutors would have been allowed to continue with additional peremptory challenges.

Judge Lance Ito's approach to jury selection contributed greatly to the lawyers having sufficient information to exercise their peremptory challenges intelligently, rather than on the basis of mere guesses. Both sides probably knew more about the prospective jurors than in any other modern trial. This was because Judge Ito administered an extensive juror questionnaire, allowed the attorneys to personally conduct the questioning of prospective jurors, known as *voir dire*, and applied a fair standard on challenges for cause. With respect to jury selection, Judge Ito deserved an A+ for fairness. Most defense lawyers would agree that if a judge is going to put the screws to you, better that it should be on evidentiary rulings or jury instructions than in jury selection. The last place you want judicial bias to show up is in jury selection, because the bias inevitably infects the jurors themselves.

The jury questionnaire was necessary because of the unprecedented barrage of pretrial publicity. The lawyers needed to know what information a prospective juror had been exposed to, and what impact it was likely to have on his or her attitude. In finding that out, they also learned much about the lifestyles and attitudes of the jurors. Both sides submitted proposed questions, and Judge Ito composed the final questionnaire, allowing most of the items requested by both sides, as well as a fair selection of items requested only by one side or the other. Both sides had equal access to the information in the questionnaires before questioning the jurors, permitting the questioning to be much more focused and expeditious.

The judge did not have to permit the lawyers to conduct *voir dire* questioning. Another clause in the far-reaching criminal justice initiative known as Proposition 115 repealed a statute giving lawyers the absolute right to question jurors. Although this "reform" was pushed by prosecutors, many of them began to have second thoughts after the proposition went into effect in 1990. The rate of hung juries went up, because on occasion the antiprosecution bias of a juror was not being exposed by the perfunctory *voir dire* questioning conducted by many judges. Ironically, some prosecutors are now using the slight increase in the rate of hung juries to justify abolition of the requirement of jury unanimity. Judges simply are not in a position to engage in probing questioning that will expose the bias of jurors. Typically, they simply ask the jurors who are prejudiced to raise their hands. Even the most biased jurors will rarely recognize or admit that they are prejudiced.

The Simpson case required skillful questioning by the lawyers because nearly all of the prospective jurors acknowledged they had been exposed to prejudicial pretrial publicity. The question was whether they could ignore its impact and follow the judge's instructions to decide the case based on the evidence.

The *voir dire* questioning was the only phase of the trial that was not televised. While I was not present for all of it, the several days of it I watched were fascinating. I remember wishing that we had video, so I could use it to instruct law students on how a jury should be selected. Each side was given a limited opportunity (fifteen to twenty minutes) to question an individual juror. The lawyers took turns with successive jurors. Johnnie Cochran and Bob Shapiro alternated for the defense, while Marcia Clark and Bill Hodgman alternated for the prosecution. Chris Darden had not yet been assigned to the prosecution's trial team. Each of the four lawyers had their own unique style in engaging the prospective jurors, and all four were very effective in getting the jurors to "open up." I had never seen better *voir dire* questioning. It was my first opportunity to see Johnnie Cochran in action, and I found it to be a remarkable performance. His relaxed charm and humor were genuine and fully engaging. The jurors warmed up to him immediately. A bond of trust was established.

One reason neither side used more than half of their peremptory challenges was because Judge Ito readily excused jurors on challenges for cause. Even though the legal standard for a challenge for cause appears to be a clear and objective one, judges differ widely in their willingness to accept assurances of objectivity. Lawyers who do not want to lose a juror biased in their favor can easily elicit the juror's assurance she can be "fair." In a recent Louisiana Supreme Court decision, the court held a judge was not required to excuse from the jury a prison guard who had gone to the funeral home to visit the body of the murder victim, because she "assured the trial court of her impartiality." Another case from North Carolina allowed a fellow prosecutor from the same District Attorney's office as the prosecutor trying the case to sit as a juror because he told the judge he could "overcome the difficulty" to remain objective. When I read decisions like these, I can only say, "Who's kidding who here?" This is the main reason peremptory challenges should not be abolished. They serve as a safety valve, so lawyers can get rid of biased jurors that judges will not get rid of, because they do not want to offend anyone. While the number of peremptory challenges currently allowed may give the lawyers too much opportunity to shape the jury, the appropriate solution is not to abolish them altogether.

The final person on the list of those O.J. Simpson can thank for the jury he got is Jo-Ellan Dimetrius, who served the defense team as jury consultant. The role of the jury consultant is widely misconstrued by those who attribute magical powers of prediction to behavioral scientists. What jury consultants do is the same thing lawyers have always done: They make educated guesses. Lawyers know they are just guessing when it comes to predicting how any particular juror will decide the case. But a good lawyer will want the guesses to be informed by as much information as can be legally gathered. A good jury consultant is able to methodically collect valuable information about jurors, and concisely present it in a way that the lawyer can effectively use in questioning prospective jurors, challenging them, and ultimately persuading the jurors who are selected.

Bob Shapiro presided over the rigorous process of interviewing several potential jury consultants. The choice of Jo-Ellan Dimetrius was obvious and unanimous. She had extensive experience in several high-profile trials in Los Angeles, including the Rodney King case. Most important, she was well acquainted with the central district of Los Angeles and proposed to focus her energy and research on the true "peers" of our jurors. All the public opinion polls done by the defense to reveal community attitudes toward the case and toward its participants were done in the central district. The occasional "focus groups" in which a cross section of laypersons were gathered to give firsthand reactions to proposed evidence or trial strategy, were conducted in the central district. When the prosecutors did a pretrial "focus group," they went to Phoenix, Arizona!

Jo-Ellan prepared the defense's proposed jury questionnaire and tabulated the responses to the questionnaire administered by Judge Ito. She briefed the lawyers before their *voir dire* questioning and closely observed the body language and reactions of prospective jurors as they were questioned. At key points throughout the trial, she was in court to assess juror reactions to the evidence and the witnesses. She continued to poll public reaction in the central district during the trial, and the data produced were helpful even in deciding which lawyers should play which roles as the trial unfolded. When issues came up regarding juror misconduct, she was a knowlegeable and well-informed strategist. But everything she did was directed toward assisting the lawyers to do the job they had to do and make the decisions they had to make, empowered by more reliable information. Suggesting that lawyers should not be permitted to employ jury consultants is like suggesting lawyers should not be permitted to employ secretaries or investigators or paralegals.

Ultimately, both sides were still guessing, right up to the return of the verdict. Predicting human behavior will never be an exact science, but keeping what progress we have made from being used in the courtroom is imprudent. A lot more can be done for defendants who can't afford a jury consultant. Jury questionnaires should be standardized, and the information they gather should be readily available to both sides in every jury trial. Those we train as trial lawyers should be familiar with the tools of modern psychology, rather than with the racial stereotypes of old wives' tales. If we impose a regimen of ignorance upon the jury selection process, as many advocate by restricting lawyer participation in *voir dire*, we end up with greater deference to prejudices and stereotypes. The lesson from the jury selection process in *People v. O.J. Simpson* is that diversity on juries does make a difference, and many of the decisions and strategies employed by the lawyers can drastically affect that diversity. Some of these decisions are political decisions, such as where the case will be tried, or whether the death penalty will be sought. Those decisions remain in the exclusive domain of prosecutorial discretion and are unchecked by our adversary process. Although these decisions in the Simpson case actually benefited the defendant, these are still the decisions with the greatest potential for abuse. We have little to fear from the decisions and strategies that are equally accessible to both sides and constantly checked by the adversary process.

EIGHT

CAMERAS IN COURT

*I*t is hard for me to think seriously about the issue of televising criminal trials without ambivalence. The professor and educator in me want to embrace the concept. Television is a powerful teaching tool. In teaching law students the skills of advocacy, I have seen the power of a video demonstration outperform even the most dynamic lecture, again and again. If only some of Clarence Darrow's trials had been televised, we would have a treasure trove from which to learn. The criminal defense lawyer in me, however, is repelled by the concept. The television camera seduces us into thinking we can be unseen observers, but it subtly transforms the events it transmits. Our courtrooms are among the last refuges for rational discourse in a world drowning in hype. Once we convert the courtroom to a "set," we transform the lawyers, witnesses, and judges into "performers."

During the course of the past two years, I have actually shifted my position on this issue twice. I started out as an enthusiastic proponent. When I went to Los Angeles to participate in the preliminary hearing, I was excited about the opportunity to take part in a national colloquium on our criminal justice system. The tiny courtroom would accommodate less than 100 observers, but the television camera allowed millions to watch the system in action. The motion to suppress could spark a national debate, reacquainting the whole country with the Fourth Amendment and the values it protects. Halfway through the trial, I realized that the behavior of the participants was different from the conduct I'd observed in other trials. Everyone thought they were seeing the "system" in action, but this was not the "system" at all. It was a distortion. The television camera was transforming what it observed into something different. I decided the cameras were a mistake.

Since the verdict, I've reconsidered my position. I find the opponents of televised trials espousing a rigid, all-or-nothing approach that ignores some of the potential benefits of cameras in court. While I remain convinced that the harm outweighed the benefits in the Simpson trial, I do not see how that justifies a flat prohibition of televised coverage of all future trials. The excesses of the Simpson trial were baggage that comes with a "trial of the century" and may not be a problem in a more routine case.

With tongue in cheek, I offered a practical guide to enable lawyers to ascertain at an early stage whether a case will be a "trial of the century," so they will be on guard against the dangers of television cameras. Here are my "top ten indicators" that a case is likely to become a "trial of the century":

10. The cops are filing copies of their investigative reports with *Hard Copy*.
9. The potential jurors already have book deals.
8. The District Attorney issues a press release announcing the case will be handled just like any other case in the office, then assigns fourteen deputies to handle pretrial motions.
7. Your voice mail contains an urgent message to call Gerry Spence.
6. Your trash Dumpster is emptied on Tuesday, although the trash man comes on Thursdays.
5. The judge stops going to the barbershop, and starts going to a hair salon.
4. You receive affectionate letters from law school classmates you haven't seen in twenty years.

3.   You notice less than affectionate messages from the pub-
     lic scrawled in the dirt of your unwashed car.

2.   All of the witnesses you subpoena retain their own law-
     yers, including the defendant's mother.

1.   The judge takes all of your motions under submission,
     so the rulings can be timed for the prime-time newscasts.

For a "trial of the century," adding television cameras in the
courtroom is like throwing gasoline on a fire. It transforms the proceedings into a sort of "hype heaven," where exaggeration knows
no limits. Like a presidential campaign. When I found time to watch
the evening talk shows after a day in court, I often found it hard to
believe these were intelligent adults speaking. The events were being reported like a football game, with the same testimony being
characterized as a touchdown for the defense or a twenty-yard loss,
depending on the commentator. The television coverage enabled all
the pundits and commentators to speak with authority, as though
they had been there. I realized many of them had not even watched
the proceedings but were relying on a ten-minute "briefing" on the
day's events they received just before going on the air.

I will never forget the day I argued a motion regarding the scope
of cross-examination of the coroner. The prosecution filed a motion
to prevent us from cross-examining Dr. Irwin Golden about mistakes he had made in other autopsies, and about an incident after
his testimony at the preliminary hearing in which he displayed a
gun and made threats against the Simpson defense lawyers. Judge
Ito ruled that the mistakes could come in but the threats could
not. Ultimately, the prosecution never called Dr. Golden. That
evening, I watched Gerry Spence pontificating on the *Geraldo*
show. He took the defense to task for "making a motion first."
"They should just get up and ask the questions," he said, without
seeking the judge's permission first. Obviously he never looked at
any of the papers filed in the case, or he would have known that the
defense did not even file a motion; we were responding to a motion
filed by the prosecution to *prevent* us from asking questions they
anticipated. Apparently, he had not watched the argument.

Most of the regular commentators and pundits had an obvious bias. They had decided which way the case should turn out, and the "spin" they placed on the day's events invariably led to the result they favored. It was most amusing to hear all the predictions of a conviction on the night before the verdict came in. For us, it was relatively simple to figure out that the verdict was very likely to be an acquittal. Only seven minutes had elapsed between the time the jury asked to have the verdict forms, and the time they signaled they were ready to return their verdicts. The forms required the jurors to decide a lot more that just guilt or innocence. If the verdict had been "guilty," they would have had to determine whether it was first or second degree, whether the "special circumstances" were proven, and whether the enhancement for use of a weapon was established. Just the mechanics of filling out a "guilty" verdict form would have taken longer than seven minutes. The commentators were all grasping at straws to bolster a conclusion that was consistent with their own bias.

Some of the television coverage was objective and well balanced. Court TV did especially well in presenting well-informed and balanced commentary by guests who were actually watching the proceedings or reading the motions and responses. But television is subject to the same inexorable law that seems to govern all journalism: Bad journalism drives out the good. Just as tabloids set the tone of press coverage, the television tabloids set the tone of television coverage. Once the cameras are admitted to the courtroom, you can't control the coverage and limit it to Court TV.

I realize that the argument I am making is equally applicable to the print media. The law is clear that we cannot exclude the press from court proceedings except in highly unusual circumstances. And we cannot pick and choose, saying we will let the *New York Times* in because their coverage is objective and balanced, but we'll keep the *National Enquirer* out because their coverage is sensationalistic and tasteless. Presently, however, the law recognizes a distinction between television cameras and print media. The television cameras may be excluded even when the news reporters are admitted. In federal courts, from the United States Supreme Court on down, television cameras have been completely excluded. In California, current rules leave it to the discretion and control of the trial judge. Since the Simpson trial, virtually every request to televise courtroom proceedings has been denied.

In most cases, television cameras will have no greater impact on the proceedings than any other media intrusion. When a newspaper reporter walks into a courtroom, everyone knows it. The lawyers carefully spell their names for the judge, and they argue with a little more flourish. The judges rule with a little more caution and explain their rulings with greater care. One may even argue that the prospect of public exposure enhances the quality of justice. In a routine case, a single television camera will not affect the behavior of the participants any more than a reporter whose pencil is poised.

Long before television, many trials were the object of intense public interest. In rural America, trials were scheduled on "market day," when all the local farmers converged on the county seat. Courtrooms were built to accommodate huge crowds of two or three hundred observers. There were pundits and commentators, too. Reading some of the early newspaper reports of court proceedings is almost like reading theater reviews, in which lawyers are lavishly praised or roundly castigated for their performances. One of my favorite examples is a story that ran in the *San Francisco Call* on September 29, 1864. Under the headline ADVICE TO WITNESSES, it described the ineptitude of a prosecutor who was obsessed with asking every witness six times if the events "took place in the City and County of San Francisco?" The reporter concluded:

> The prosecuting attorney may mean well enough, but meaning well and doing well are two different things. His abilities are of the mildest description, and do not fit him for a position like the one he holds, where energy, industry, tact, shrewdness, and some little smattering of law, are indispensable to the proper fulfillment of its duties. Criminals leak through his fingers every day like water through a seive. He affords a great deal less than no assistance to the

judge, who could convict sometimes if the district attorney would remain silent, or if the law had not hired him at a salary of two hundred and fifty dollars a month to unearth the dark and ominous fact that the offense was committed in the city and county of San Francisco. The man means well enough, but he don't know how; he makes of the proceedings in behalf of a sacred right and justice in the police court, a driveling farce, and he ought to show his regard for the public welfare by resigning.

The police court reporter who authored that devastating critique went on to a distinguished literary career. His name was Mark Twain. Occasionally I felt a kinship to the prosecutor who was his victim. At one point in the trial, Johnnie Cochran strongly suggested that the lawyers not watch television after a day in court, lest they be totally deflated by their bad reviews.

The chief proponent of courtroom television is Steve Brill, who directs the operations of Court TV. I have noticed a subtle shift in his pitch since the Simpson trial. He used to argue that television cameras should be allowed in court because it will educate the public about the justice system and increase public support for the courts. Now he argues that the cameras should be allowed in court because they can show America what's wrong with our justice system and what needs to be fixed. To borrow a term from the trial, the argument is disingenuous. The cameras in the Simpson courtroom may not have been broadcasting "what's wrong with our justice system," but rather "what can go wrong with our justice system when television cameras are present." Most of the criticism I have heard of the trial involved conduct exacerbated by the presence of the cameras. For example, many have suggested the trial simply went on too long. I'm convinced the trial would have been over much sooner if it had not been televised. There were frequent interruptions just to deal with problems created by the cameras. A long parade of media lawyers marched into court every time Judge Ito threatened to pull the plug, filed motions and presented arguments, while the prosecution and defense lawyers watched from the sidelines Without exception, the media lawyers were excellent. I thought the advocacy of Floyd Abrams and Kelly Sager was superb and a pleasure to watch. But it did nothing to advance the case of *People v. O.J. Simpson* to an expeditious conclusion. Some of the interminable testimony seemed to have no other purpose than to showcase the talent of a lawyer for the camera. I managed to sneak off for a two-week trip to Europe to visit my daughters right in the middle of the trial. I left when the coroner was being sworn in. When I returned, he was still on the witness stand. And I hadn't missed a thing. Bob Shapiro's cursory cross-examination was a high point of the trial, because it demonstrated how little two weeks of testimony had advanced the resolution of anything at issue in the case. Brian Kelberg is a brilliant lawyer, but apparently fifteen minutes of fame was not enough for him. He needed sixty hours.

Another valid criticism was the sniping and snarling among the lawyers. The level of petulance and personal vituperation achieved a new low for the American bar. There were lots of reasons for this besides the presence of television cameras. I am convinced that the unique culture of the Los Angeles Criminal Courts Building is also to blame. I had never encountered a District Attorney's office which seems to apply a universal, irrebutable presumption that all defense lawyers, without exception, are amoral sleazoids who are beneath contempt. This level of affection seems to be fully reciprocated by the Los Angeles criminal defense bar. It was a telling moment for me when Deputy District Attorney Shari Lewis responded to some courtroom repartee about how the prosecutors would have no appreciation of the pressures defense lawyers faced until they became defense lawyers themselves. She said she would never consider becoming a defense lawyer. The British system, where barristers represent the prosecution one day and the defense the next day has much to recommend it. The adversary system thrives when advocates have mutual respect for each other's roles. In Los Angeles, however, a "we're the good guys, you're the bad guys" mentality pervades the prosecutor's office.

In any event, the television camera exacerbated the problem. Winning and losing became a daily event, and the lawyers were motivated to capture the momentum for the evening news with a dramatic "put-down" of the other side. It was a sure sound bite and an easy way to regain momentum on a bad day.

The witnesses bore the greatest brunt of media intrusion into their lives, and we may never be able to sort out all of the ways their credibility was enhanced or diminished by their celebrity. Some may profit, while others will bear lifelong scars. But we have lost our sense of proportion when we strip away any claims to privacy for anyone who approaches the witness box. Candidates for public office invite public scrutiny of their private lives by seeking a public trust. But citizens who simply turn out to be in the right place at the wrong time by walking their dogs hardly deserve to be treated with the same indignity and insult ordinarily reserved for nominees for the Supreme Court or Surgeon General. While some witnesses testified as though they were auditioning for a gig, others sought to avoid service of a subpoena because they didn't want to come near the courtroom.

It is no answer to blame all of the excesses of the trial on Judge Ito in order to absolve the television cameras. It is clear, however, that the presence of the cameras made Judge Ito's job more difficult. Some have suggested Judge Ito enjoyed his celebrity, basking in the warm glow of the television cameras. I did not believe that for a minute. I think he sincerely felt that a valuable educational mission was being accomplished by televising the trial. But he created enormous pressure for himself, and I am sure he was aware that at times he too found himself performing in ways he might not have if the cameras had not been there. Despite his courtroom becoming a theater for an audience of forty million, though, it remained a comfortable and hospitable environment for the lawyers to work. That was attributable to his unflappable judicial patience and fundamental decency.

On the other side of the ledger, some tremendous benefits accrued from the television coverage. Both sides were the beneficiaries of evidence that might never have come to light but for the television cameras. Kathleen Bell, one of the key defense witnesses available to impeach Detective Mark Fuhrman, stepped forward after she recognized Fuhrman when she saw his testimony on television during the preliminary hearing. Dozens of viewers volunteered photographs of O.J. Simpson wearing gloves during halftime telecasts at football games, and several of them even testified as witnesses for the prosecution. The ability to tune in the trial enabled many of the lawyers and investigators to follow the case without being in the courtroom. I certainly appreciated being able to stay on top of the case even while I was teaching a course at Stanford University School of Law four hundred miles away. Alan Dershowitz kept abreast of the daily proceedings while teaching at Harvard and would frequently fax ideas or suggestions right into the courtroom. The video of the trial will continue to be a valuable teaching resource, not only for law schools but for other educational programs as well. There might even have been an improvement in our national vocabulary, with expressions like "plaintive wail," "disingenuous," and "waxing and waning" becoming part of our lexicon. And although the dialogue was much too brief, we began some serious public discussion of the problems of spousal abuse, police perjury, and racism.

Ultimately, it boils down to a question of degree. It is certainly possible for a trial to be televised without completely losing our sense of proportion. Television coverage can provide a valuable public resource for educational purposes. But some cases present a greater risk that the proceedings will be converted to a circus. Television cameras greatly exacerbate that risk. Rather than a flat prohibition of television cameras, we need guidelines to refine the exercise of discretion by judges. We need to identify the risk factors that should counsel against television coverage. The lesson from the cameras in the courtroom at the Simpson trial is that television cameras come equipped with a little button to turn them on and off. There are cases when we should leave the button on, and cases when we should switch it off. We have the intelligence to figure out when we should push the button. After all, our television sets have such buttons too. During the trial, I was accosted at an airport by a lady who wanted to complain about how much time she had to spend watching the trial. She seemed taken aback when

I asked her if her remote control had one of those little red buttons labeled "power." We all have the power in our hands to turn our television sets on and off. All we lack is the discipline.

In a presentation to the Los Angeles County Board of Supervisors, it was seriously proposed that if a retrial of the Simpson case was required, it be booked into the Schubert Theater, and tickets be sold to the public for fifty dollars a seat. This would raise funds to meet the estimated ten million dollars the trial cost the public. Another suggestion was that the county claim the authority to sell television rights to the highest bidder, much like television rights are sold for sporting events. There is a certain irony to the suggestion that the government cash in on the entertainment value of trials. How long would it be before police and prosecutors went looking for cases that would have greater earning potential as entertainment events? We could end up with a trial of the century every month, instead of the current rate of one every three years.

I stubbornly cling to the vision of our courts as bastions of thoughtful reflection and dispassionate analysis. Television cameras do little to enhance either, and can do much to corrupt both.

DOMESTIC DISCORD

I first learned about the power of labels as a young prosecutor in the U.S. Attorney's office in Los Angeles in the 1960s. I was assigned to a special section of the office to investigate and prosecute "organized crime." It was amazing to observe the transformation that took place when the label "organized crime" was affixed to a case. Across the street in the state courts, a routine bookmaking case typically was disposed of with a quick guilty plea and a fine of $1,000. When the same case was brought into federal court and called an "organized crime" case, suddenly there was press interest, high-powered defense lawyers, and judges ready to throw the book at the defendant. We had a rubber stamp to affix the label to our files in three-inch-high red letters: ORGANIZED CRIME & RACKETEERING. I was always careful to carry the files into court with the label showing. There were lots of subtle ways to communicate the label to the jury as well. The indictment could be packed with aliases, so each time it was read, the jury would be reminded that the defendant was "also known as Ice Pick Willie" or "Bankroll Bill." An "expert witness" could be called to explain the "secret code words" used to communicate within the syndicate, and the law of "omerta" that bound the conspirators to a pledge of silence.

Today, the process is much the same. Only the labels have changed. The labels a prosecutor loves to affix to the defendant's forehead in a homicide case are "batterer" and "stalker." From the outset, the prosecution labeled the murders of Nicole Brown Simpson and Ronald Goldman a case of domestic violence. That label had abolutely nothing to do with any evidence found at the scene of the crime. Domestic violence homicides rarely present two victims with their throats slashed. Domestic violence homicides are most often preceded by loud, angry arguments. Domestic violence homicides usually occur inside the home, not on the front walk. Turning the case into a domestic violence homicide, however, offered some obvious advantages for the prosecution. The most obvious was the incredible power of the label. Portraying O.J. Simpson as a wife-batterer was a quick and easy way to demonize him and neutralize his image as a sports hero. The overnight shift in public opinion when the 911 tapes were released fully vindicated the strategy, and that strategy became the linchpin of the prosecution's case.

As we sifted through the pretrial discovery and saw the investigative trail the prosecution was pursuing, we realized that much of it would not be admissible under the California Evidence Code. The prosecution was delving into every crevice of a sixteen-year relationship, looking for witnesses to every harsh word that ever passed between O.J. Simpson and Nicole Brown Simpson. And they weren't stopping there. Simpson's prior marriage, which ended in divorce seventeen years earlier, was also being scrutinized. Neighbors who lived next door to Simpson and his first wife twenty years before were being asked to dredge up any loud arguments they might have heard. Most alarming was their reliance upon a sleazy tabloid book as the source of most of the investigative leads they were pursuing. Within four months after the murders, Dove Books published Nicole Brown Simpson, *The Private Diary of a Life Interrupted*, by Faye Resnick. Resnick was a close friend of Nicole Brown Simpson, who had actually been living in Nicole's condo. Shortly before the murders, she was placed in a drug rehabilitation program. The book was a trashy "exposé," purporting to describe intimate details of the relationship between Nicole and O.J. Simpson. I wanted to take a shower after reading it. Faye Resnick was never called as a witness by the prosecution, because they knew her credibility would have been shredded. She had no personal knowledge of what happened the night of June 12, but she was willing to speculate based on half-baked rumors, hearsay, and a lot of imagination. Her exploitive book provided the blueprint for the prosecution's investigation, however.

The motions challenging the admissibility of all of the "evidence" of domestic discord the prosecution was amassing would have to be heard prior to trial. We had opposed sequestration of the jury and were gravely concerned that the hearing of our motions would expose all of these allegations to media attention, risking that they would then seep through to the jury. We would gain little by winning a ruling that much of this evidence was inadmissible, if the jury had learned of its existence anyway. We resolved the dilemma by reversing our position on sequestration. Locking up the jury was not a happy prospect, but we liked the jury we had, and saw grave risk of losing many of them if they were exposed to the media feeding frenzy that would accompany the litigation of the domestic discord evidence.

The use of the term "domestic discord" itself engendered controversy. Knowing the power of labels, we certainly didn't want to assist the prosecution in pasting the labels "batterer," "stalker," or "abuser" on our client. We didn't even want to call our motion a motion to exclude evidence of "battering," "stalking," or "abusing." Those are value-loaded conclusions that didn't even fit the evidence in question. We labeled our motion a motion "to exclude evidence of domestic discord," and included in the motion itself a request that the prosecution be precluded from using terms like "battering" and "stalking" in front of the jury.

The evidence we sought to exclude could legally be admitted for only one purpose at trial. That purpose is defined by Section 1101 of the California Evidence Code. Section 1101 preserves a fundamental principle of criminal law that is centuries old. That principle is that we punish people only for the criminal act with which they are charged. We may not punish them because we conclude they are "bad persons," or have done other bad things in the past.

O.J. Simpson was charged with the brutal murders of two people. He was not charged with being a "wife batterer" or a bad husband. Any prior incidents involving Simpson and his wife would be relevant evidence only if they helped prove what happened on the night of June 12. The prosecution's argument was based on exceptions spelled out in Section 1101(b) of the Evidence Code, which allows evidence of prior bad acts "when relevant to prove some fact (such as motive, opportunity, intent, preparation, plan, knowledge, identity, absence of mistake or accident) other than the defendant's disposition to commit such acts." The key to these exceptions is the similarity between the prior bad acts and the act for which the defendant is on trial. If, for example, on a prior occasion, O.J. Simpson had slashed his wife with a knife, or threatened to do so, that might be relevant to prove he was the person who slashed the victims on June 12. If on a prior occasion O.J. Simpson had become uncontrollably enraged and homicidal when seeing his wife in a romantic interlude with another man, that might be relevant to show he had a motive to kill the victims on June 12. But if the only thing the evidence of prior bad acts showed was that O.J. Simpson was a bad person, and bad persons are more likely to murder than good persons, it was irrelevant. Not because that is an illogical inference. Bad persons are more likely to murder than good persons. But we do not want to take the risk that a person might be convicted of a serious crime simply because the jury believes he's a bad person. We want to insist on evidence he actually did the bad act he is charged with.

Viewed from this perspective, the prior incidents of domestic discord the prosecution wanted to offer proved very little about what happened on the night of June 12. There was only one incident of physical assault, where O.J. Simpson actually laid a hand on Nicole Brown Simpson. That occurred January 1, 1989, more than five years prior to the homicide. After a New Year's Eve that included drinking by both Mr. Simpson and his wife, they got into a loud argument in the bedroom of their Rockingham residence. Simpson allegedly struck Nicole on the forehead and slapped her several times. Police responded to a 911 call and found Nicole in the bushes near the house. Although three days later she stated she did not wish to prosecute, misdemeanor battery charges were filed, and Mr. Simpson entered a plea of "no contest." He was sentenced to probation conditional on counseling, and he successfully completed all the terms and conditions of probation. Those terms included over 100 hours of community service, which he completed by visiting homes for abandoned and abused children and speaking to community groups.

This incident is certainly nothing for O.J. Simpson to be proud of. But to turn it into a prelude to murder five years later stretches credulity to the breaking point. Studies of domestic violence in America confirm that approximately two and a half million incidents very similar to this take place every year. One recent study revealed that 31.6 percent of married women report that their husbands have pushed, grabbed, or shoved them, 17.6 percent reported slapping, and 16 percent reported a husband throwing something at them. Women should not tolerate that kind of abuse. They should report it and seek intervention. But what is the likelihood that the angry husband who slapped them will subsequently slash their throats with a knife? Mathematically, the probability is easy to compute. There are 1,500 murders of women by husbands or boyfriends each year, compared to 2,500,000 "batterings." That's a ratio of .0006 to 1. Where the identity of a murderer is not known, evidence that the victim was struck by her husband five years before does not take us very far in establishing the identity of the murderer.

Contrary to all the hype about the "system" failing Nicole Brown Simpson, the "system" performed remarkably well in the wake of the 1989 incident. O.J. Simpson learned an important lesson. He never laid a hand on Nicole Brown Simpson again. Not one shred of evidence was ever produced to suggest any physical assault after January 1, 1989. Part of the motivation may have been an agreement Simpson signed, that if he ever assaulted Nicole Brown Simpson again, he would waive any rights he had under their prenuptial contract. When they divorced three years later, Nicole never made any claim that the agreement had been broken. If it had, it would have had significant financial consequences in the divorce.

Actually, much of the so-called "evidence" of abuse by Simpson was compiled as ammunition to bolster Nicole's position in the divorce. The prosecutors quoted from what they called a "diary" prepared by Nicole. Far from a diary prepared contemporaneously with the events it purports to describe, it was a summary prepared to gain an advantage in divorce litigation, compiled years after the events took place. It was clearly inadmissible because it was hearsay evidence, not subject to cross-examination.

The prosecution also offered two incidents involving damage to property as "prior bad acts." The first occurred in late 1984 or early 1985, before O.J. and Nicole were even married. Police were summoned to the Rockingham residence and encountered O.J. and Nicole in the driveway. Nicole claimed that O.J. had broken the windshield of her Mercedes-Benz with a baseball bat. She declined to press charges, and the police did not even bother to file a report about the incident. It came to light only because the L.A.P.D. officer who responded to that call, and later claimed to have an "indelible memory" of it, was Mark Fuhrman. The second incident resulted in the infamous 911 call in October 1993. By then, the Simpsons had divorced, but were attempting a reconciliation while Nicole maintained her separate residence. Mr. Simpson objected to a display of photos of persons with whom Nicole had romantic relationships during their separation. O.J. Simpson left her residence, and when he returned later, found the doors locked. He kicked in a french door to gain entry, and then berated Nicole over her relationship with Keith Zlomsowitch. No physical assault occurred, and the entire incident was witnessed by Kato Kaelin, who was living in Nicole's guest house at the time.

Neither of these incidents bore any resemblance to what happened the evening of June 12, 1994. If they proved anything, they proved that O.J. Simpson occasionally displayed a bad temper and a foul mouth. Under the Evidence Code, evidence showing a bad temper and a foul mouth is irrelevant. These incidents were inadmissible unless they showed the identity of the killer or his motive or intent. For that purpose, they were useless. If the murderer had broken the windshield of Nicole's car with a baseball bat, or left a french door unhinged, a plausible argument might have been made that these incidents were relevant. But the murders bore no resemblance to anything O.J. Simpson had ever done or threatened to do.

The Keith Zlomsowitch incident came as close as the prosecution ever got to a relevant prior incident. In April 1992, O.J. Simpson observed Nicole and Keith engaged in sexual activity on the couch in her living room. The activity, which included oral copulation, was fully visible to anyone approaching the front door. Mr. Simpson did not interrupt them. The following day, in an angry but nonphysical exchange when he encountered Mr. Zlomsowitch giving Nicole a massage, Mr. Simpson expressed his concern that their sexual activity was occurring in the presence of his children.

The prosecution attempted to characterize this as "stalking." If their theory was that the June 12 murders occurred while Mr. Simpson was stalking his ex-wife, the Zlomsowitch incident really refuted their theory. If Mr. Simpson could restrain himself while observing his ex-wife engaged in sexual activity with another man, why would he fly into uncontrollable rage upon seeing her talking to Ronald Goldman on the sidewalk?

When we filed our pretrial motion to exclude the evidence of domestic discord, we included every conceivable incident that might be offered, including many from Faye Resnick's book and events stretching back fifteen or sixteen years. It was doubtful the prosecution could even produce credible evidence of many of these incidents, but we wanted our objections clear on the record. Judge Ito's ruling gave the most expansive reading ever given to the exceptions in Section 1101(b) of the Evidence Code. He ruled that in any case where the one accused of a violent crime had a previous relationship with the victim, *any* prior assaults against the same victim are admissible. The only similarity he required was that the victim and the accused were identical.

The only authority cited was a court of appeal ruling that prior assults upon the same victim were admissible to rebut the defendant's testimony that he had an amicable relationship with the victim. Judge Ito's ruling was a triumph of law by label. All the prosecution has to do is label a homicide a "domestic violence" case.

They can then offer any evidence they can find of any prior assault of the victim by the accused.

This ruling permitted the 1989 New Year's incident to be offered in evidence. Judge Ito ruled it even covered the 1985 windshield incident, because it involved "physical violence" against Nicole despite the absence of any assault. Neither the 1993 french door incident, nor the Keith Zlomsowitch incident, however, involved any assault or physical violence in Nicole's presence. The Zlomsowitch incident, he ruled, was "stalking" behavior, and thus relevant to show motive, intent, premeditation, and identity. The 1993 french door incident, he ruled, had "significant probative value as it relates to the nature and quality of the relationship in late 1993 and expressions of anger and jealousy by defendant." Again, these rulings obliterated any protection against evidence of prior bad acts in a domestic violence case. Any prior arguments will show the "nature and quality" of the relationship.

The ruling thus permitted all 911 tapes to be played for the jury. While prior precedents offered little support for that ruling, it had the virtue of avoiding a serious problem for the prosecution. The release of the 911 tapes prior to trial could now be deemed a "harmless error." Where jurors are exposed to prejudicial, inadmissible evidence by the misconduct of police or prosecutors, a defendant has a strong claim he was denied a fair trial. But if the evidence is admissible at trial anyway, the defendant cannot claim he was prejudiced by the jury's exposure to the same evidence prematurely. Frankly, I wondered whether that explained why Judge Ito was willing to stretch the law so far to allow the prosecutors to use this evidence. The questionnaires completed by our prospective jurors confirmed the impact that the premature release of the 911 tapes had on the attitudes of the jurors. Seventy-eight percent of the jurors indicated they had heard the 911 tapes before trial. Among those who heard the tapes, 15 percent indicated they thought O.J. Simpson was guilty, or more likely guilty than not guilty. Among the remaining jurors who had *not* heard the 911 tapes, only 10 percent expressed a belief that O.J. Simpson was guilty, or more likely guilty than not guilty.

Judge Ito did grant our motion to exclude some of the evidence of domestic discord. For the most part, he excluded incidents prior to 1985, on the grounds they were too remote to be relevant. There was consistency in this ruling, since he had already precluded the defense from discovering any complaints against Detective Mark Fuhrman prior to 1985. He appeared to be establishing a clear line limiting how far back either side could go in offering evidence of other events. Most important, Judge Ito ruled that any statements made by Nicole Brown Simpson, expressing fear of O.J. Simpson, were inadmissible hearsay. Her state of mind was not relevant to any issue in the case. The law and precedents were so clearly on our side on that issue that Judge Ito couldn't find any way around them. Not that he did not want to. As he put it in a very revealing passage in his ruling, "It seems only just and right that a crime victim's own words be heard, especially in the court where the facts and circumstances of her demise are to be presented. However, the laws and appellate court decisions that must be applied by the trial court hold otherwise." I felt a cold chill when I read those sentences. It was obvious Judge Ito would be looking for any opportunity the evidence might present to let in the hearsay that emanated from Nicole Brown Simpson herself. The one opportunity that might have been presented for him to do so was if O.J. Simpson took the witness stand. On cross-examination, he could be questioned about statements Nicole Brown Simpson made in his presence.

Judge Ito's ruling on the domestic discord motions opened the door wide for the prosecution to try the case of *People v. O.J. Simpson* as a domestic violence case, rather than a murder case. The problem, of course, is that this theory worked only if you assumed O.J. Simpson was the murderer. The evidence of prior domestic discord simply did not take the case very far down the road of proving Simpson's identity as the murderer, or even establishing a motive for the murder. There was no escalating pattern to it. In fact, there was not any pattern to it at all. All it showed was that O.J. and Nicole occasionally had some very loud arguments, and on one occasion the argument got physical. Frequently, things got broken.

Often, they'd been drinking. None of these things had happened the night of June 12, 1994.

As it turned out, the prosecution did not even offer all of the evidence Judge Ito's ruling permitted them to offer. Keith Zlomsowitch was never called to the witness stand. Many other witnesses identified as the source of domestic discord evidence in the pretrial motions were never produced at trial. They may not have been as persuasive in person as they looked on paper, or they may have been vulnerable to damaging cross-examination. I strongly suspect that the prosecutors were so confident that O.J. Simpson would take the witness stand, that they were saving some of the evidence for cross-examination or rebuttal. That was a miscalculation, and Simpson's decision not to testify was strongly influenced by the fact that it would leave the door closed to additional evidence of domestic discord that had not been presented in the case in chief.

Judge Ito summarily denied our request to preclude the prosecutors from using terms such as "battered spouse" and "stalking," concluding "such restriction is not warranted." We heard those labels a lot, in opening statements, closing arguments, and throughout the trial. The prosecutors truly overplayed their hand, stretching the evidence far beyond anything it proved. One of the jurors, in a postverdict interview, commented, "this wasn't a domestic violence case; this was a murder case." To me, that confirmed that the jurors were paying closer attention to the jury instructions than the prosecutors. At the conclusion of the case, the jury was given the standard, formula instruction on the use of evidence of other bad acts. That instruction provides:

> Evidence has been introduced for the purpose of showing that the defendant committed crimes other than that for which he is on trial. Such evidence, if believed, was not received and may not be considered by you to prove that defendant is a person of bad character or that he has a disposition to commit crimes. Such evidence was received and may be considered by you only for the limited purpose of determining if it tends to show:

A characteristic method, plan or scheme in the commission of criminal acts similar to the method, plan or scheme used in the commission of the offense in this case which would further tend to show the existence of the intent which is a necessary element of the crime charged, the identity of the person who committed the crime, if any, of which the defendant is accused or a clear connection between the other offense and the one of which the defendant is accused so that it may be inferred that if defendant committed the other offenses defendant also committed the crimes charged in this case;

The existence of the intent which is a necessary element of the crime charged;

The identity of the person who committed the crime, if any, of which the defendant is accused;

A motive for the commission of the crime charged.

For the limited purpose for which you may consider such evidence, you must weigh it in the same manner as you do all other evidence in the case. You are not permitted to consider such evidence for any other purpose.

The prose may be convoluted and complex, but the message is clear. It's a message the prosecutors consistently sought to avoid, constantly replaying the tapes and rehashing the evidence to strip away the public image and portray O.J. Simpson as a bad person, who would have a propensity to violence. The jurors saw through it, and applied the law as the judge instructed them.

One thing the jury never heard during the trial was "expert testimony" about the "battered women's syndrome." Such evidence is frequently offered in criminal cases to explain why a woman who is in a battering relationship would not simply walk away, and why she might be in reasonable fear for her life even though no overt threats are being made. Such evidence is highly relevant when a woman is on trial for killing her batterer, to explain why she simply didn't walk away before resorting to the use of deadly force. Such evidence is not relevant, however, to prove that a female victim was a battered spouse, therefore it is more likely that the perpetrator of her murder was her husband or ex-spouse. The reason it is not relevant for that purpose is because there is no scientific research to back up any inference that prior battering and subsequent murder are likely to have been perpetrated by the same person. The California Evidence Code addresses the admissibility of evidence of the "battered women's syndrome" quite specifically, and it allows such evidence to show "the physical, emotional, or mental effects upon the beliefs, perceptions or behavior of victims of domestic violence," but prohibits the use of such evidence "to prove the occurrence of the act or acts of abuse which form the basis of the criminal charge." In other words, the expert can explain the conduct of the victim, but can't be called simply to portray the defendant as a "batterer" who is more likely to engage in violence. The conduct of the victim was never an issue in the Simpson trial, and the only purpose for which the prosecution could have called an expert was to paste the "batterer" label on O.J. Simpson. We had our own expert waiting in the wings. Dr. Lenore Walker, who actually developed the concept of "battered women's syndrome," was prepared to testify that O.J. Simpson did not fit the criteria of the typical battering spouse. Although Johnnie Cochran referred to her potential testimony in his opening statement, we thought better of it when it came time to present the defense case. At that point, it was clear that presenting an expert ourselves would have opened the door to a prosecution counter expert, and brought the whole issue of spousal abuse back to center stage of the trial, at the very point we were succeeding in putting the real issue in the case on center stage: Was O.J. Simpson the perpetrator of these murders? The message we wanted to deliver consistently was that the evidence of domestic discord was irrelevant and would not assist the jury in resolving the real issue in the case.

The lesson from the domestic discord issue as it was presented in the trial of *People v. O.J. Simpson* is the need to get past the labels. Spousal abuse is a serious problem, just as organized crime is a serious problem, and urban street gangs are a serious problem. Too often, as soon as someone pastes a label on a case, and the accused is identified as "mafia" related, or a member of a "gang," or a "wife batterer," the case takes off in a different orbit, and everyone views it differently. The judge makes assumptions, the media jumps to conclusions, and the jury brings lots of baggage into the jury room. There is a real risk that the accused will be convicted not because of evidence he committed the crime he is charged with, but because the "label" the prosecutors have pasted on him suggests he should be in jail whether he did it or not.

Among the chilling words that Detective Mark Fuhrman uttered on the Fuhrman tapes is an apt description of the danger of guilt by label. He was explaining why he was never bothered by the thought that he might be arresting an innocent person:

> "There's a thing I've always said too, 'Even if you get the wrong guy, this guy's done something before, or he's thought about doing something.'"

In the Simpson case, the "domestic violence" label put on the case from the beginning led in only one direction, and that was the only direction the police and prosecution seriously pursued: toward the prosecution of O.J. Simpson. If someone had questioned the appropriateness of that label at an early stage, and suggested that perhaps this was a drug-related killing, or a random act of violence, the investigators might have pursued other leads pointing in a different direction. The phenomenon of prematurely labeling a case is closely related to the fatal mistake of a rush to judgment.

THE MOUNTAIN
OF EVIDENCE

Marcia Clark frequently characterized the prosecution's case
as a "mountain of evidence." When good defense lawyers encounter a "mountain," however, they realize climbing over it is only
one alternative. They must also consider tunneling under it, or simply walking around it. We decided that the wisest course in the case
of *People v. O.J. Simpson* was to pursue all three alternatives. Barry
Scheck came up with some colorful alliteration to describe our
route: We would argue the "mountain" of evidence was a molehill
that was "contaminated, compromised, and corrupted."

The incredible extent to which the L.A.P.D. had botched the
collection of blood evidence became apparent soon after the preliminary hearing. At the preliminary hearing, the prosecution had
only preliminary DNA testing results available, so they relied on
conventional serology to prove that blood drops found at the Bundy
crime scene were of the same type as O.J. Simpson's blood. The conventional serology results didn't take them very far. O.J. Simpson
and Nicole Brown Simpson both had Type A blood, and they were
both Type 1 on the ESD Enzyme test. The only test that distinguished them was a PGM enzyme test. She was sub-type 1+, while
he was sub-type 2+2−. By multiplying the frequency of Type A,
Type 1 ESD, and sub-type 2+2− PGM, the serologist calculated that
.48 percent of the population had the same characteristics as O.J.

Simpson and the blood found in the blood drops at the scene. There were three problems with that, however. The possibility that the drops were a mixture of more than one person's blood could not be excluded, the time when the blood drops were deposited could not be ascertained, and there were 40,000 other persons in Los Angeles with the same markers in their blood. DNA testing was essential to get more specific identification.

When DNA results finally began trickling in, we were surprised how many came back "inconclusive," because the samples had deteriorated. The drops were large enough, and if, in fact, they had been left the night of the murders, should have been fresh enough to give strong DNA results. The explanation for inconclusive results was how the samples were handled after collection. Blood samples are collected by wetting small fabric swatches and applying them to the bloodstain to moisten and absorb the blood. The key to preserving DNA is to dry the swatches as soon as possible after collection. While they remain moist, bacteria can actually consume the DNA fragments.

All of the blood samples had been collected by criminalists Dennis Fung and Andrea Mazzola. Ms. Mazzola was a recent hire who was still being trained, and the Simpson case was the first time she had actually done evidence collection at a crime scene. Rather than go to a single scene and return the evidence promptly to the laboratory, Fung and Mazzola were summoned first to the Rockingham scene at 7 A.M., finished collecting the evidence outside the Simpson house, then went to the Bundy crime scene, collected all the blood samples there, and then went *back* to Rockingham to assist in execution of the search warrant. They put their samples in plastic bags and stored them in the back of their van without refrigeration. They did not return to the laboratory until after 7 P.M. that evening, to begin drying out their samples. By that time, many of their swatches had been cooking like a stew in the sunshine of a warm June day for twelve hours.

DNA testing has powerful potential for law enforcement. Like any other new technology, however, it requires a heavy initial investment in equipment and training of personnel. Law enforcement agencies are like any other bureaucracy: they rarely invest in new technology until they are absolutely compelled. L.A.P.D. is certainly no exception to this principle.

The Simpson case involved extensive use of the latest innovation in DNA technology, the Polymerase Chain Reaction, or PCR test. PCR testing was necessary because so many of the blood samples were deteriorated. If more DNA were in the samples, more precise RFLP results could have been obtained. The heavy reliance on PCR rather than RFLP tests created two big problems for the prosecution. First, the risk of contamination was greatly magnified, because of the greater sensitivity of the tests. PCR works by "amplifying" the DNA, duplicating very small fragments over and over. Any contaminant is also amplified, however, meaning a very minute contaminant can yield a false positive result. Second, the admissibility of PCR tests had rarely been litigated in court. There were a growing number of appellate court decisions around the country upholding the admission of RFLP results, but PCR was so new that courts had yet to consider its admissibility.

California is among the states that require a showing of "general acceptance" in the scientific community before evidence derived from new technology can be admitted in court. The United States Supreme Court recently abandoned this more conservative test of admissibility for the federal courts. The test was first devised to exclude evidence of polygraph, or "lie detector" results in the case of *Frye v. United States.* Generally known as the *Frye* test, in California it is called the *Kelly-Frye* test to incorporate the name of the California Supreme Court decision recognizing it, the case of *People v. Kelly.* In the early stages of the Simpson case, the California Supreme Court considered a case raising the question whether California should join the federal courts and reject the *Kelly-Frye* test for a more liberal standard of admissibility of scientific evidence. The case was closely watched for its potential impact on the Simpson case, and when the conservative California Supreme Court opted to preserve the more conservative *Kelly-Frye* test, both sides geared up for a contentious hearing on whether PCR testing met the standard of general acceptance in the scientific community. That issue would be decided by the judge, who would hear the evidence and arguments outside the presence of the jury.

Barry Scheck lined up an impressive list of expert witnesses to challenge the admissibility of the PCR test results, but we anticipated the prosecution would have little difficulty prevailing on the admissibility of the limited RFLP results they achieved. Our witnesses included Dr. Kary Mullis, the scientist who won the Nobel Prize for inventing the PCR technology, who has serious misgivings about the use to which law enforcement was putting the technology to "match" and include a suspect, rather than to exclude someone.

As the time for the *Kelly-Frye* hearing approached, however, we faced a real dilemma. The prosecution had vigorously resisted our efforts to streamline the hearing by limiting the number of witnesses who could be called. The hearing would consume a minimum of two weeks and could easily stretch out to a month. That meant our jury would be kept "on ice" for a long delay before the first witness was even called for the trial. We began a serious reassessment of what we had to gain and what we had to lose by mounting the *Kelly-Frye* challenge. Judge Ito's other pretrial rulings had convinced us that he would not exclude *any* DNA test results, even PCR. Unless there was clear and unavoidable precedent that compelled him to rule against the prosecution, he gave the prosecutors every benefit the law allowed. While there was no precedent holding PCR was admissible, neither was there any holding it was inadmissible. Judge Ito, we were certain, would let it all come in and leave the precedent setting to a higher court. If we waived the *Kelly-Frye* hearing, however, we could not even present the issue to a higher court. We might be giving up a strong issue for appeal, to win a reversal if the trial resulted in a conviction.

Some of us on the team considered ourselves primarily "appellate" lawyers, rather than "trial" lawyers. We revel in the heady intellectualism of legal argument to appellate courts, while the "trial" lawyers grovel in the nitty-gritty of factual issues decided by juries. The appellate lawyers on our team were reluctant to give up an issue for potential appeal that could go either way. The trial lawyers on the team saw lots of advantages to waiving the hearing besides speeding up the trial and avoiding having to put the jury "on ice." The strongest evidence we would have to challenge the DNA results would be the sloppy way in which the samples were collected and processed even before the testing was done. Many of the same witnesses we were planning to call for the *Kelly-Frye* hearing would reappear during the trial to support our arguments relating to contamination. Why give the prosecution the advantage of probing our evidence in a "warm-up" outside the presence of the jury? We would also gain an advantage in compelling the prosecutors to begin presenting their case to the jury sooner that they anticipated. Marcia Clark and Chris Darden were planning on turning over the *Kelly-Frye* hearing to a team of prosecutors with DNA experience assembled from D.A.'s offices all over the state, while they disappeared to prepare their opening statements and their lead-off witnesses so they could start the case with a bang in front of the jury.

We debated the strategy of waiving the *Kelly-Frye* hearing more vigorously than any other tactical call during the entire trial, and ultimately everyone was convinced that the potential advantages of the waiver outweighed the disadvantages. Before agreeing to an outright waiver, however, we decided to propose a compromise. We proposed having the *Kelly-Frye* hearing contemporaneous with the presentation of the evidence to the jury! Usually the hearing is held outside the presence of the jury before the jury hears the evidence in order to avoid prejudicing the jury by exposing them to evidence that may subsequently be excluded. Juries have difficulty putting out of their minds something they have already heard. We argued that protection is to benefit the defendant. We were prepared to give up that protection. Let the jury hear the DNA evidence, we argued, rather than presenting the same evidence twice, first to the judge, then to the jury. After the evidence came in, Judge Ito could hear any additional evidence that was relevant only for the *Kelly-Frye* determination, and then decide whether it should be struck from the record and the jury instructed to disregard it. This course of action would give us the advantage of preserving the issue for appeal, without the delay of a pretrial hearing and a prosecutorial "preview" of our evidence. Since we anticipated an unfavorable ruling from Judge Ito anyway, we would risk little by allowing the jury to hear the evidence prior to his ruling.

The prosecutorial response to this suggestion was predictable. They squealed like stuck pigs. They did not want us to gain any procedural advantages without paying the price of a complete waiver. The court, however, had nothing to lose and much to gain from our proposal. It would avoid needless duplication, speed up the trial, and preserve the legal issues for orderly review by an appellate court. It was creative and innovative, and soundly based in the law of evidence. More than any other exercise of discretion by Judge Ito, his ruling on this proposal supported our belief he was biased toward the prosecution. He rejected the proposal to conduct the *Kelly-Frye* hearing contemporaneously with the admission of the DNA evidence, and the reason he rejected it was readily transparent. He didn't want to give the defense an advantage unless he had to, even if it meant a longer trial.

We then proceeded in our determination to go "around" the "mountain." We waived the *Kelly-Frye* hearing and agreed that all DNA test results could be admitted. Our challenge would not be a frontal attack on DNA technology. It would rather be "garbage in–garbage out." The testing of even the most sophisticated laboratories could not be trusted if what they were testing had been contaminated, compromised, and corrupted before it arrived.

The prosecutors hoped to avoid a challenge to the accuracy of their test results by employing two different outside laboratories to conduct the tests. They believed that if two different laboratories independently came up with consistent test results, the claim of errors in the testing procedures could be easily refuted. Some of the samples were sent to Cellmark Laboratories, a private laboratory that has actively promoted DNA testing and profited from its employment, while other samples were sent to a laboratory operated by the State of California Department of Justice in Berkeley, California.

The greatest vulnerability of their test results, however, was not in the testing procedures, but in the collection and handling of the samples by the Los Angeles Police Department before they were sent out for testing. The L.A.P.D. was the "black hole" through which *all* of the evidence passed, and if it was contaminated, compromised, and corrupted, the responsibility fell right in the lap of the L.A.P.D.

Many commentators suggested that this defense strategy required acceptance of a highly improbable scenario, that there was a "conspiracy" in the L.A.P.D. to "frame" O.J. Simpson, and that many officers and civilian employees were willing to risk their careers to accomplish this nefarious goal. That was never the defense theory at all. By going around, under, and over the "mountain" of evidence, we were suggesting that some evidence could not be trusted because those who handled it were incompetent or negligent; some evidence could not be trusted because the procedures and facilities utilized to preserve it were inadequate, and some evidence could not be trusted because it had been corruptly altered or manufactured. Once you accepted these three premises, you were left in a state of reasonable doubt about *all* of the evidence. None of it could be trusted. Even with respect to the "corruption," there was no need to prove it was part of a conspiracy to "frame" Simpson. It could just as easily have been motivated by a sincere belief in his guilt, and the need to shore up a disintegrating case by covering up prior mistakes and enhancing the persuasiveness of the evidence. Mark Fuhrman summed up the process well on the Fuhrman tapes, in words the jury never heard: "You do what you have to do to put these . . . assholes in jail. If you don't, you . . . get out of the . . . game."

Regardless of whether it was carelessness or corruption, the bottom line was that the evidence could not be trusted, because those who collected and handled it could not be trusted. If you turn a mountain on its head, it resembles a funnel. The real problem the prosecution had to contend with was the mouth of the funnel, the Los Angeles Police Department.

The first opportunity the defense had to probe the handling of the blood evidence was in motions to require "splitting" of the evidence so the defense could conduct its own independent testing.

Courts have recognized that the prosecution cannot deprive the defendant of a reasonable opportunity to conduct independent testing of blood evidence, in order to challenge prosecution tests. The prosecution argued, in essence, that the defense was entitled to test only what was "left over" after they completed all of the tests they wanted to conduct. DNA testing consumes the material tested, so by scheduling testing in two different laboratories, there was a substantial likelihood that for some samples, there would be *nothing* left when the prosecution was through. Thus, our motion challenged the prosecution's right to do two identical tests, when that could deprive the defense of material necessary to do a different variety of testing. In order to rule on the motion, the court had to be apprised of a precise inventory of how much of each sample was available and how much would be needed to conduct the testing proposed by the prosecution. That gave us the opportunity to visibly inspect the swatches and how they were packaged. We discovered that L.A.P.D. criminalists Fung and Mazzola kept no records of how many swatches were taken for each of the stains they collected. Some stains produced as many as seven swatches, others as few as two or three. Nor were the swatches of uniform size. The swatches themselves were not tagged or identified, but simply dropped into coin envelopes that were marked. After they were dried, they were then placed in paper bindles. Although Mazzola testified that the bindles were initialed, no initials were found on any of the paper bindles produced. Some of the bindles also had transfer stains matching the swatches, suggesting they were still damp when they were supposed to have been already dried. In short, the physical evidence simply did not match up with the testimony as to how the blood swatches were handled. As Dr. Henry Lee put it in his trial testimony, "something is wrong here." What easily could have been wrong was the prosecution's attribution of testing results to particular stains. If a swatch was switched or misidentified, either deliberately or accidentally, there was no way to verify that what was tested actually came from any particular bloodstain.

Judge Ito denied our split motion, essentially buying the prosecutors' argument that we had to wait until they were done, and then we could have what remained to conduct our own tests. We then asked him to at least set a deadline for the completion of all prosecution testing, so we were not left in a position of not getting material we had a right to test until a point in time when testing was no longer feasible because it would delay completion of the trial. This too was denied, and the prosecution was allowed to delay some testing of samples until the trial was nearly over. Thus, the prosecutors were given a free hand to set up whatever testing regimen and schedule they felt would most benefit their case. The defense was left with a few useless shreds, the leftover crumbs that remained.

As it turned out, we found all the ammunition we needed to establish reasonable doubt in the results of the prosecution's *own* tests. When we made the suggestion in Johnnie Cochran's opening statement that actual blood from the vial of O.J. Simpson's blood extracted by a nurse on June 13, 1994, was missing and unaccounted for, and could have been used to "spike" the samples submitted for testing, the prosecution scrambled for the evidence it needed to foreclose that possibility. The more the prosecutors scrambled, the deeper they dug their own hole.

They submitted samples of blood allegedly recovered from the back gate and from the sock found in Mr. Simpson's bedroom to the FBI, for a unique series of tests to detect the presence of EDTA. EDTA is used as a preservative in test tubes and collection vials, to prevent the coagulation of blood samples. If it appeared in the blood found on the back gate or the socks, stains that were allegedly discovered weeks after the crime, it would suggest that those bloodstains came from a test tube, rather than from Mr. Simpson or the victims of the homicides. If it did not appear, it would be powerful evidence to refute the suggestion that those samples had been "planted."

These two bloodstains were highly suspicious for other reasons. Fung puportedly returned to the Bundy crime scene three weeks after the murders, after the scene had been hosed down and cleaned up, and found a large stain that had previously been overlooked on the bottom rung of the rear gate, leading to the alley behind Nicole Brown Simpson's condo. Despite its exposure to the elements, the stain turned out to have higher concentrations of DNA than any of the stains collected immediately after the homicides.

The sock stain was equally suspicious, as already noted. It, too, had unusually high concentrations of DNA, and it, too, was belatedly discovered long after seizure of the sock.

The EDTA test was *positive* for both of these samples. The FBI expert who conducted the tests testified that the "trace" levels of EDTA could have been attributable to "environmental" factors (e.g., it was already on the gate before the bloodstain, or it was already on the sock from prior exposure to detergents), or even to concentration in the natural blood. Both of these hypotheses were rejected by the experts called by the defense, who pointed out that since FBI testing provided no basis to quantify the amount of EDTA that was present, it could not be determined whether the quantities exceeded the "trace" levels that might be attributed to "environmental" factors. Judge Ito precluded a defense attempt to impeach the FBI agent who conducted the EDTA tests by showing he was reprimanded by his superiors for not preserving records and by showing his bias to favor the prosecution in other cases.

The prosecution also sought to refute the suggestion of "planted" evidence by seeking a retraction from the male nurse who drew Mr. Simpson's blood sample. Thano Peratis testified both before the grand jury and at the preliminary hearing that he extracted approximately 8 cc's of blood from Mr. Simpson. When we totaled up all of the blood removed from the vial to provide reference samples and to be tested for drugs or alcohol (with negative results), only 6.5 cc's could be accounted for. The missing 1.5 cc's, we suggested, would have supplied all the blood needed to provide the stain on the gate and plant other samples as well. Even accidental spillage could have contaminated other swatches.

The blood vial itself had been handled in a most unusual manner. The nurse gave the blood to Detective Philip Vannatter immediately after he placed it in the vial, and placed the vial in an envelope with a certificate printed on it. For some unexplained reason, the certificate bore the wrong date. Vannatter, instead of then booking the blood in evidence right at Parker Center, where he received it, stuck it in his pocket and brought it with him when he returned to Simpson's Rockingham home later that afternoon. He testified he delivered it to Fung that evening, as Fung and Mazzola were finally leaving to return to the laboratory with the blood samples they had collected. Mazzola testified she never saw the blood vial. Fung's explanation was that it was put into a large plastic bag while she was not looking!

Although they had called Thano Peratis as a witness at both the grand jury hearing and the preliminary hearing, the prosecution refused to call him at trial. Instead, they relied on the faulty certificate and the testimony of detectives Vannatter and Tom Lange that they observed the blood being drawn from Mr. Simpson's arm. The prosecution was going to great lengths to avoid having to explain the discrepancy in the amount of blood Peratis said he had drawn and the amount that could subsequently be accounted for. We argued that the failure to call the nurse should result in exclusion of all tests utilizing the Simpson blood sample, but Judge Ito ruled the observation of the police officers was sufficient.

That left us in the position of having to call the nurse ourselves if we wanted to prove that 8 cc's of blood had been drawn. At this point, we learned that the nurse might not be available to testify. He had recently undergone open heart surgery, replacing a quadruple bypass, and was recovering from the surgery. In one of the more remarkable coincidences of the trial, Thano Peratis was a cousin of our jury consultant, Jo-Ellan Dimetrius. His unavailability actually enabled us to use a hearsay exception for former testimony. We simply offered the previous sworn testimony he had given at both the grand jury hearing and the preliminary hearing, to establish that 8 cc's of blood had been drawn. In response, the prosecution presented one of the most bizarre evidentiary presentations ever offered in an American court of law. One of the prosecutors went to

Mr. Peratis's home with a video camera, and recorded an interview in which he was carefully coached through a repudiation of the testimony he had previously given under oath on two occasions. The video was made without notice to the defense, and there was no cross-examination. In the video, Paratis said his prior testimony that 8 cc's had been drawn was just an estimate, and now he was sure that he had only drawn 6.5 cc's! Judge Ito relied on an obscure provision of the California Evidence Code to admit the videotape in evidence. Section 1202 of the Evidence Code provides that an inconsistent statement by a hearsay declarant may be offered to attack his credibility, even though he was not confronted with the inconsistency. It is an exception to the normal rule that a witness must be given an opportunity to explain an inconsistency between his present testimony and any prior statements. Where the witness is not present to be examined because he is unavailable or a hearsay exception applies, it makes sense to permit the prior inconsistencies as well. But this exception should not permit the deliberate eliciting of a repudiation in the absence of cross-examination. The ruling admitting the videotape was a gross violation of the defendant's right to confront and cross-examine the witnesses against him. Ultimately, the tactic of using it may have backfired for the prosecution, however. It was such an obvious "put-up" that it was almost laughable. The prosecutors presented themselves as panic-struck amateurs desperately grasping for straws as their ship was sinking. The reality of their desperation offered a sharp contrast to the bold "mountain of evidence" image that Marcia Clark sought to project.

The lesson from the so-called "mountain of evidence" is that if the messengers who bring the evidence can't be trusted, the evidence itself won't be trusted. Technology is only as good as the people who operate it.

Law enforcement must invest in the training and equipment needed to reduce the risks of contamination before new testing regimens will be accepted as reliable. Police departments that are hard put to keep gasoline in their patrol cars will be hard put to invest in new technology for their laboratories. Perhaps it's time for statewide consolidation of police laboratories, with statewide standards for training and qualification of technicians. Dr. Henry Lee's Connecticut laboratory could provide a national model of how to provide top-quality laboratory personnel and equipment to law enforcement on a statewide basis.

THE FUHRMAN TAPES

*D*etective Mark Fuhrman presented the prosecution with a dilemma that is common for any trial lawyer. The ethical constraints that apply to *both* sides in our adversary system prohibit the *knowing* use of perjured testimony. Lawyers most often avoid any ethical problem in presenting the testimony of witnesses whom they *doubt* by saying to themselves, "I don't really *know* whether this witness is being truthful or not. It's not my role to judge his credibility. That's up to the jury." Whatever information the prosecutor has that would undermine the credibility of an important witness, however, must be turned over to the defense.

The leading U.S. Supreme Court decision imposing this obligation on the prosecutor is the 1963 case of *Brady v. Maryland*. The Court held that the Constitution requires that any exculpatory evidence in the possession of the prosecutor must be turned over to the accused, including evidence that might be used to impeach the credibility of prosecution witnesses. Lawyers often refer to this as the *Brady* duty or obligation. Most often, the issue arises after a defendant has been convicted, and evidence comes to light that the prosecution failed to disclose prior to trial. If the prosecution made promises to a prosecution witness to get him to cooperate, for example, those promises could provide fruitful cross-examination to show the bias of the witness in favor of the prosecution. Failure to disclose such promises has led to the reversal of convictions in several Supreme Court decisions since *Brady*.

There is no corresponding duty imposed on defense lawyers, however. While a witness's previous statements may have to be turned over pursuant to a reciprocal discovery law, there is no general obligation to turn over all evidence that might be used to challenge the credibility of defense witnesses.

The dilemma that the *Brady* obligation creates for prosecutors is that if their skepticism about a witness motivates them to do some digging, whatever negative material they dig up will have to be handed over to the defense. As a result, the only digging many prosecutors do is to dig holes in which to insert their heads. They believe what they don't know can't hurt them. In the case of Detective Mark Fuhrman, there were lots of "danger signals" that should have flashed a warning to prosecutors not to build their case on his credibility. Those signals were ignored, however, in a studied and calculated effort to bolster Detective Fuhrman and discredit all defense efforts to challenge his credibility.

The "Fuhrman tapes" are the most devastating evidence ever presented in an American court of law to completely destroy the credibility of a police officer. If the prosecution had known of the existence of the tapes before they put Fuhrman on the stand, they would have had to disclose the tapes to the defense. More important, they might have decided to avoid the problem altogether by not even calling Detective Fuhrman to the witness stand, and not offering any of the evidence he observed. The prosecutors were completely blindsided by the discovery of the tapes near the end of the trial. At that point, their tactical options were much more limited, because they had already presented Fuhrman as a credible witness. To candidly admit they had been "taken in" by Fuhrman at that point would concede the underlying premise of the defense case: that Detective Fuhrman was capable of fooling the prosecutors and framing an innocent man.

But the prosecutors had only themselves to blame. The choice they made to ignore the "danger signals" and forge ahead with a strategy designed to portray Fuhrman as the innocent victim of defense bombast was made to gain a tactical advantage. That strategy blew up in their faces. If they were truly interested in pursuing the "truth," they might have undertaken a thorough investigation of Fuhrman that could have led them to the tapes.

The initial efforts by the defense to investigate Fuhrman's background were met with a combination of stonewalling, public relations hype, and castigation of the defense for "character assassination." In August of 1994, a month after the preliminary hearing, the defense filed a "Pitchess Motion" to gain access to any complaints filed against Detective Fuhrman by others he might have arrested, and any personnel records maintained by the Los Angeles Police Department that would substantiate his racial animosity toward African-Americans. The defense's right of access to such materials was established in a 1974 California Supreme Court decision in the case of *Pitchess v. Superior Court,* hence the name Pitchess motion. Peter Pitchess was the sheriff of Los Angeles County at the time, and the case recognized that the privacy of police personnel records did not preclude access by an accused upon a showing that the records could produce relevant evidence, such as an officer's prior use of excessive force, ethnic or racial bias, or the falsifying of police reports or planting of evidence. Subsequently, the California legislature enacted the procedure for Pitchess motions into the California Evidence Code. The code provides that once a defendant makes a plausible showing of why the information is needed, the judge is required to review the files and turn over any relevant material to the defense. It sets a time limit, however, excluding any complaints concerning conduct "occurring more than five years before the event or transaction which is the subject of the litigation."

Our Pitchess motion was supported by three documents raising serious questions about Detective Fuhrman's credibility. First was the City Attorney's response to a lawsuit filed by Mark Fuhrman in 1983, in which Fuhrman sought a disability pension on the basis of stress. In the course of medical and psychiatric evaluations of his disability claim, Fuhrman made derogatory comments about racial minorities. His disability claim was rejected on the grounds he was "consciously exaggerating problems or malingering."

Second, a lawsuit naming Fuhrman as a defendant was filed by an African-American robbery suspect who had been shot by police. He alleged that arresting officers placed a knife next to him after he was shot, to make it appear he was armed and dangerous, and when he asked for some help with his bleeding wounds, an officer said, "Why don't you die and save us the paperwork." The suspect was unable to identify Fuhrman as the arresting officer, although police reports identified Fuhrman as one of the officers who opened fire and as the officer who recovered a butcher's knife adjacent to the suspect's feet.

The third item was an affidavit from Kathleen Bell. Kathleen Bell wrote a letter to Johnnie Cochran after seeing a news story about the defense allegation that Detective Mark Fuhrman was a racist. She reported an incident in 1985 or 1986 in which she encountered Fuhrman in a Marine Recruiting Office in Redondo Beach and was shocked by the virulence of his racist rantings. In the affidavit filed with our Pitchess motion, she quoted Fuhrman as stating he would "pull over any vehicle that was occupied by a black man and a white woman." When she asked what if he didn't have a good reason to pull them over, he replied, "I'd make one up." When she responded that they might be "in love," Fuhrman appeared to become disgusted, and said, "If I had my way, they would take all the niggers, put them together in a big group, and burn them."

Based on these three items, Judge Ito required Fuhrman's personnel file to be produced for his inspection. After examining it, however, he announced that none of the relevant material came within the five-year time period specified by the statute. If the "event or transaction which is the subject of the litigation" was the murder of Nicole Brown Simpson and Ronald Goldman, Judge Ito's ruling was correct. Any information prior to June 12, 1989, would be protected against defense discovery. A more fair interpretation, however, would be that the "event or transaction" which was the subject of the litigation was the encounter between Mark Fuhrman and O.J. Simpson in 1985, when he responded to the complaint that Simpson smashed the windshield of Nicole's automobile with a baseball bat. We were seeking evidence that would corroborate Kathleen Bell's account, which was contemporaneous with the baseball bat incident. Since Simpson and Nicole were obviously an interracial couple, the animosity expressed by Fuhrman toward interracial couples could provide key evidence as to his motivation to lie or plant evidence.

Judge Ito was not about to give the statute a broad reading that would benefit the defense, however. In the trial of *People v. O.J. Simpson*, the Pitchess motion statute was construed in a way to assist police in covering up Mark Fuhrman's record. Ironically, in admitting evidence of prior incidents of domestic discord involving O.J. Simpson and Nicole Brown Simpson, no artificial five-year barrier was created for the prosecution. They were permitted to offer evidence of events going back ten years. But the prior record of Detective Mark Fuhrman was protected by the five-year barrier created by the legislature, even though the statute could have been read to permit greater access. Judge Ito applied the limitation mechanistically.

The prosecution then filed a motion, seeking to prevent the defense from even using the three items attached to our Pitchess motion. They asked Judge Ito, in advance of trial, to rule that in cross-examining Detective Fuhrman, we could make no reference to his disability claim, the lawsuit alleging evidence planting, or the racist comments to Kathleen Bell. In an overt play for sympathy for Detective Fuhrman, their motion asserted:

> Detective Fuhrman has been repeatedly maligned by the defense in this case. Because of the clever defense manipulation of the media, the undue harassment and undue embarrassment he has undergone can never be completely undone.

The brass of L.A.P.D. were also mounting a public relations campaign to enlist popular support for Detective Fuhrman. He was extolled as a model officer, one of L.A.P.D.'s finest, who was being maligned by unscrupulous defense lawyers. Fuhrman retained lawyer James Toutellot to file a lawsuit against Bob Shapiro for libel, claiming Shapiro leaked a false accusation that he planted evidence in the Simpson case. Tourtellot made frequent television appearances to assert Fuhrman's claim that all of the defense allegations about his racism were fabricated. A "Mark Fuhrman Defense Fund" was created, and contributions were solicited from police groups all over the country.

The arguments surrounding the prosecution's motion inspired some of the most impassioned oratory of the entire trial. Deputy District Attorney Chris Darden argued that the jury should never hear the "N-word," because it would arouse such strong passions among African-American jurors that they would be blinded to the evidence and be unable to fairly and objectively evaluate the credibility of Detective Fuhrman. Johnnie Cochran responded that Darden's argument was an insult to African-American jurors. He said African Americans had been hearing the "N-word" for centuries, and to suggest that they could not be fair when presented with evidence of racial animosity was itself racial stereotyping of the worst sort. Deputy District Attorney Marcia Clark described the defense strategy as the playing of a "race card," a deliberate attempt to inject issues of racism into the trial to inflame the jury.

The law, however, was clearly with the defense. The California courts had long since resolved the issue of the relevance of a witness's racial attitudes to his bias. Where the racial animosity was specifically directed to interracial couples, it was highly relevant to the assessment of credibility. Judge Ito ruled, "Assuming Bell's statement to be true, a direct inference of a credibility problem is apparent. If the defendant can make an offer of proof as to what evidence they will produce to suggest the moving of evidence and the court is satisfied by that offer of proof, the prosecution's objections will be denied." He also addressed the admissibility of the "N-word," reaffirming his faith in the ability of jurors to put their passions aside in evaluating the evidence:

The racial divisions that exist in this country remain the last great challenge to us as a nation. How we evolve and hopefully solve this problem will be our memorial in history. When meritorious arguments are raised on both sides, the court must always remember this process is a search for the truth and that it depends upon the sound judgment of our jurors. If the challenged racial epithet was used in a relevant incident, it will be heard in court.

At the same time, however, he ruled that the disability claim was too remote, and the knife-planting incident was too ambiguous. Both were excluded from evidence.

The defense offer of proof was found sufficient, and when Detective Fuhrman was sworn in as a witness at trial, the prosecution knew he would be confronted with the Kathleen Bell incident. His testimony was carefully choreographed in an unusual "prep" session. Six prosecutors met with Fuhrman in a grand jury room at the courthouse on a Sunday morning, and conducted a "mock" examination and cross-examination. When Fuhrman took the witness stand in front of the jurors, Marcia Clark made sympathetic references to the "ordeal" he had been subjected to. In an effort to "take the sting out" of the anticipated cross-examination, she elicited a flat denial the Kathleen Bell incident ever took place. The prosecution position would be that Detective Mark Fuhrman was an honest and upright officer who was being unjustifiably maligned. He had no racial animosity. The only way to explain Kathleen Bell's allegations was that she was a liar.

At the time it took place, F. Lee Bailey's cross-examination of Detective Fuhrman was widely regarded as ineffectual. For six days he hammered away, and Fuhrman never wavered. He testified like a choirboy, looking Bailey in the eye and flatly denying the accusations of racism and the suggestions he may have planted evidence. Bailey did what a good cross-examiner should do in that situation: He pinned Fuhrman down with precise questions probing every detail of his denials. Surely, if the Bell incident had occurred,

Fuhrman would remember it? Surely, he would remember uttering the words Bell claimed he said, if he had ever uttered such words? With the climax of his cross-examination, F. Lee Bailey was at his best. As long as lawyers are allowed to cross-examine witnesses, they will look to the questions which Bailey put to Detective Mark Fuhrman on March 15, 1995, as examples to emulate:

Q: Do you use the word "nigger" in describing people?

A: No, sir.

Q: Have you ever used that word in the past ten years?

A: Not that I recall, no.

Q: You mean if you called someone a nigger you have forgotten it?

A: I'm not sure I can answer the question the way you phrased it, sir.

Q: You have difficulty understanding the question?

A: Yes.

Q: I will rephrase it. I want you to assume that perhaps at some time since 1985 or 1986, you addressed a member of the African American race as a nigger. It is possible that you have forgotten that act on your part?

A: No, it is not possible.

Q: Are you therefore saying that you have not used that word in the past ten years, Detective Fuhrman?

A: Yes, that is what I'm saying.

Q: And you say under oath that you have not addressed any black person as a nigger or spoken about black people as niggers in the past ten years, Detective Fuhrman?

A: That's what I'm saying, sir.

Q: So that anyone who comes to this court and quotes you as using that word in dealing with African Americans would be a liar, would they not, Detective Fuhrman?

A: Yes, they would.

Q: All of them, correct?

A: All of them.

Detective Fuhrman was willing to put his credibility head to head against the credibility of Kathleen Bell. So was the prosecution. It is interesting to speculate how the trial might have ended if the Fuhrman tapes had never surfaced. Kathleen Bell would have been subjected to a searing cross-examination, suggesting that she was some sort of Simpson case "groupie" who was making the whole thing up in order to gain her fifteen minutes of fame. The jury might have been asked to find the "truth" by weighing the denials of Mark Fuhrman against the accusations of Kathleen Bell. Actually, the breadth of Fuhrman's denial opened the door to impeachment by other witnesses besides Kathleen Bell. Even before Fuhrman left the witness stand, the defense was assembling a list of others who could testify they heard Fuhrman use the "N-word" in the previous ten years. Judge Ito precluded any questioning of Detective Fuhrman regarding these other incidents until he had an opportunity to consider their admissibility. That meant Detective Fuhrman was not excused as a witness. He left the courtroom subject to recall for further cross-examination. As it turned out, the right to recall Fuhrman as a witness became a powerful advantage for the defense after the Fuhrman tapes surfaced.

The prosecution sought every opportunity to bolster Fuhrman in presenting their case. They hoped to paint a scenario in which it would have been physically impossible for Fuhrman to have picked up a glove at the Bundy scene, because he would have been seen by other officers. Another officer was called to testify that Fuhrman was never alone, and he never went near the physical evidence surrounding the bodies. The jury was told that a photograph which clearly depicted Mark Fuhrman kneeling between the bodies, pointing to a glove and cap at Ron Goldman's feet, had been taken later in the day, after Fuhrman returned from Simpson's Rockingham residence. Close to the end of the trial, the defense called the photographer who took that photo, and produced his "contact prints," which indicated the order in which his photographs were taken. There was no doubt that the photo in question had been taken in the early morning hours, *prior* to Fuhrman leaving the

Bundy scene. The photographer also testified he found Fuhrman alone before the photo was taken.

After Fuhrman left the witness stand, defense investigators went to work to locate and interview witnesses who could impeach his denial of the use of the "N-word." But it was not until July 7, 1995, that we had any inkling tape recordings of Fuhrman's voice uttering the epithet might be available. Investigator Pat McKenna received a call from an informant that a woman named "Laura" had tape recorded conversations with Mark Fuhrman in which he talked about "planting evidence and getting niggers." By that time, we had received thousands of anonymous "tips" about "blockbuster" evidence that didn't pan out. But Pat McKenna's keen instincts told him this one was worth checking out. He called the North Carolina telephone number he had been given, and asked for "Laura." He was told she was out. He left a message and number for her to call back. Within thirty minutes, a woman called back and identified herself as Laura Hart McKinny. McKenna explained that he was seeking her help with respect to information about Detective Mark Fuhrman for the Simpson defense. She responded that she would contact her attorney, and hung up the telephone. Thirty minutes later, McKenna received a call from Matthew Schwartz, a Los Angeles attorney with offices in Century City. Schwartz confirmed that the tapes existed, that he had heard them, and that the voice on the tapes sounded to him like the voice of Detective Mark Fuhrman. The defense requests to examine the tapes were rebuffed, however. Ms. McKinny took the position that she did not want to volunteer to assist either side in the Simpson case, but she would surrender the tapes and testify if lawful process was served on her.

"Lawful process" to secure the testimony of an out-of-state witness is surprisingly complex and convoluted. Witnesses within the borders of the state can be summoned to court by serving them with a subpoena, which orders them to appear at a designated time and place. Failure to appear can result in the issuance of a warrant, to actually arrest the person and bring him to court. But no state has the power to reach across its borders and physically compel a citizen of another state to come to its courts. It must rely on the cooperation of the authorities in the state where the witness resides. The problem was addressed many years ago by a compact, or agreement, among the states, and the enactment by every state legislature of the Uniform Act to Secure the Attendance of Witnesses from Without the State in Criminal Cases. The first step under the act was the issuance of an out-of-state subpoena by Judge Ito, together with a certificate declaring his finding that the testimony of the witness was material and necessary to the case. Judge Ito had no hesitation in concluding that Ms. McKinny was a material and necessary witness, and the papers were issued by him on July 18, 1995, and forwarded to North Carolina. Ms. McKinny's attorneys advised her that the validity of the subpoena could be challenged in the courts of North Carolina, and a hearing was set before Judge William Z. Wood on July 28, 1995. Johnnie Cochran and F. Lee Bailey flew to North Carolina, and they heard the tapes played for the first time in the chambers of Judge Wood. There was no doubt they were hearing the voice of Detective Mark Fuhrman, and that the word "nigger" was repeatedly spoken. As the tape turned and the voice filled the room, they realized that conclusive evidence was within their grasp to prove that Detective Mark Fuhrman had committed perjury in the trial of *People v. O.J. Simpson*. Ms. McKinny was reluctant to turn over the tapes, however, because she realized once they became evidence in the Simpson trial, any rights she had to exclusive control of their distribution would be lost. She had no intention to exploit the tapes herself, but the reason she had made the tapes was to develop a screenplay, the culmination of years of hard work.

Laura McKinny first met Mark Fuhrman in a Westwood restaurant in February 1985. At the time, she was employed by UCLA, assisting in a tutoring program for athletes. She was also a fledgling writer, interested in writing a screenplay and a novel about the experiences of women police officers. There was intense public interest in the difficulties encountered by women joining metropolitan police departments at the time. *Cagney and Lacey,* a television series portraying the travails of female cops, was at the height of its popularity. Fuhrman, who was not in uniform, struck up a conversation by inquiring about Ms. McKinny's laptop computer, a novelty in 1985. After learning that Fuhrman, who was a patrol officer in Westwood at that time, had strong views against the employment of women as L.A.P.D. officers, Ms. McKinny arranged subsequent meetings to get background information about the reality of the experience of L.A.P.D. officers working with female colleagues. She had been interviewing a number of police personnel, going on "ride-alongs" in patrol cars, and generally immersing herself in the unique culture of the Los Angeles Police Department. Fuhrman saw an opportunity, as well. He agreed to serve as a consultant and technical adviser in the development of Laura McKinny's screenplay, for a percentage of the profits.

Laura McKinny met with Fuhrman for a series of taped interviews spread over a ten-year period, between April 1985 and July 1994. Their last meeting occurred after O.J. Simpson had been arrested and Fuhrman testified at the preliminary hearing. She transcribed the tapes into typewritten manuscripts soon after the interviews. With two exceptions, she retained the tapes as well. Two of the tapes had been subsequently reused and taped over. The transcripts reflected the development of Ms. McKinny's project. She was a skilled interviewer, with whom Mark Fuhrman had no reluctance to bare his soul. The earlier transcripts were background interviews, in which Fuhrman was asked to recount personal experiences and give his personal point of view. He was asked for "mundane details" and his "sequence of daily events." Fuhrman was told the tapes would be transcribed verbatim, and was actually sent copies of the transcripts. One taped exchange confirmed this:

MCKINNY: I just transcribe you.

FUHRMAN: Verbatim.

MCKINNY: I have to.

FUHRMAN: All the cocksuckers. Everything. That's important. That's policeman's talk.

MCKINNY: It's life talk. It's not just policeman's talk.

FUHRMAN: But, we have mastered it. No, the marine corps mastered it.

Again and again, McKinny emphasized her goal of documenting realistic situations, so she could portray the fictional events in her screenplay with the ring of truth. The interviews included Fuhrman's reactions to drafts of the screenplay and the characters and dialogue presented. But the occasions when he was making suggestions regarding fictional portrayals were easily identifiable from the context of the interviews. Most often, he was reacting to the portrayals in terms of whether they realistically reflected his own experiences.

Laura McKinny was called as the only witness in the hearing before Judge Wood on July 18, 1995. Based on her testimony, and listening to the few brief excerpts of the tapes in chambers, Judge Wood rejected Judge Ito's determination that she was a material witness. He ruled that the taped and transcribed statements of Detective Fuhrman were mere fiction, to assist in the creation of a movie script. The ruling was a stunning blow to the defense. Judge Wood was making factual determinations that could only be made after careful examination of all the transcripts and tapes in the context of the testimony that Fuhrman had presented in the Simpson trial. Those determinations should only have been made by Judge Ito after Laura McKinny was ordered to appear as a witness in the Simpson trial and produced the tapes and transcripts.

Within thirty minutes after Judge Wood's ruling, a group of North Carolina lawyers directed by Kenneth Spaulding of Raleigh, North Carolina, were hard at work, perfecting an expedited appeal to the North Carolina Court of Appeals. It was a race against the clock. The Simpson trial was winding down to its close, and if the tapes could not be secured, the defense would lose the most potent evidence available. The petition was filed on the morning of August 1, 1995, in the North Carolina Court of Appeals at Raleigh. That afternoon a three-judge panel was appointed, and issued an order that all responsive pleadings be filed by noon on August 7. A decision would issue forthwith, without oral argument.

Just before 3 P.M. on the afternoon of August 7, the North Carolina Court of Appeals announced their decision. They reversed the ruling of Judge Wood and ordered Laura McKinny to honor the subpoena. Her lawyers announced there would be no further appeals, and arrangements were immediately made to copy the tapes and transcripts and deliver them to California. Prosecutors actually attempted to then seize the tapes in California with a subpoena, before they could be delivered to the defense, but Judge Ito ruled they would be turned over to the defense pursuant to the defense subpoena.

A team of stenographers was put to work to prepare new transcriptions of the tapes as quickly as possible. I was given a set of the transcripts Laura McKinny had made, to begin assembling an "offer of proof" to seek admission of the tapes into evidence. It is hard to describe the emotions that surged through me as I read the transcripts for the first time. There was certainly triumphant glee that such compelling evidence of Fuhrman's true character was now in our hands. But it was tempered by a repellent sense of horror. I'd known a fair number of cops in my years as a proseccutor and defense lawyer. My own brother and my favorite cousin both had distinguished careers as police officers, and are two of the gentlest and kindest people I know. I've certainly known police I'd rather not socialize with, and some were undoubtedly racists. But I'd never even imagined the level of hatefulness and bigotry that oozed from those pages. The transcripts contained forty-two instances of Detective Fuhrman uttering the word "nigger." They were not casual slips of the tongue. In only one case was he assuming the role of a fictional character when the word was used. Some of the phrases were eerily reminiscent of the words Kathleen Bell reported hearing in the Marine Recruiting Station in Redondo Beach. At one point, Fuhrman was discussing American aid to drought victims in Ethiopia with Laura McKinny. I recalled the anguish I felt at the time of the Ethiopian drought, viewing the heartrending images of starving black infants. Mark Fuhrman's reaction was chilling:

"... we got all this money going to Ethiopia for what. To feed a bunch of dumb niggers that their own government won't

even feed. . . . Let 'em die. Use 'em for fertilizer. I mean,
who cares."

His contempt knew no bounds, but most of his venom was directed
close to home. Referring to an L.A.P.D. commander as a "dickhead,"
he said, "He should be shot. He did that for one thing. He wants to
be chief, so he wants the city council, and the police commissioner,
and all these niggers in L.A. city government and all of 'em should
be lined up against a wall and fuckin' shot." At another point, they
were discussing the construction of a new police headquarters
building for the 77th District in South Central Los Angeles, and
Fuhrman explained his opposition to the construction of a new
building:

"Leave that old station. Man, it has the smell of niggers that
have been beaten and killed in there for years."

From an evidentiary standpoint, however, I was most interested in Fuhrman's candid accounts of his evidence-gathering
techniques. Not only could we show he deliberately lied when he
denied use of the "N-word," we could now prove from his own lips
that he had no hestitation about planting evidence, falsifying reports, and lying in court if it accomplished his goal of "putting a
criminal in jail." When I compiled the offer of proof, I not only
cited and excerpted each occasion where Fuhrman uttered the "N-
word," but collected eighteen examples of Fuhrman admitting
participation in police misconduct, including the use of deadly
force, beating suspects to extract confessions, planting evidence,
framing innocent persons, and lying or covering up misconduct by
other officers. Several of these examples closely paralleled evidence
and events in the O.J. Simpson case. When confronted with Kathleen Bell's statement that he said he would "find a reason" to pull
over any "nigger" he saw in a car with a white woman, Fuhrman
had testified that he had never made such a statement, and would
remember it if he had. In one exchange with Laura McKinny, Fuhr-

man described the arrest he had made of a black man in Westwood the previous evening:

MCKINNY: So under what did you arrest him?

FUHRMAN: I didn't arrest him under anything, just took him to the station, ran him for prints, gave them to the detectives to compare with what they've got in the area. I'll probably arrest a criminal that way.

MCKINNY: So you're allowed to just pick somebody up that you think doesn't belong in an area and arrest him?

FUHRMAN: I don't know.

MCKINNY: Well, I mean, you did, so—

FUHRMAN: I don't know. I don't know what the Supreme Court or the Superior Court says, and I don't really give a shit. If I was pushed into saying why I did it, I'd say suspicion of burglary. I'd be able to correlate exactly what I said into a rea sonable probable cause for arrest.

At another point, he explains to McKinny his impatience with his partner's unwillingness to "play the game" by making up lies to "put these fucking assholes in jail":

"Well, I really love being a policeman when I can be a policeman. It's like my partner now. He's so hung up with the rules and stuff. I get pissed sometimes, and go, 'You just don't fucking even understand. This job is not rules. This is a feeling. Fuck the rules, we'll make them up later.' He's a college graduate, a Catholic college. He was going to be a fucking priest. He's got more morals than he's got hair on his head. He doesn't know what to do about it. . . . He doesn't know how to be a policeman. 'I can't lie.' Oh, you make me fucking sick to my guts. You know, you do what you have

to do to put these fucking assholes in jail. If you don't, you
fucking get out of the fucking game."

The evidence of tampering with blood samples in the Simpson case
immediately came to mind when I encountered an exchange in
which Fuhrman explained that he did not consider the manipula-
tion of a scab on a heroin addict to appear fresher than it was to be
the falsification of grounds for arrest:

> "So if that's considered falsifying a report, and if some hype,
> you know, says, Ah, you know, whatever, I shot two days
> ago, and you find a mark that looks like three days ago, pick
> the scab, squeeze it, looks like serum's coming out, as if it
> were hours old. That's a hard find. You just can't find the
> mark, 'cause he's down. His eyes don't lie. That's not falsi-
> fying a report. That's putting a criminal in jail. That's
> being a policeman."

The "code of silence," by which police officers have a tacit understanding they will lie for each other to cover up allegations of misconduct, was described by Fuhrman in full detail. He boasted that
he must have "three or four thousand pages" of complaints and
investigations of his conduct by the Internal Affairs Division of
L.A.P.D. (Not one page was ever produced in response to the defense's Pitchess motion to gain access to these complaints and reports.) He bragged that he got away with brutally beating several
suspects in a police shooting incident, because the officers all stuck
together and told the same false story:

> "Well, they knew I did it. They knew damn well I did it.
> There's nothing they could do about it. Most of those guys
> work the 77th together. We came in as a gang unit. We were
> tight. I mean, we could have murdered people and got away
> with it. We were tight. We all knew what to say. We didn't
> have to call each other at home, and say, 'okay.' We all knew
> what to say."

He described an argument with his partner (the one who was going to be a "fucking priest") about his unwillingness to adhere to the code of silence:

> "He goes, 'I got a wife and kid to think of.' I says, 'Fuck you. Don't tell me because you've got a wife and kid . . . you're either my partner all the way or get the fuck out of this car. We die for each other. We live for each other, that's how it is in the car. You lie for me, up to six months suspension. Don't ever get fired for me. Don't get indicted for me. But you'll take six months for me, 'cause I'll take it for you. If you don't, get the fuck out of here. It shouldn't have to be said.'"

While we were compiling our offer of proof, the prosecutors were given their copy of the tapes and transcripts, and began to strategize their response. I suspect as they read and listened to Mark Fuhrman's words, they heard the faint echo of a toilet flushing. If the jury ever heard any of this, their entire case would go right down the tubes. Panic set in. Their response took us completely by surprise. I'm convinced it was a calculated effort to abort the proceedings and cause a mistrial so they could start all over again. They made a motion to throw Judge Ito off the case!

The basis of their motion was that the Fuhrman tapes included some unflattering references to Judge Ito's wife, Captain Margaret York of the Los Angeles Police Department. Captain York was at one time a watch commander in West Los Angeles, and Mark Fuhrman was among the officers under her command. We were aware of that coincidence and had actually raised the issue ourselves before the Fuhrman tapes came to light. When we were investigating Fuhrman's background, we heard of an incident in which he had allegedly been reprimanded for an anti-Semitic incident. We were concerned that Judge Ito's wife would have to be called as a witness if we were allowed to present evidence of that incident. The matter was resolved by sending the issue to another judge. Captain York submitted an affidavit swearing that she had little contact with

Fuhrman and did not recall any occasion on which she reprimanded him.

The tapes were replete with insulting references to women police officers, which was, after all, the whole focus of Laura McKinny's project. We did not include any of the evidence of hostility toward women in our offer of proof, since it was essentially irrelevant. The issue we were presenting was Fuhrman's credibility in denying his racism and use of racial ephithets, and his past participation in planting evidence and covering up police misconduct. The use of the references to Captain York at this point were a ruse, a ploy to cause Judge Ito's embarrassment and disqualification, and ultimately abort the trial. At this point, there were only two alternate jurors left, and the jurors were chafing under the long, unexplained delays made necessary by the motions and issues raised by the Fuhrman tapes. If Judge Ito were forced off the case, it would take a new judge weeks to prepare to step in and resume the trial. He would have to read 20,000 pages of transcripts of prior proceedings. He would have to familiarize himself with all of the prior evidentiary rulings. Still ahead were key rulings on the permissible scope of rebuttal evidence, as well as rulings on proposed jury instructions, including over forty special requests that were tailored to particular evidentiary rulings. Meanwhile, the jury would have to be put "on ice," perhaps as long as a month. If three more jurors had to be excused, it was all over. A mistrial would be declared, and the prosecution would get a second chance to try to salvage their case.

From a personal standpoint, the crisis over Judge Ito's removal could not have come at a worse time. The motion to disqualify Judge Ito was made on August 15. That evening, I made my long-awaited "debut" as a playwright! The one sabbatical project I had managed to complete was the fulfillment of a lifelong ambition. For many years, I have pursued a fascination with the life and career of William Jennings Bryan. I amassed a personal collection of buttons and other campaign items from his three runs as Democratic nominee for the presidency. I collected and read every biography ever written, and most of his personal writings. The more I read and learned, the more

I became convinced he had been misjudged. His portrayal as a misguided zealot at the Scopes Trial in *Inherit the Wind* ruined his reputation. I resolved to attempt to resurrect and rehabilitate him by the same device that ruined him: a play! Timing was essential. Since 1996 would be the centenary of his famous "Cross of Gold" speech, which won Bryan his first presidential nomination at the age of thirty-six, it would be an opportune time to unveil a new play about his life. My fantasy was to have a production mounted in Chicago, during the 1996 Democratic convention, since the "Cross of Gold" had been delivered in Chicago at the Democratic convention of 1896. I had never written a play, much less had one staged. Ed Asner, an actor I greatly admire, agreed to do a reading of the play at a Los Angeles theater, and an audience of 100 friends and family had been invited. I was looking forward to the thrill of seeing my work come to life on stage. At that very moment, we were faced with a trial crisis of momentous proportions. Right up until the minute we left for the theater, I was furiously reading cases and statutes on judicial disqualification.

We got to the theater shortly before the reading, and my jaw dropped when I saw every one of my co-counsel march through the door: Cochran, Douglas, Chapman, Bailey, Shapiro, Scheck, and Neufeld—they were all there to share this moment. Barry Scheck had his copy of the transcripts of the Fuhrman tapes under his arm, so he could work on the case during the intermission. The reading went splendidly, and it was the thrill of a lifetime to see my work come to life. But the thrill did not match the spirit of camaraderie I felt that night. Knowing that all of my fellow lawyers would be burning the midnight oil to make up for a couple hours off, I was deeply gratified by the team's show of support.

Our response to the disqualification move was swift and sure. We were by this time quite unhappy with the drift of Judge Ito's rulings. Time and again, he was caving in to the prosecution's efforts to restrict the presentation of defense evidence. We were precluded from any showing of Faye Resnick's extensive drug use at Nicole Brown Simpson's condo, in an effort to suggest an alternative motive for the killings. The impeachment we offered against Detective Fuhrman was being sanitized and restricted at every turn. If there were a way to replace Judge Ito and resume the trial the next day, we might have jumped at the chance. But it was clear to us that this move was a prelude, to set in motion events that would inevitably lead to a mistrial. We opposed the disqualification move with vigor. What was especially galling was the prosecutorial suggestion we could avoid the whole problem by not offering the Fuhrman tapes in evidence. That clearly exposed the cynical nature of their motion.

We argued that the disqualification statute had no application to this situation, that it could be dealt with the same way the issue had been dealt with before: Let another judge decide whether the portion of the Fuhrman tapes which referred to Judge Ito's wife had any possible relevancy to the case. If it was determined they did not, the problem was resolved without Judge Ito ever having to even look at those portions of the transcript. We also argued that the failure of the prosecution to object when the issue of Captain York was previously raised was a waiver of any conflict that might be presented. The prosecution made a rather lame argument about the "appearance of impropriety," having a judge decide whether tapes could be used to impeach a witness, when the tapes contained disparaging remarks about the judge's wife. Ironically, no impropriety appeared from anything Judge Ito had said or done. The Fuhrman transcripts remained under seal, the portions referring to his wife had been excised, and the public would never have even been aware of any problem but for the prosecution's disqualification motion.

The crisis was resolved in an unanticipated way. The prosecution relented and agreed that another judge could rule on the relevancy of the transcript reference to Captain Margaret York. We never learned the full story behind their change of position. Before it was publicly announced, however, we were treated to a spectacle such as I had never seen before, nor hope to ever see again. First thing that morning, the prosecution requested a meeting in chambers with Judge Ito, off the record. That meant the court stenographer who took down every word spoken at a trial was not present. Such meetings are ordinarily limited to mundane procedural mechanics that have no impact on the trial. I accompanied Johnnie Cochran and Bob Shapiro back to Judge Ito's chambers, and Chris Darden came in with Marcia Clark. We all sat down. Chris leaned across Judge Ito's desk and told him how unhappy those in the District Attorney's office were with some of his rulings. It was a very heavy-handed attempt to deliver a not-so-subtle message: We've decided to let you stay on the case, but you better shape up! I had never heard a lawyer talk to a judge that way, and couldn't believe it was being done so brazenly in our presence. Johnnie Cochran immediately stood up and announced we were simply not going to participate in this. The defense lawyers stormed out of chambers and returned to the courtroom. When court resumed that morning, Cochran complained bitterly about what had happened and announced he would file a complaint against Darden with the state bar. The complaint was prepared and filed within days. Darden responded with accusations against the defense lawyers, suggesting that his "grand jury" investigation uncovered information about the defense lawyers that would be turned over to the U.S. Attorney's office. It was like watching a little boy caught with his hand in the cookie jar, desperately looking for someone else to blame. If anyone had any doubt about the true motivations behind the prosecution's aborted effort to disqualify Judge Ito, Chris Darden's disgusting performance that day removed them.

The question of whether the references to Captain Margaret York in the Fuhrman tapes had any relevance to the trial of *People v. O.J. Simpson* was referred to Judge John Reid. Judge Reid made short shrift of the issue. On Friday, August 25, he ruled that they were irrelevant, and the decks were cleared for Judge Ito to consider how much, if any, of the Fuhrman tapes would be heard by the jury.

The day we spent arguing the admissibility of the Fuhrman tapes was the most memorable day I have ever spent in a courtroom. At first Judge Ito seemed reluctant to allow each of the excerpts we were offering to be displayed and heard in the courtroom. Marcia Clark offered to stipulate that the voice on the tapes was Fuhrman's and argued there was no need to air the tapes in court.

We responded that the tone and inflection of his voice were essential considerations in assessing the tapes to impeach his testimony. After a brief recess, Judge Ito announced, "I think that there is an overriding public interest in the nature of the offer that you are making, and I don't want this court to ever be in a position where there is any indication that this court would participate in suppressing information that is of vital public interest." It was such a dramatic shift of position that we concluded something must have happened during the recess to convince him to let the tapes be played. It was one occasion where I would have liked to have been a fly on the wall of the judge's chambers. The tapes and transcripts were the best example I've seen of evidence that speaks more eloquently than a lawyer ever could. With little interruption or explanation, I offered one excerpt after another, a total of sixty-one excerpts. The effect was stunning. The courtroom was absolutely silent as everyone strained to hear the words. As the depth of hate and bigotry they conveyed seared into the consciousness of the courtroom audience, one could sense a heavy resignation in the air. It truly was Los Angeles's worst nightmare, indisputable proof that all the years of abuse that L.A. blacks had endured at the hands of rogue police officers were not figments of overactive imaginations. It was impossible to feel any sense of self-satisfaction, to gloat or say "we told you so." We could only share the sense of shame that such a man had ever worn a badge.

We anticipated that the prosecutors would argue that Fuhrman's statements were a charade for Laura McKinny's benefit, that he was not expressing his actual opinions and beliefs. The testimony of Laura McKinny laid that argument to rest, if it had any plausibility left after Fuhrman's voice was heard. Ms. McKinny's reluctance to testify only added to her credibility, and the concise way she had gone about researching her screenplay and transcribing the tapes left no doubts as to the accuracy of her transcripts. She testified Fuhrman was not "role playing"; he was providing her with precisely what she asked him to provide: his "truth," his perceptions, his frame of reference, and his experience. Judge Ito took the offer of evidence under submission. We anticipated he would pare the offer down substantially, but we seriously underestimated Judge Ito's willingness to help the prosecution salvage their case. The ruling he issued on August 31, 1995, was an outrage. While I believe that it is generally inappropriate for lawyers to publicly criticize the rulings of a judge while the trial is still pending, I feel no reluctance to now express the anger that's still there. Lawyers who whine when they lose are doing a disservice to their profession and may even be hurting their clients. Especially with Judge Ito, I realized that there were always going to be lots more issues he would have to decide, and it would be suicidal to publicly castigate his rulings, even when convinced they were dead wrong. But the ruling on the Fuhrman tapes was so transparent in its purpose, so disingenuous in its reasoning, and so devastating in its impact, a lawyer would be remiss to simply accept it and move on. The entire defense team read it in disbelief, then agonized about how to react. Johnnie Cochran blistered the judge in a press conference. I went to work on a motion for reconsideration, with little hope the judge would even read it.

Judge Ito ruled that only two excerpts from the tapes and transcripts could be presented to the jury: (1) An eight-word statement—"We have no niggers where I grew up,"—removed from the context of the following excerpt:

> "People there don't want niggers in their town. People there don't want Mexicans in their town. They don't want anybody but good people in their town, and anyway you can do to get them out of there that's fine with them. We have no niggers where I grew up."

And (2) a question and answer with no explanation as to its context (a discussion of where black Muslims congregated): "Q: Why do they live in that area? A: That's where niggers live." In addition, Laura McKinny would be allowed to testify as to the total number of times she heard Mark Fuhrman use the word "nigger" in her tapes and transcripts: Forty-one. (She actually testified there were forty-two, including one belatedly discovered example that had not been inserted in the offer of proof.) In the most devastating portion of his ruling, Judge Ito held that *none* of the incidents of evidence planting, lying, or covering up police misconduct could be offered before the jury.

The first excerpt Judge Ito allowed was not on tape, but had been transcribed from one of the tapes that was taped over and destroyed. The second excerpt was on tape, but the background noise and sound quality rendered it the least audible of all of the tape extracts we offered. Fuhrman's voice was barely recognizable. I assumed that was a deliberate choice on Judge Ito's part, consistent with the tenor of the rest of the ruling. It was the only aspect of the ruling on which he was willing to relent, permitting the substitution of a more audible excerpt when Laura McKinny finally testified in front of the jury.

What was infuriating was the dishonest portrait of Detective Mark Fuhrman this presented to the jury. The relevance of Fuhrman's racial attitudes lay in their virulence. One who listened to the tapes was left with little doubt that this man would be motivated and fully capable of framing an innocent man purely for racial spite. The sanitized version of the tapes that Judge Ito was permitting portrayed Fuhrman as an insensitive boob who said naughty words when he shouldn't have. It even offered a sweet explanation for his insensitivity: "We have no niggers where I grew up." All we were left with was a little corroboration of Kathleen Bell's testimony that, indeed, Fuhrman had used the word "nigger" in the past ten years despite his denial.

The jury would never hear Detective Fuhrman's explanation of how he made up evidence to provide probable cause for arrests of blacks who were in the wrong part of town. Judge Ito's explanation for that portion of the ruling was hypocritical, when compared to his willingness to admit evidence of prior incidents of alleged spousal abuse against O.J. Simpson. The same evidentiary principle was at stake. But prior incidents of Detective Fuhrman's misconduct could not be admitted unless and until the defense offered independent proof that Fuhrman "planted" the glove found on the Rockingham premises. No case authority was cited for such a "threshold" requirement, and it certainly had not been imposed on the prosecution. The evidence of prior incidents of alleged spousal abuse was the first evidence they offered in their case in chief. Judge Ito rejected the specific incidents where Fuhrman made up probable cause for an arrest by finding there was not sufficient similarity between those incidents and the Simpson case, because Fuhrman did not make the arrest of O.J. Simpson! In other words, the fact that an officer planted blood on another suspect he arrested is irrelevant to show he planted blood on this suspect, because this suspect was subsequently arrested by some other officer. This reasoning was patently specious.

The concerns that the Fuhrman tapes were so inflammatory they might have prejudiced the jury were legitimate concerns, and Judge Ito's ruling excluding the excerpts about letting Ethiopians be used as fertilizer, or lining up African-American city council members and shooting them were probably appropriate. But he went far beyond those concerns in his transparent effort to bail out the prosecution's sinking ship. He invited them to present Mark Fuhrman to the jury as a misguided zealot, rather than a cunning liar.

The sanitized testimony of Laura McKinny that was finally presented to the jury had none of the dramatic impact of the actual tapes and transcripts. The prosecutors could not resist taking some of their frustrations out on Laura McKinny, however. In his cross-examination of Laura McKinny, Chris Darden snidely suggested she was a failure as a playwright, she wrote scripts for "soft porn," and her relationship with Mark Fuhrman was not "only professional." "I don't understand," she protested; "I don't feel adversarial toward you, but I felt there was something negative coming from some of your questions." It was a classic example of attacking the messenger when you don't like the message. Darden's performance didn't appear to sit well with the jury.

Even the minimum damage inflicted by the brief excerpts from the Fuhrman tapes that Judge Ito admitted required the prosecutors to shift their strategy regarding the other witnesses called to impeach Mark Fuhrman. Rather than the previously planned "slash and burn" attack to brand as liars Kathleen Bell, Natalie Singer, and Roderic Hodge, all of whom testified to hearing Fuhrman use the "N-word," those witnesses were quickly excused after perfunctory cross-examinations.

The lesson of the Fuhrman tapes will resound in American courtrooms, perhaps even longer than the lesson of the Rodney King tapes. The lesson is that racism is alive and well, and it does affect the way citizens are treated by police officers. We ignore that lesson at our peril. The fact that Mark Fuhrman so freely shared his venom with women he casually met belies the claim of the L.A.P.D. that they never knew they had a viper in their midst. It's no stretch to conclude there are a host of fellow officers who were well aware of who Mark Fuhrman was and what he represented. That he was not only tolerated, but protected and promoted to a position of great responsiblity does not speak well for the L.A.P.D. Chilling evidence of a "code of silence" can be heard loud and clear on the Fuhrman tapes. Rooting out racism in American police departments will be no easier than rooting it out of our other institutions. It has to start with the recognition that we still have a serious problem. If the Fuhrman tapes weren't enough to deliver that message, the public reaction to the jury's verdict should have been. It doesn't seem to be a message many people want to hear. Not only is racism alive and well in America; so is denial.

T W E L V E

THE SOUND

OF SILENCE

*I*f O.J. Simpson is innocent, why doesn't he get up on the witness stand and say so, and be cross-examined?" This is the kind of question defense lawyers expect to hear from the public. Those who haven't been to law school have little appreciation of the Fifth Amendment, much less the values it preserves in our adversary system. But it is not the kind of question you expect to hear from a prosecutor. Unless the prosecutor asking it already knows the answer but wants to plant doubts in the minds of television viewers. Unless the prosecutor asking it has been badly stung by the spectacle of her star witness himself taking the Fifth Amendment to avoid cross-examination. There is an essential difference, however, between the privilege invoked by O.J. Simpson in declining to testify in his own behalf, and the privilege invoked by Detective Mark Fuhrman, to avoid further cross-examination. In both cases, the result was silence. In the case of O.J. Simpson, however, the silence was by nature ambiguous. In the case of Mark Fuhrman, it was not. It spoke volumes.

The Fifth Amendment of the United States Constitution has always guaranteed to the accused in a criminal trial the privilege of declining to testify, on the grounds that his testimony might tend to incriminate him. For many years, the invocation of that privilege carried a cost, however. The prosecutor would get up in closing argument, and say to the jury, "What have we heard from the defendant, the one person who has the most at stake in this case? Nothing. If he's as innocent as his lawyer says he is, why didn't he get up on the witness stand and say so?" A telling argument, but not unanswerable. The problem is that the answer most often would have dug an even deeper hole for the defendant. Most often, the real answer would have been, "The defendant would love to get up and tell his side of the story. But if he does, the prosecutor can impeach him with his prior convictions. The defendant doesn't want you to know about those prior convictions, because he's afraid you'll be more likely to convict him, regardless of the evidence that's been presented with respect to the crime he's on trial for." That's not a telling argument. True, but not telling.

The United States Supreme Court finally addressed this hypocrisy in 1965, in the landmark case of *Griffin v. California.* They declared that prosecutors could no longer comment on the defendant's invocation of the Fifth Amendment privilege, because such comment undercuts the privilege itself. It imposes an impermissible price on the exercise of a constitutional right. The *Griffin* rule has since been applied even to a suspect who invokes his *Miranda* rights by refusing to respond to interrogation when he is placed in custody. Ordinarily a suspect's silence is treated as an implied admission of guilt, but the court ruled that where the silence follows a warning of his Fifth Amendment right to remain silent, the silence is ambiguous. It may imply guilt, but on the other hand, it may simply imply the caution that the Fifth Amendment respects, and suggest the suspect wants to see his lawyer before he speaks.

In 1981, the U.S. Supreme Court went a step further and declared that the defendant has a right to have the jury instructed they should *not* draw any adverse inference from the defendant's failure to testify. Such an instruction was requested and given in the trial of *People v. O.J. Simpson.* The jury was told:

"A defendant in a criminal trial has a constitutional right not to be compelled to testify. You must not draw any inference from the fact that a defendant does not testify. Further, you must neither discuss this matter nor permit it to enter into your deliberations in any way."

Obviously, it was not the fear of impeachment by prior convictions that kept O.J. Simpson off the witness stand. His only prior conviction was the misdemeanor assault in 1989, and the jury heard about that during the first week of the trial. Nor was he kept off the witness stand by the ethical rule that precludes a lawyer from allowing his client to lie when he "knows" his client is guilty. All of O.J. Simpson's lawyers believed in his claim of innocence. What kept O.J. Simpson off the witness stand was a simple principle of economics. He had more to lose that he had to gain by testifying.

The decision not to testify was made late in the trial. Prosecutors listen very closely to a defense lawyer's opening statement, because it gives them the first clue whether the defendant will take the witness stand. Anyone listening to Johnnie Cochran's opening statement would have bet that O.J. Simpson would testify as a witness. Cochran previewed evidence that could only come from the lips of Simpson himself. At that point in the trial, the defense fully intended to call Simpson to the stand. In fact, two very experienced women lawyers from San Francisco, Christina Arguedas and Penelope Cooper, were engaged to prepare him for cross-examination. It was felt that lawyers who were not part of the defense team could more realistically simulate the kind of cross-examination Mr. Simpson would be subjected to, and these particular lawyers could best emulate the aggressive style of Marcia Clark. Preparing a client for cross-examination is an important aspect of any criminal defense lawyer's trial strategy. In 1973, I was engaged to assist in preparing Daniel Ellsberg for cross-examination in part because I had worked closely with the prosecutor who would cross-examine him, and could emulate his style. O.J. Simpson withstood the exercise quite well. He confidently and fully explained his whereabouts on the night of June 12, 1994, just as he had in his interview with the detectives on June 13, 1994. The only concern related to all of the doors that would be opened to the previous events in his sixteen-year relationship with Nicole Brown Simpson. Simpson would be the last witness called by the defense. From a tactical standpoint, there was a real risk to ending the trial with a rehash of all of the domestic discord evidence with which the trial had begun. Not only would all of that evidence be replayed, but a good deal of additional evidence of discord that had been excluded by our pretrial motion was excluded only from the prosecution's opening case and could still be used to rebut the defense case. Cross-examination would open new doors and bring much of that evidence before the jury for the first time.

We also were very pleased with the state of the evidence with respect to the cut on O.J. Simpson's finger when he returned from Chicago on June 13, 1994. The prosecution's decision not to offer the twenty-page statement that O.J. Simpson gave to the police on June 13 left a hole in their case. In the statement, he admitted that he may have cut his finger before he left Los Angeles, while he was rushing around to get things out of his Bronco and get packed, and then cut it again in Chicago. But none of the witnesses who saw him that night—including Kato Kaelin, limo driver Allan Park, and fellow passengers on the flight to Chicago, had observed any cuts or injuries to his hand. The evidence of a broken glass and bloody towel in his Chicago hotel room established his explanation that he accidentally cut himself in Chicago.

Most important, we realized that if he took the witness stand, Marcia Clark would drag out his cross-examination for weeks. Extending the trial for even two more weeks was a high-risk venture, in terms of the dwindling jury and the possibility of a mistrial.

Ultimately, the choice was left to O.J. Simpson himself. The decision whether to testify is a decision the lawyers cannot make for the client. All the lawyers can do is make sure the client understands all of the pros and cons of either choice, and offer their own recommendations. Once again, the recommendation of the entire team of lawyers was unanimous. It was not in O.J. Simpson's best interests to take the witness stand. O.J. Simpson badly wanted to tell his side of the story, and it was with great reluctance that he heeded his attorneys' advice. He trusted the jury and felt confident they would follow the judge's instruction not to draw any inference from his failure to testify.

O.J. Simpson was not the only person to rely on the Fifth Amendment in the case of *People v. O.J. Simpson.* So did Mark Fuhrman. What's sauce for the goose is sauce for the gander. Is chutzpah the only explanation for the defense suggestion that, even though no adverse inference should be drawn from the invocation of the Fifth Amendment privilege by O.J. Simpson, an adverse inference *could* be drawn from Detective Mark Fuhrman's reliance on the same privilege? Actually, the defense position was well reasoned and strongly supported by the law.

Detective Mark Fuhrman was recalled to the witness stand when we renewed our motion to suppress, based on the revelations in the Fuhrman tapes. We argued that the newly discovered evidence of Fuhrman's perjury undercut the credibility of his testimony at the preliminary hearing so substantially that the evidence he allegedly found in the warrantless search the morning of June 12, 1994, should now be suppressed. Judge Ito was hard put to conclude that Fuhrman was still credible, so he took refuge in a finding that the testimony of Detective Vannatter alone was sufficient to uphold the reasonableness of the search. During the hearing, I put three questions to Detective Fuhrman:

Was the testimony that you gave at the preliminary hearing
  in this case completely truthful?
Have you ever falsified a police report?
Did you plant or manufacture any evidence in this case?

To each question, after consulting with counsel, he responded, "I wish to assert my Fifth Amendment privilege." I then asked whether he intended to assert the privilege in response to every question I asked, and he answered "Yes." The motion, of course, was outside the presence of the jury. We still had reserved the right to call Detective Fuhrman for further cross-examination in front of the jury, but his invocation of the Fifth Amendment privilege would also render him unavailable as a witness for that purpose.

Ordinarily, a witness who wishes to rely upon the Fifth Amendment privilege must invoke it on direct examination, before he testifies. Giving testimony on direct examination has been held to be a waiver of the protection of the Fifth Amendment privilege, so that it cannot be invoked to preclude appropriate cross-examination. That principle was applied in a famous case handled by F. Lee Bailey, the prosecution of Patty Hearst for assisting her kidnappers in the perpetration of a series of robberies. Bailey put Ms. Hearst on the witness stand to describe the circumstances of her kidnapping and confinement, but advised her to invoke the Fifth Amendment with respect to the robberies. The court overruled her claim, and she ended up asserting the privilege repeatedly in front of the jury. There is an important exception to this rule, however, where a witness who previously testified *can* invoke the Fifth Amendment privilege. If the witness is concerned that further testimony may incriminate him of the crime of *perjury* in his earlier testimony, that protection will not have been waived by the prior testimony, and the privilege can be invoked. Thus, the *only* legal basis for Detective Fuhrman to invoke the protection of the Fifth Amendment was fear of a perjury prosecution for the testimony he had already given.

Surprisingly, one division of the California Court of Appeal had already addressed a situation very similar to the one we faced with Detective Fuhrman. A key witness who testified against the defendant at his preliminary hearing was called again as a witness at his trial. The witness said his prior testimony was false, and he refused to give testimony at the trial on the grounds of the Fifth Amendment. The trial court upheld the claim of the privilege, allowed the previous preliminary hearing testimony to be read to the jury, and then instructed the jury with the same instruction our jury received regarding O.J. Simpson's failure to testify. They were told, "When a witness refuses to testify as to any matter, basing his refusal on the constitutional privilege against self-incrimination, you are not to draw from that fact any inference as to the credibility of the witness, or as to the guilt or innocence of the defendant." The court of appeal overturned the conviction and ruled as follows:

> When the People wish to go forward in reliance upon the testimony of a recanting witness, fundamental fairness would require, at a minimum, that the jury (1) be advised precisely why the witness is being allowed to refuse to testify, i.e., an alleged fear of a perjury prosecution, and (2) be instructed that they should draw all reasonable and appropriate inferences therefrom concerning the witness's credibility and the guilt or innocence of the accused.

Judge Ito was not prepared to go that far with Detective Fuhrman. He ruled that Fuhrman could not be called in front of the jury, and the jury could not be told that he took the Fifth Amendment, but the jury would be instructed as follows:

> Detective Mark Fuhrman is not available for further testimony as a witness in this case. His unavailability for further testimony in cross-examination is a factor you may consider in evaluating his testimony as a witness.

The prosecutors immediately sought a ruling from the court of appeal, to forbid Judge Ito from giving that instruction. They argued the instruction would violate Section 913 of the California Evidence Code, which provides "no presumption shall arise because of the exercise of [a] privilege, and the trier of fact may not draw any inference therefrom as to the credibility of the witness or as to any matter at issue in the proceeding." We were confident Judge Ito had carefully avoided any problem with Section 913. His instruction offered no explanation why Fuhrman's testimony was unavailable and made no mention of his invocation of any privilege. It told the jury it could consider his *unavailability* for cross-examination in assessing his credibility. We thought the instruction was essential to avoid the jury drawing an adverse inference

against the *defendant,* because he did not recall Fuhrman for further cross-examination when the jury knew he had the right to do
so. We felt sure the court of appeal would decline to inject itself
into an ongoing trial, or would at least give us an opportunity to be
heard before doing so. To our surprise, an immediate ruling came
from the court of appeal. It ordered Judge Ito to either withdraw his
ruling granting the instruction, or make a showing why the court
of appeal should not order him to do so on the following Monday.
With the assistance of Dennis Fischer, one of the best appellate
lawyers in California, we prepared to appear in the court of appeal
to defend Judge Ito's ruling. Without notice or hearing, however,
Judge Ito promptly withdrew his ruling.

The process of review was somewhat bizarre. Completely ig-
noring precedent from another division of the same court of appeal, and without any opportunity for the defendant to be heard,
the California Court of Appeal had injected itself into an ongoing
trial to reverse a trial court's ruling. Judge Ito's conduct was equally
bizarre. Apparently, he didn't even have enough confidence in his
ruling to let it stand long enough so we could go to the court of appeal on Monday and defend it.

Having been deprived of any explanation to the jury as to why
Detective Fuhrman was not being recalled for further cross-
examination, we went back to Judge Ito to seek alternative remedies.
We asked, alternatively, that Fuhrman's earlier testimony describing the finding of the glove be stricken from the record, that he be
required to testify under a grant of use immunity that would
preclude his use of the Fifth Amendment (the privilege becomes
unnecessary if the state is precluded from using the testimony
against the witness in future proceedings), that he be recalled to
testify as to matters as to which the privilege had been waived, or
that his unavailability be remedied by admitting in evidence his
prior admissions of planting evidence contained in the Fuhrman
tapes. All of these requests were denied, and a subsequent petition
to have the California Supreme Court intervene was also denied.
We were left with no further recourse. I secretly wished we could
have gone back to North Carolina to seek some justice!

Unlike the silence of O.J. Simpson, which was explained to the jury with the instruction they should not consider it, the silence of Detective Mark Fuhrman was never explained. As far as the jury was concerned, he simply disappeared from the case. They were never instructed they should *not* speculate or draw inferences. They were simply left to their own devices.

There is one other element of silence in the trial of *People v. O.J. Simpson* that merits further explanation: the silence of Reverend Roosevelt Grier. While O.J. Simpson was in jail awaiting his trial, Reverend Grier became a frequent visitor to offer spiritual counseling. Grier became a minister after a stellar football career and the disillusionment of cradling the body of a dying Robert F. Kennedy after his assassination on the eve of his presidential primary election victory in California in 1968. Rosie Grier was a personal hero of mine, however, for a more obscure reason. Our children were profoundly touched by a remarkable television special in the 1970s called "Free to Be You and Me." Rosie Grier appeared in that special to sing a catchy little tune called "It's All Right to Cry." The tune became a little ritual in our family, and I recall countless special moments when singing it gave us some consolation in difficult circumstances. I counted it a special privilege to finally meet Rosie Grier personally and get to know him. He's a remarkable person, and devotes his life to inspiring young people to look to their Bibles for the answers they need. O.J. Simpson found great consolation in his visits.

Among every defense lawyer's greatest fears is that a client in confinement will be victimized by snitches who are planted in jails, or guards with ears on a stick, who will make every effort to overhear snatches of private conversations and report them to gain some favor or reward. We took special precautions to insure that the attorneys and clergy who visited O.J. Simpson would have complete privacy. The arrangement for weekend visits was somewhat awkward, however. The room set aside was right next to a control booth staffed by deputies, and Simpson could only communicate through a telephone headset from behind a glassed-in enclosure.

Shortly before the trial testimony began, in December of 1994, we were informed that a jail deputy had reported overhearing a portion of a conversation between O.J. Simpson and Roosevelt Grier during a weekend visit. A report had been transmitted by the sheriff's office to the court, and Judge Ito ordered it sealed. The prosecution filed a motion to have it unsealed and turned over to them. The hearing of this matter consumed several court days, requiring testimony by Roosevelt Grier and the jail deputy, who claimed O.J. Simpson was "yelling" and could be overheard in the control booth. There was intense press speculation about the nature of the statement as some sort of confession or admission. We were confident it was not, and could be fully explained if put into context. But the prospect of having to *explain* a conversation between a prisoner and his spiritual counselor in a trial before a jury was particularly odious. California has a very broad statutory privilege for clergy-penitent communications, and this conversation clearly fell within the privilege. The prosecution argued that the privilege only protects confidential communications, and the fact that Mr. Simpson was "yelling" waived the privilege. Both Mr. Simpson and Reverend Grier insisted they spoke in normal tones, but we realized we would not succeed in challenging the credibility of the deputy's claim that he could only overhear snatches of conversation when voices were raised. Ultimately, Judge Ito ruled that in fact the privilege *had* been waived:

> [C]lergy/penitent communications must be made in confidence. Yelling defeats this purpose and renders the privilege waived, especially where it is apparent there are third persons nearby whose job requires them to pay attention to any behavior that is out of the ordinary.

Nonetheless, Judge Ito protected the conversation from disclosure because of the assurances that had been given to the defense that the special visiting area was secure and private. He concluded that Simpson was lulled into a false sense of security in regard to the confidentiality of his communications. The prosecution never learned the contents of the deputy's report, and O.J. Simpson never had to explain to the jury what he and Reverend Grier were discussing. The entire incident sent a cold December chill through the defense camp. Prosecutors who would seek to use a snatches of a defendant's consultations with his minister in an effort to incriminate him would go to any lengths to gain a conviction. Our attorneys and investigators took extraordinary precautions to protect the confidentiality of all communications. For the first time, I installed a shredder in my office, and declined to discuss the case in any telephone calls utilizing cellular telephones. Paranoia became an occupational necessity.

The lesson from the invocation of privileges during the trial of *People v. O.J. Simpson* is that inferences should not be drawn from silence, unless the silence is unambiguous. The principle is one that is frequently ignored by the press and the public. I still find that the question I am most frequently asked when speaking about the case is, "If O.J. Simpson is innocent, why didn't he get up on the witness stand and say so, and be cross-examined?" Now, at least I have a more compact response. I can say, "Read my book."

IF IT DOESN'T FIT

*T*he courtroom experiment to test the fit of the bloody glove found on the Rockingham premises on the hand of O.J. Simpson was a turning point in the trial. From that point on, the prosecution was scrambling to undo the damage they had done to their own case, to try to explain why the glove was obviously too small. They demanded that Mr. Simpson try on a pair of brand-new gloves of the same size. They called a glove salesman as an "expert witness" to suggest the glove may have shrunk. (He was impeached with a letter he had written asking that he be invited to the prosecution's "victory party.") They brought in a parade of witnesses in an attempt to link the gloves in evidence with gloves worn by O.J. Simpson during football game telecasts.

I thought the misfit was a paradigm for the entire prosecution case and could provide a "theme" for our final argument. I found the theme could even be expressed in a rhyme: "If it doesn't fit, you must acquit." This phrase would not only remind the jurors of the dramatic failure of the glove experiment, it summarized what was certainly the most important jury instruction the jury would hear: the instruction on circumstantial evidence.

California judges rarely depart from the standardized "formula" jury instructions approved by the Committee on Standard Jury Instructions, Criminal, of the Los Angeles County Superior Court, generally known as "CALJIC" instructions. These instructions have been tried and tested, and are frequently updated to reflect the latest decisions of the appellate courts. Even though we submitted numerous requests for "special" instructions that did not appear in CALJIC, we had little hope these requests would be granted. With rare exceptions, they were denied. But we knew we could count on Judge Ito giving the standard CALJIC instruction on circumstantial evidence, and that became the foundation of our entire final argument.

This instruction informs the jury in a case based on circumstantial evidence, as the Simpson case was, that if the evidence is susceptible of two reasonable interpretations, one pointing to guilt, the other pointing to innocence, the jury must acquit, because the defendant must be given the benefit of the doubt. It also says that, before the jury can convict, the proved circumstances must not only be consistent with the theory that the defendant is guilty, but they must be irreconcilable with any other conclusion.

The prosecution's case was built on "circumstantial" evidence, evidence which proves a fact from which an "inference" of another fact may be drawn. There was no "direct" evidence, such as an eyewitness who observed the killings. Even if all the witnesses who testified for the prosecution were believed, none of them had any personal knowledge of what happened at the Bundy location on the night of June 12, 1994. The jury had to "infer" that O.J. Simpson sneaked over to his ex-wife's house during a twenty-minute interlude, and while their children were asleep in an upstairs bedroom, stabbed and slashed Nicole Brown Simpson and Ronald Goldman, then rushed back to his home, got rid of a knife and bloody clothing, and packed for a business trip to Chicago.

There were lots of circumstances that didn't "fit" this scenario, and were more consistent with Mr. Simpson's claim that he was at home, and as he told the limousine driver, he was rushing around to get showered and packed. His demeanor both before and after the crime, and the narrow corridor of time in which the crime could have been committed, all gave rise to substantial doubt. These circumstances, we would argue, were equally consistent with innocence as with guilt. Just as the "fit" of the glove didn't match the theory of the prosecution's case, neither did the "fit" of other circumstantial evidence.

Many lawyers suggest that cases are won or lost when the jury is selected; that the predisposition of the jurors will determine the outcome of the case. Others argue that cases are won or lost in the opening statement; that the first impression jurors form of the relative strengths and weaknesses of the opposing sides will ultimately control their decision. Then there are those who insist that jurors do, in fact, struggle to keep an open mind throughout a trial, and it is the final arguments that will convince them one way or the other.

I believe the case of *People v. O.J. Simpson* was "won" in the final arguments. That is not to say that many of the jurors were not already convinced before the arguments commenced. "Winning," however, meant convincing all twelve jurors that their doubts were reasonable ones. Before the final arguments, most of the lawyers on the defense team thought there was a substantial risk the case would end with a "hung" jury. We felt we had two or three jurors who remained unconvinced. The closing arguments would be our last opportunity to convince them.

The question of who should argue the case for the defense was a difficult one. There was no question but that Johnnie Cochran should argue, but Judge Ito was willing to let the argument be split between two lawyers, and the choice of the second lawyer set off some jockeying for position. Bob Shapiro imagined himself giving a final argument from day one of the case, as any good defense lawyer would. Many of the tactical moves made in the earliest stages of the case are made with final argument in mind. The most difficult aspect of our final arguments, however, would be effectively dealing with the scientific evidence. No one understood that evidence better than Barry Scheck. The only question was whether Barry Scheck was having the same effect on the jurors that he was having on Judge Ito. Judge Ito seemed to keep both Barry Scheck and Peter Neufeld on a shorter leash than the other lawyers, as though he did not trust them to the same extent he trusted Johnnie Cochran or Bob Shapiro. Bob thought that Barry was affecting the jurors in the same way, that Barry's aggressive manner and New York accent would annoy some jurors. The polling done by our jury consultant, however, confirmed that Barry had a very high "trust" level among viewers who matched the demographics of our jurors. I thought that Barry's logical and methodical carving up of the evidence would complement Johnnie's more emotional style, and it was extremely important that we appeal to *both* the hearts and minds of our jurors. At times, I felt Johnnie and Barry were speaking to entirely different personalities on the jury, and it was absolutely essential that we reach both the jurors to whom Johnnie was speaking and the ones to whom Barry was speaking if we were to get a unanimous verdict. The final choice was left to O.J. Simpson, and he decided to go with Johnnie and Barry.

Johnnie Cochran and Barry Scheck have very different styles, and those differences were reflected in how they prepared their final arguments. Johnnie sought lots of input from everyone on the team. Charles Lindner, who had not previously participated on the defense team, was asked to put together an outline for Johnnie, and he pulled together all of the suggestions that had been made and organized them into a structured presentation. His fresh perspective was useful, so the argument would not just replay things the jury had already heard. But the outline was often just a jumping-off point. Cochran is most effective when he is extemporizing, and he frequently departed from the structure of the outline.

Barry Scheck is almost surgical in his logical precision. He had excellent recall of the precise details of the evidence and could weave a tapestry that pulled it all together in a very credible way. He also knew where we were vulnerable and anticipated the prosecution's arguments effectively. He delivered a scathing attack on the prosecution's case that would be remembered by the jurors as they listened to the prosecution's closing summation, to which we could not respond.

The structure of final arguments gives the prosecution a significant advantage. They get to open and close the argument. The defense can respond to their opening argument but never gets the opportunity to respond to their closing argument. Many prosecutors take full advantage of having the final word, saving their most powerful appeal to the jury for the end of their argument.

Viewers may have observed that the defense made few objections to the prosecution's opening argument, because we knew we would have a full opportunity to respond to their arguments, point by point. But Marcia Clark's closing argument was frequently interrupted by defense objections. The most serious objection was that she was "vouching" for her case. The personal beliefs of lawyers about the guilt or innocence of the accused are irrelevant, and improper "vouching" consists of conveying one's own personal convictions in an attempt to persuade the jury. It's like saying, "I wouldn't be here if I wasn't personally convinced the defendant is guilty, so your trust in me should allay your doubts." At several points, Ms. Clark seemed to be saying precisely that in ways that were hardly subtle. Judge Ito ruled that, while she came close to the line that defines proper argument, she hadn't crossed it.

Some commentators have suggested that Johnnie Cochran crossed the line of ethical propriety in his final argument by comparing Mark Fuhrman to Adolf Hitler, by frequently quoting the Bible, and by urging the jury to "send a message" to the Los Angeles Police Department. The latter argument, it was suggested, verged on what is called "jury nullification," in which a jury disregards the law to pursue its own vision of justice. I don't believe any of these criticisms are valid, when the arguments are placed in the context in which they were made.

The strongest reaction to Cochran's allusion to Adolf Hitler seemed to come from the Jewish community, as if Cochran was appropriating their proprietary villain. The reaction might have been appropriate if Cochran had compared the evil done by Detective Mark Fuhrman to the evil done by Adolf Hitler. There is, of course, no comparison, and even the attempt to draw a parallel would be an insult to those who know of the devastation of the Holocaust. That's not the point Johnnie Cochran was making, however. He was alluding to the fact that Adolf Hitler's genocidal and racist rantings were not taken very seriously, prior to his rise to power. Once

Fuhrman had been exposed, and his genocidal rantings to Kathleen Bell had been admitted into evidence ("If I had my way, they would take all the niggers, put them together in a big group, and burn them"), the prosecution had shifted from a spirited defense of Fuhrman's integrity to a dismissive posture, as if to suggest he was some sort of aberration from the lunatic fringe who could be isolated and ignored. Cochran was simply suggesting that cancer spreads, and it is not irrational to believe that Fuhrman infected those around him, at least to the extent that they protected him and covered up his wrongdoing.

I suspect that some of the negative reaction from the Jewish community was traceable less to the Hitler allusion than to the fact that Johnnie Cochran entered the courtroom that morning with a phalanx of guards borrowed from Louis Farrakhan's Nation of Islam. The nature of the threats that Cochran was receiving as the trial wound down to the final moments have not been disclosed, but they were threats that had to be taken seriously. They were virulently racist, and extremely graphic. They were coming from persons who could obviously penetrate the security we had established to protect communications within the defense camp. We had a fax machine in the courtroom so the lawyers on the team who were not in court could fax suggestions and citations during court recesses. To our chagrin, messages started appearing on the courtroom fax that contained physical threats to Cochran. Cochran had to keep his focus on giving the most important final argument of his career, and the liberty of his client that depended on it. He could not let himself be distracted by threats to his own life or the lives of his family. While he might not have given full consideration to the "public relations" impact of appearing with Farrakhan's phalanx, he can hardly be blamed for not putting "public relations" first at such a critical time.

The quotations from the Bible were vintage Cochran. Some people seem surprised that Johnnie Cochran is a serious student of the Bible. They prefer to view biblical references with cynicism, as though quoting the Bible is a cheap ploy from the criminal defense lawyer's "bag of tricks." Using the Bible in that way can be extremely dangerous for a lawyer. Jurors who know their Bibles will be extemely suspicious of a lawyer who abuses it, quoting it for arguments it doesn't really support. The use of Bible quotations as instruments of persuasion in arguments to a jury has become highly controversial in recent years. Most often it is used by prosecutors, quoting passages out of context to argue that the death penalty is appropriate punishment. In 1991, the Supreme Court of Pennsylvania admonished prosecutors that "reliance in any manner upon the Bible or any other religious writing in support of the imposition of a penalty of death is reversible error *per se* and may subject violators to disciplinary action." I thought it was one of the dumbest appellate decisions I ever read. The best cure for Bible-thumping prosecutors is Bible-thumping defense lawyers.

If Clarence Darrow were defending, and a prosecutor argued that the Bible demanded an eye for an eye, Darrow would not even have objected. He simply would have pulled his own Bible out of a battered briefcase and turned to Exodus. He would have reminded the jurors that the same Bible that commands the death of murderers also commands the execution of adulterers, witches, those who have sex with animals, and anyone who reviles or curses his mother or father. He would have noted that the Bible contains some curious exceptions, such as the one for a man who beats his slave to death. "If the slave does not die for a couple days, then the man shall not be punished, for the slave is his property." Finally, Darrow would have turned to the New Testament, and read to the jurors the words of Jesus Christ when he was invited to participate in an execution: "Let anyone among you who is without sin be the first to cast a stone at her."

The point is not whether the Bible supports or condemns capital punishment. The point is that jurors are intelligent enough to give the Bible the weight it deserves, and lawyers should be free to address jurors as though they are intelligent human beings. As former California Court of Appeal Justice Robert Gardner put it: "A juror is not some kind of a dithering nincompoop, brought in from never-never land and exposed to the harsh realities of life for the first time in the jury box."

I borrowed a biblical allusion from Clarence Darrow for one of the arguments I made to Judge Ito. In the 1907 trial of labor leader Bill Haywood for the murder of Idaho governor Frank Steunenberg, Darrow denounced police informant Harry Orchard as "the Ananias of the age." When I compared Detective Fuhrman to Ananias, I saw a lot of quizzical expressions in the courtroom. Ananias was struck dead upon lying to the apostle Peter. Most modern lawyers lack familiarity with the Bible. The jurors they speak to do not. We observed at least one of the jurors carrying her Bible with her in and out of court.

On the Sunday before the final arguments began, I was stunned to hear a familiar refrain from the trial as I sat in church listening to that Sunday's gospel reading. It was from the book of Luke, and it was a warning that if your servant deceives you in small things, you cannot trust him in big things. That's precisely what our jury would be instructed to do in evaluating the credibility of witnesses. One of the key jury instructions we would rely upon in our attack on the testimony of Detective Fuhrman was a CALJIC instruction of ancient vintage:

> A witness, who is willfully false in one material part of his or her testimony, is to be distrusted in others. You may reject the whole testimony of a witness who willfully has testified falsely as to a material point, unless, from all the evidence, you believe the probability of truth favors his or her testimony in other particulars.

When I got home, I checked the passage and suggested to Johnnie Cochran that he refer to it in the final argument. He made effective use of it.

Shortly before the final arguments were to commence, the California Supreme Court handed down a decision upholding a conviction despite the defense objection that the prosecutor improp-

erly used a biblical passage in his final argument. The passage was
from Chapter 24 of Proverbs:

> It is wrong to sentence the poor and let the rich go free.
> Whoever says to the truly guilty you are innocent, peoples
> will curse him and nations denounce him.

When we read the decision and passed it around the table at one of
the defense team strategy meetings, a collective groan was heard.
We were sure the prosecutors would read the same decision and
insert the same biblical passage into their final arguments. Johnnie Cochran found another passage in Proverbs that stressed the
importance of protecting the innocent and used it effectively in
his final argument. I was waiting for the other shoe to drop during
the closing arguments of the prosecutors. Instead, they casually
tossed the shoe out the window. Chris Darden made an oblique reference to Proverbs, without even quoting it. It was as though he
were embarrassed to mention the Bible.

The most serious criticism of Johnnie Cochran's final argument
came from those who believed he was arguing "jury nullification."
Juries certainly have the power to ignore the law and return a verdict that they believe is just even though the instructions on the
law given to them by the judge would not permit that verdict. They
cannot be called to account for their verdict. That is not what the
Simpson jury did, and at no time in his final argument did Johnnie
Cochran suggest that they do that. Was he implicity and indirectly
suggesting jury nullification by arguing that a verdict of "not guilty"
would send a message to the Los Angeles Police Department?

Shortly after the verdict, as I scanned the most recently published law review articles, an intriguing title caught my eye. It was,
"What Message Are We Sending Juries When We Urge Juries to Send
a Message?" At first, I was surprised that someone had picked up
on this issue so quickly and got an article in print discussing it so
fast. When I read the article, I found it was not a discussion of the
Simpson case at all. It was addressing the frequency with which
prosecutors were arguing to juries that a verdict of guilty would

"send a message to terrorists" or "send a message to drug dealers." It made the valid point that such arguments are improper, because they ask juries to consider extraneous factors outside the evidence in the case in reaching their verdict. Juries are routinely instructed, as the Simpson jury was, that they are not to be influenced by "mere sentiment, conjecture, sympathy, passion, prejudice, public opinion or public feeling." Urging juries to "send messages" suggests that a verdict serves some broader public purpose than resolving the issue of the guilt or innocence of the accused.

But inevitably, the verdict delivers a message to the parties who are in court. An appeal to "send a message" to the prosecutors who tried the case, or to the police who investigated it, is *not* an appeal to decide the case on the basis of extraneous factors apart from the evidence. The "message" Johnnie Cochran asked jurors to deliver is that "we don't trust the messengers you sent into this courtroom. They lied to us." For the Los Angeles Police Department, that's a fair reading of the verdict. That's a "message" that should be taken to heart. But if history repeats itself, it's a message that will be blithely ignored.

In looking at all the other "trials of the century," I found some parallels to the public uproar over the content of final arguments that the Simpson case engendered. The case that comes closest is the 1906 trial of Harry Thaw for the murder of New York architect Stanford White. White was shot to death during a theater performance in Madison Square Garden, which he himself had designed and built. The trial had everything. The motive was revenge for White's seduction of Thaw's wife, Broadway showgirl Evelyn Nesbit. She had frolicked in the nude on a red velvet swing in White's love nest. The sexual escapades were so titillating that President Theodore Roosevelt sought to have newspapers reporting the testimony banned from the U.S. mail.

The defendant was wealthy enough to afford a team of seven defense lawyers, who publicly fought with each other almost as vigorously as they fought the prosecution. The lawyers were celebrities before the trial even began. The prosecution was headed by William Travers Jerome, the Manhattan District Attorney, whose

cousin Jennie was the mother of Winston Churchill. The lead lawyer for the defense was Delphin Delmas, brought to New York from
my hometown of San Jose, California, where he had graduated from
Santa Clara University. He was known as "The Napoleon of the
Pacific Bar," since he had been born in France. He encouraged the
nickname by combing his forelock like Napoleon and frequently
inserting his hand between his coat buttons.

The closing argument that Delphin Delmas presented in the
Thaw trial caused an even bigger reaction than Johnnie Cochran's
final argument in the Simpson trial. Delmas urged the jury to acquit Thaw on a theory of insanity that was not recognized by the
law. He called it "Dementia Americana," the unwritten law that
would allow an outraged husband to avenge the seduction of his
wife. Delmas didn't compare any police officers to Adolf Hitler,
since Hitler was only fifteen years old at the time, but he did compare the defendant to Jesus Christ. Delmas told the jury that after
he shot Stanford White in the face, "Thaw spread out his arms making of his body the sign of the cross, a circumstance which denoted
the character of the act. His arms were spread out like the arms of
a priest after the sacrifice of the mass has been consummated and
he has turned to the worshippers to bid them depart." The press labeled it an obvious play for the sympathy of Catholic jurors!

The jury was unable to reach a verdict in the first Thaw trial.
Delphin Delmas was sent back to San Jose, and his replacement
presented a more traditional insanity defense. It succeeded. The
many friends and admirers of Stanford White were outraged. The
jurors received so much hate mail that they formed a special association to provide mutual support for each other.

Cases like the Harry Thaw trial still have much to teach lawyers about the art of persuasion. So does the case of *People v. O.J.
Simpson*. Cases are still won or lost in final arguments by the simple art of persuasion. For the defense lawyer, the challenge is to persuade jurors that their doubts are reasonable ones. The final arguments presented by all of the lawyers, on both sides of the case of
People v. O.J. Simpson, were classic examples of advocacy at its best.
No arguments were overlooked. All of the evidence was analyzed.

Every tool of persuasion was employed. As each lawyer sat down, exhausted and spent, he or she had the satisfaction of knowing they had given it their best.

The lesson drawn from the final arguments in the case of *People v. O.J. Simpson* by the critics of the verdict is that the "race card" trumped the evidence. The critics were not listening. The defense employed very traditional tools of persuasion. We did not appeal to "racism," but appealed to reason. The reasoning power of jurors, however, is not exercised in a vacuum. Jurors bring their real-life experiences with them and use their common sense in evaluating the evidence. A persuasive final argument cannot be sterile, colorless, and divorced from the real flesh and blood lives of ordinary people. Nor can a jury's verdict.

FOURTEEN

WALKING AWAY

*T*he news that the jury had reached a verdict during their first day of deliberation took everyone by surprise. I had confidently predicted that deliberations would take two weeks, and returned to my office at Santa Clara University. In the course of our meetings in chambers to review jury instructions, Judge Ito and the prosecutors concurred in similar expectations. Everyone anticipated a lengthy process of deliberation, because everyone assumed the jury would be deeply divided. It turned out that whatever division existed was quickly resolved. The initial vote of the jurors was 10–2 for acquittal. They requested that the testimony of Allan Park, the limousine driver, be read back. Almost immediately thereafter, they asked for the verdict forms and announced they had reached a decision. Judge Ito delayed announcing the decision until the next day, to allow time for the lawyers and families to reassemble. I booked an immediate flight back to Los Angeles. It was a moment I did not want to miss.

Speculation about the verdict was intense, with most commentators assuming that the testimony the jurors asked to have read back signaled a guilty verdict. The defense lawyers felt confident that the speed of the verdict favored an acquittal, but one can never be absolutely sure. The tension continued to build, right up to the moment the jury filed into the courtroom and delivered their ver-

dict. The later report of how many sets of eyes and ears were seeing and hearing the verdict at the same time we were was beyond
belief. It was a rare moment in American history, when millions of
Americans interrupted the ordinary routine of their lives to experience an event together. Even beyond our national borders, a world
was watching. In a way, it seemed bizarre that only the small clus-
ter of us gathered in the courtroom actually saw the jury as they
filed in and out of the courtroom. They did not smile. They were
deadly serious, and greatly relieved that their own ordeal was drawing to a close. I sensed a deep pride in their bearing, as they delivered the "verdict of the century," awaited by so many of their fellow citizens.

Apparently, the television coverage observed intently by so
many Americans included lots of "reaction shots" as the verdict
was announced in different public settings. As the verdicts of "Not
Guilty" were read aloud, black audiences reacted with cheers and
jubilation. White audiences reacted with stunned silence. The racial
divide that the verdict would reveal was being defined.

The prosecutors quietly left the courtroom. The defense lawyers embraced each other and O.J. Simpson. Johnnie Cochran gathered all of us in a tight circle, and asked me to lead a prayer of
thanksgiving. It was a simple prayer. Not a prayer of gratitude for
a "victory." More like the prayer of Job, expressing gratitude for de-
liverance and recognition of a power we can never understand.

Judge Ito came back into the courtroom and shook hands with
each of the lawyers. A brief press conference was held in the courtroom. There was no gloating. We gathered up our books and papers
for the final time. That tiny courtroom had been a fulcrum for the
turning of a lever that groaned and lurched for sixteen months, finally grinding out a just result. It was hard to believe it was over.
It had been a "trial" in every sense of the word, and the greatest sense
of relief I felt was that there had been a final resolution, that we
wouldn't have to go through it all again.

The celebration at Mr. Simpson's Rockingham home that afternoon was subdued. It is sobering to see a client in chains in a jail
cell in the morning, and then see him embraced by his family in

his own home that same afternoon. The helicopters hovering over-
head and the hordes of television cameras outside the gate were constant reminders that a process of public judgment was still underway. The "spin" was being spun, and the media appetite for
"insight" was being fueled.

The public reaction to the verdict was a source of profound disappointment. I remember Bob Blasier joking that there were reports
of riots in Beverly Hills, with angry crowds throwing croissants at
passing limousines. Rather than a vindication of reasonable doubt,
the verdict was being interpreted as some sort of perverse racial
message, that this was "payback" for centuries of racial oppression.
Certainly nothing the jurors said or did provided any confirmation
of that hypothesis. Those jurors who submitted to postverdict interviews confirmed that their vote was compelled by the reasonable doubts they had about the prosecution's case. One summed it
up by paraphrasing the testimony of Dr. Henry Lee: There was
"something wrong" with the prosecution's case. Another juror candidly stated she thought O.J. "probably did it," but she understood
that "probably" wasn't good enough, that she had to be convinced
beyond a reasonable doubt. I wanted to jump up and cheer when I
heard that. What a splendid testament to the American jury, to have
understood the law so clearly and followed it so faithfully.

The media, however, saw it differently. The jubilant cheers of
African-Americans were portrayed as a celebration that O.J. Simpson "beat the system." Apparently, it did not occur to many white
observers that the cheers may have been because the system
worked, and those who were cheering knew how seldom the system works for a black man in America.

The day after the verdict, the *Wall Street Journal* ran a lead story
under the headline, COLOR BLINDED. It was not even a story about
the O.J. Simpson verdict. But no one could read it without making
the obvious connection. The story reported that race was playing
an increasing role in jury verdicts around the country, and that it
fit "neatly into a tradition of political activism by U.S. juries." An
acquittal rate of 47.6 percent for black defendants in the Bronx was
attributed to the fact that juries there are 80 percent black and His-

panic. In Washington, D.C., it was reported, where more than 95 percent of defendants and 70 percent of jurors are black, the acquittal rate of 28.7% was "significantly above the national average." The article concluded that this phenomenon may reflect an increase in "jury nullification" by black juries:

> Some jury-nullification advocates now say blacks are justified in using their jury-room vote to fight what they perceive as a national crisis: a justice system that is skewed against them by courts, prosecutors and racist police such as former Los Angeles Detective Mark Fuhrman.

Those who disagreed with the Simpson verdict were quick to attribute the verdict to the racial composition of the jury. I myself must confess to yielding to the same temptation to criticize verdicts I disagreed with. In commenting upon the first Rodney King verdict, acquitting the police officers after their Simi Valley trial, I wrote, "Apparently, it was easy to convince a jury of white suburbanites to disconnect their eyeballs from their brains, and not be satisfied with seeing." To quote a Latin maxim I wish I had taken to heart, *"verba volant, scripta manent."* "Spoken words fly away, written words remain to haunt you." I was certainly convinced that my observation of what was going on in the Rodney King video was just as good as the observation of the jury. Why shouldn't those who tuned in to the O.J. trial on their TV sets assume they were just as capable as the jurors of deciding his guilt or innocence? It's a long leap from the conclusion that the Simpson jurors got it wrong, however, to the conclusion that their race biased them in favor of the defendant, or that they were motivated to "send a message" to the white community. In reading the "hate mail" sent to my university address after the verdict, I was surprised how many were ready to make that leap, based on nothing other than the fact that O.J. Simpson is black, and nine of his twelve jurors were black. The fact I had made the same leap myself in the Rodney King case offered no consolation.

Our right to disagree with the verdict of a jury is absolute, although it should be tempered by the realization that we never see exactly what the jury sees. Even when we are watching the case on television, we are victims of an illusion: the illusion of actually being there, when we are not. Throughout the trial, we would often see the camera zoom in on the face of the defendant or the families of the victims in the audience, to record their reaction to testimony. During the direct or cross-examination of a witness, whether the camera was trained on the lawyer or the witness depended on who was making the most telegenic faces, a point that was not lost on the lawyers. Every fifteen minutes there was a station break, along with some "spin" from the commentators. Even more important, the jury was *not* hearing, seeing, or reading much of what the public was hearing, seeing, or reading thoughout the trial. It was as though we were all in a large coliseum, watching a three-ring circus. But the jury was wearing blinders that permitted them to watch only the center ring. In second-guessing the jury, which is the right of every American, we need to remember that the jurors are the only ones among us who kept their eyes on the center ring, and who took an oath to decide the case only on the evidence presented in the courtroom.

There is a big difference between disagreeing with the jury and disparaging the jury. The phenomenon of "jury-bashing" assumes another dimension, attributing motives to the jurors which question their intelligence and their integrity. In recent years the phenomenon has grown, with howling mobs of indignant citizens protesting verdicts and harassing jurors. The trial of Dan White for the murders of San Francisco Mayor George Moscone and Supervisor Harvey Milk, the trial of the police officers in the first Rodney King trial, and the first trial of the Menendez brothers in Los Angeles for the murder of their parents, are all recent examples. Even my esteemed co-counsel in the Simpson case, Alan Dershowitz, joined in, saying of the Menendez case: "What I am criticizing is . . . the foolish juries who fall for the sob stories told by the lawyers." *Verba volant, scripta manent.*

Many Americans focused on the quickness of the Simpson verdict to justify a conclusion that the jurors did not base their verdict on the evidence. They assumed that the jurors were not considering and weighing the evidence throughout the nine months of the trial. Being sequestered, they had little else to do. The admonition that they should not come to any conclusions until all the evidence was in certainly did not mean they should turn off their brains until the trial was over. Just the process of hearing the jury instructions and listening to final arguments consumed ten full days. Ordinarily, the first thing any jury does when they retire to deliberate is to take a vote, and discover how far apart they actually are. Deliberation is a process in which jurors seek to persuade each other, not a process in which twelve empty receptacles are filled.

The Simpson jury was ready to come to a decision. They had bonded. They picked a foreperson immediately, with no disagreement. They discovered that they were not very far apart in their final conclusions, and the minority were quickly and easily persuaded that the doubts of the majority were reasonable ones. What if, at that point, they had said to themselves, "It's not going to look right for us to return a verdict so quickly. Let's shuffle through the exhibits for a couple days." They would then have been violating the instructions Judge Ito read to them. They were told not to be swayed by what others might think of their verdict.

The jurors who sat through the case of *People v. O.J. Simpson* made a tremendous sacrifice. They permitted the lawyers and the judge to probe every crevice of their hearts and minds, to pass judgment on whether they could be fair and open. Both sides agreed to each of them serving, before they were sworn in as jurors. They gave up ten months of their lives to live in sequestered isolation. They sat through a tedious and contentious trial, listening to the testimony of hundreds of witnesses and examining over 800 exhibits. All for the magnificent sum of five dollars per day. They should be hailed as public heroes. Instead, many of their fellow Americans have dismissed them as racist morons. Adding injury to insult, many are now ready to seriously consider radical surgery to "reform" our system of trial by jury.

In California, the public dissatisfaction with the Simpson verdict is now being used by the proponents of a measure to abolish the requirement of unanimity for jury verdicts. When a campaign was launched to qualify this measure as a ballot initiative, the "poster boy" trotted out at a press conference was Fred Goldman, the anguished father of Ron Goldman. For Californians, it was *déjà vu*. The campaign for the "Three Strikes" sentencing measure adopted in 1994 was initiated with a press conference graced by the presence of the grieving family of Polly Klaas. They later denounced the measure, and campaigned against it, after realizing that they were being cynically used to promote a change that would do more harm than good. The initiative measure to abolish unanimity has been labeled "The Public Safety Protection Act of 1996." Whether it has anything whatsoever to do with public safety is a question that will be robustly debated. But there is no question that it has absolutely nothing to do with the case of *People v. O.J. Simpson*. If this measure had been in effect, the Simpson jurors would have returned a verdict in ten minutes, instead of four hours. If our concern is that jurors need to deliberate longer, then the last thing we should do is permit them to return 10–2 verdicts without even listening to the doubts of the minority. The requirement of unanimity, which is as old as the jury itself, protects the deliberative process, by requiring jurors to listen to each other and persuade each other. In one classic Massachusetts study utilizing mock juries, it was reported that juries deciding the same case deliberated an average of 138 minutes when a unanimous verdict was required, and only 103 minutes under a ten out of twelve rule. Abolishing the requirement of unanimity may get us quicker verdicts, but quicker verdicts are not necessarily more just ones. We should not assume that the doubts of a juror are unreasonable, just because that juror stands alone, or with only one companion. Those doubts should be listened to and carefully considered.

By every objective measure, it appears that the jury in the case of *People v. O.J. Simpson* did precisely what they were sworn to do. They rendered a verdict based on their evaluation of the evidence. The doubts they entertained were reasonable doubts. To say that their doubts were less than "reasonable" because nine of the jurors were African-Americans is blatant racism. The life experience of any juror will ultimately affect his or her conclusions of what is reasonable and what is not. Obviously we cannot quantify the spectrum of life experience in a community and reduce it to a quota. We cannot say that those who are a minority in the community must remain a minority on the jury. Jurors do not represent a constituency. The deliberative ideal we strive for is that all jurors will be valued, and that they will value each other. When we engage in jury-bashing, we denigrate that ideal. We deliver the message that the value of a juror's opinions are to be measured by his or her race, and the value of a verdict is to be measured by public opinion polls.

The diversity of the Simpson jury is the product of many years of struggle for racial equality. Their verdict should teach us that persons of very different backgrounds can come together and reach a unanimous conclusion at great personal cost even in the most contentious and hotly disputed cases. The fact that we might have come to a different conclusion had we been in their shoes does not diminish the value of their achievement. Nor should it diminish our faith in the institution of trial by jury.

Shortly after the verdict was rendered, the widely reported reaction of white Americans was bluntly questioned by a black law professor at George Washington University in Washington, D.C. Writing in the *Washington Post,* Paul Butler posed a provocative challenge:

> Among yourselves you ask a question like mine: Are black people racist or just stupid? We are neither. We were not applauding the release of a criminal, but rather that at least the system could work for an African-American man. Even one charged with violence against a white woman, an allegation with historical resonance in the United States—go look at the strange fruit on the limbs of Southern trees. Many of us do not doubt that O.J. bought himself that reasonable doubt with a lot of cash, but we also know that's how criminal justice works in the United States. White people didn't take it so personally when it worked that way

for rich white men like John De Lorean, William Kennedy
Smith and Claus von Bülow.

The national shunning of O.J. Simpson now being promoted on radio
talk shows is an ugly manifestation of the hypocrisy Professor Butler so eloquently denounces. Like it or not, O.J. Simpson's acquittal symbolizes the exercise of a power which makes many black
Americans rejoice, and which makes many white Americans very
uncomfortable. We need to ask ourselves why.

Much of the white discomfort emanates from simple frustra-
tion. We keep thinking we "solved" the problem of race in America, and it keeps rearing its head again. The normal human reaction
when we face a snarling, festering problem that seems insoluble is
to walk away from it. Facing it squarely is too costly, in terms of
the risk we will fall on our face. We prefer to "leave it lay, and walk
away." My own experience as a law school dean taught me that
every time I let an "insoluble" problem lay and walked away, it
ended up biting me in the ass.

Our criminal justice system is no different than our other
human institutions. The problem of racism in our system of criminal justice is a systemic problem that keeps rearing its head. And
we consistently ignore it and walk away.

That's what the United States Supreme Court did in the 1987
case of *McCleskey v. Kemp.* The Court was confronted with overwhelming evidence of racism in the administration of the death
penalty. And the Court walked away. A sophisticated statistical
analysis of over 2,000 murder cases in Georgia in the 1970s showed
that defendants charged with killing white persons received the
death penalty in 11 percent of the cases, but defendants charged
with killing blacks received the death penalty in only 1 percent of
the cases. When the race of the victim was combined with the race
of the defendant, it established that the greatest likelihood of a
death penalty being imposed was when a black defendant killed a
white victim. The death sentence was imposed in 22 percent of
those cases. When a white defendant killed a black victim, the
death penalty was imposed 3 percent of the time.

In a 5–4 decision, the Court ruled that this statistical proof of bias that permeates the system was not sufficient to require the state to offer a remedy. The defendant must prove more than that the state continues to operate a system that is discriminatory. He must show that the state enacted or maintains the discriminatory law *because* of its racially discriminatory effect. One consideration that the Court found especially persuasive was that there was no way they could limit a requirement that the state offer a remedy just in death penalty cases. "If we accepted McCleskey's claim that racial bias has impermissibly tainted the capital sentencing decision, we could soon be faced with similar claims as to other types of penalties." In other words, if we open Pandora's box, we might discover that the whole system suffers from the same pervasive cancer. It is better to leave the box closed. It is better to leave it lay, and walk away.

The Court also engaged in a classic exercise in buck-passing. Legislatures, they declared, are better equipped to weigh and evaluate the results of statistical studies with flexibility not available to the courts.

In an eloquent dissent joined by four other Justices, Justice William Brennan decried the message that the Court was sending, that systemic racial bias could be ignored:

> "It has been scarcely a generation since this Court's first decision striking down racial segregation, and barely two decades since the legislative prohibition of racial discrimination in major domains of national life. These have been honorable steps, but we cannot pretend that in three decades we have completely escaped the grip of a historical legacy spanning centuries. Warren McCleskey's evidence confronts us with the subtle and persistent influence of the past. His message is a disturbing one to a society that has formally repudiated racism, and a frustrating one to a nation accustomed to regarding its destiny as the product of its own will. Nonetheless, we ignore him at our peril, for we remain imprisoned by the past as long as we deny its influence in the present."

One could indeed hear an echo of the *McCleskey* majority in the prosecution's arguments in *People v. O.J. Simpson*. In April of 1987, while the Supreme Court was announcing its *McCleskey* decision, Detective Mark Fuhrman was explaining to Laura McKinny, "Nigger drivin' a Porsche that doesn't look like he's got a $300 suit on, you always stop him." The prosecutors in *People v. O.J. Simpson* argued in a Los Angeles courtroom that the racist attitudes of Detective Fuhrman were irrelevant and should be ignored. Mark Fuhrman's bite was about to be felt.

As the *McCleskey* Court put it, legislatures are better equipped to deal with the systemic bias demonstrated by statistical studies. The Congress of the United States had an opportunity to prove the Court's point in October of 1995, at the very moment the verdict in the case of *People v. O.J. Simpson* was being rendered. The statistical evidence of system-wide racial bias was carefully assembled and analyzed by the Federal Sentencing Commission, a body of judicial and academic experts created by Congress itself to establish guidelines for uniformity in the sentencing of federal prisoners. In the wake of a blizzard of media hype about crack cocaine in the early '80s, Congress enacted a harsh mandatory sentencing law that requires a five-year prison sentence for one convicted of possessing 5 grams of crack cocaine, and a ten-year sentence for one possessing 50 grams of crack. The corresponding thresholds for powdered cocaine, however, are set 100 times higher. A five-year sentence is not mandated for powdered cocaine unless the defendant possessed 500 grams, and a ten-year sentence is reserved for those possessing 5,000 grams. What quickly became apparent was that the harsh penalties for crack cocaine are almost exclusively falling on African-American defendants, inner-city youth in the black ghettoes where crack cocaine is most widely used. White defendants deal in powdered cocaine, much of which is later converted to "crack." The Federal Sentencing Commission documented that 90 percent of the defendants sentenced under the harsh crack cocaine law were black, while only 3.5 percent were white. In Los Angeles in 1991, every one of the twenty-four defendants charged with crack cocaine possession in federal court were black. The only white defendants charged with crack cocaine possession were prosecuted in the state courts, where sentences were substantially less. The commission urged Congress to repeal the disparity and treat crack and powdered cocaine the same. Congress rejected the recommendation by a 4–1 margin. It was more important to "send a message" they were tough on crime, than it was to respond to overwhelming evidence of racial disparity. There were riots in five federal prisons the day following the congressional vote. Most Americans were unaware there was any connection. The thousands of young African-Americans serving long sentences in federal prisons for possessing small quantities of crack cocaine know precisely what is going on. While African-Americans constitute only 13 percent of monthly drug users, they constitute 74 percent of those imprisoned for drug offenses. An even more staggering statistic is the 828 percent increase in the number of black women incarcerated for drug offenses between 1986 and 1991. The war on drugs in America has become an ugly race war. Congress prefers to leave it lay, and walk away.

It is time for a lot more candor and a lot less denial in assessing the role that race plays in our criminal justice system. At the present time, one out of three black males under the age of twenty-nine is either in jail or on probation or parole. That exceeds the number of young black males in college. Study after study verifies that color makes a difference at every stage of a criminal case. Whites do better at getting charges dropped. They are better able to get charges reduced to lesser offenses. They draw more lenient sentences for the same crimes, and go to prison less often. In California, African-Americans represent 7 percent of our population, but 35 percent of our prison population. The proportion of our black prison population is increasing dramatically as a result of the stringent "Three Strikes" repeat offender sentencing law adopted by California voters in the wake of the Polly Klaas kidnap-murder in 1994.

There may be other explanations besides racism for the disparity of treatment of minorities in our criminal justice system. But we seem determined to avoid the issue of racism altogether, lest even *discussing* it will be "divisive" or "embarrassing." There was

more than symbolism in the prosecution's characterization of the
race issue in the Simpson case as a "card" that was being "played"
in a game. The message they sought to deliver is that racism was
irrelevant, that it really didn't matter because it didn't make a difference. That begs the question. Whether it "makes a difference"
must be determined by exposure and inquiry. We are creating a climate in America in which exposure and inquiry into racism are
forbidden topics, like discussing masturbation in polite company.

Some have suggested that the power of American juries is the
only recourse left. Professor Paul Butler makes a compelling argument that, at least in drug cases, black jurors should engage in jury
nullification, and refuse to continue locking up young black men
to achieve a white agenda:

> Certainly, jury nullification is anti-democratic; that's why
> I like it. It is the only legal remedy African Americans have
> to free ourselves from the tyranny of the majority. We had
> to beg Mr. Lincoln to give us the right not to be slaves. We
> had to plead with the Congress to allow us to vote. We had
> to convince the Supreme Court to let our children go to in-
> tegrated schools. We are now busy begging white people for
> programs that will allow our children to eat and our busi-
> nesses to survive. At least when we serve as jurors we have
> real power to disagree with what the government tells us
> justice is.

The verdict in *People v. O.J. Simpson* was not an example of
black jury nullification. No one, not even Professor Butler, advocates that jury nullification would ever be appropriate in a murder
case. But the verdict in *People v. O.J. Simpson* was undeniably affected by the issue of race. Keeping the issue of race out of the trial
of *People v. O.J. Simpson* would have been like keeping the issue of
slavery out of the Civil War. It kept injecting itself, not because the
lawyers or the media were exploiting it, but simply because it was
there and it had to be confronted. The efforts to push it aside or
suppress it were ineffectual because they were dishonest. And the

suggestion that the Simpson jurors were incapable of honestly confronting the issue because nine of them were black is itself no less racist than would be the suggestion that a black justice should not participate when the Supreme Court is presented with a racial issue, or black members of Congress should not vote when a racial issue is presented to Congress.

Many white Americans simply reject the idea that a doubt based on proof that racism may have motivated the planting or alteration of evidence can be a reasonable doubt. We conveniently forget the lessons of history, in which many black Americans were sent to their deaths based on little more than racism. Why did white America slumber and yawn when the power of all-white juries was ruthlessly exercised to sentence black Americans to death, in the face of evidence that literally shouted "reasonable doubt"? We need not reach back to another century to find examples. We need only travel as far back as 1980, to Montgomery County, Texas. A sixteen-year-old white girl was raped and murdered during a high school volleyball tournament. An immediate arrest was made of a black janitor, without any investigation of leads pointing toward others. The policy of the District Attorney's office was to strike all black jurors when the defendant was black. This was before the recent U.S. Supreme Court decision ending the exercise of peremptory challenges in a racially discriminatory manner. At the first trial, an all-white jury deadlocked 11-1 for conviction. The holdout juror was denounced by the other jurors as "a Nigger lover," and he received thousands of harassing telephone calls after a mistrial was declared. Another all-white jury convicted at the retrial, and the defendant was sentenced to death. Shortly before the scheduled execution, new evidence was produced demonstrating perjury during the previous trials. Two other janitors were implicated. Many of the evidentiary leads pointing to the other suspects had been ignored in the police investigation. The conviction was set aside and denounced by the Texas Court of Criminal Appeals as a "subversion of justice" in 1989. This may be the first time many have heard or read of this case. The fact that a black janitor was unjustly condemned to death didn't get a lot of press or create an uproar. No one initiated a petition campaign to reform the jury system, and no radio talk shows expressed outrage. This is not to suggest that past injustices which victimized blacks are justification for an injustice that frees one. It is simply to suggest that the widespread conclusion of many white Americans that justice failed when O.J. Simpson was acquitted may not be based entirely on an objective evaluation of the evidence. It may be based on unfair suspicion of the motives of the jury, which is rooted in our own racial attitudes. Before we embark on an agenda of "jury reform," we need to search our souls and ask what we are proposing to reform? Are we restricting the power of the American jury, because that power is now within the grasp of those whose motives we distrust? Where does that distrust come from?

The hard lesson of the verdict in the case of *People v. O.J. Simpson* has a lot to do with the power of juries, how that power is perceived by African-Americans, and how that power is feared by white Americans. We can let the problem of racism in our criminal justice system lay, and walk away when it is presented to our Supreme Court and our Congress. But in the trial courts, where issues of guilt and innocence are decided every day, we can't walk away. Juries won't let us, and they shouldn't let us.

F I F T E E N

SEARCHING FOR
THE TRUTH

*A*gain and again, before a television audience of thirty to forty
million viewers, the trial of the case of *People v. O.J. Simpson*
was described as "a search for the truth." It became Marcia Clark's
favorite phrase, repeated like a mantra. Judge Ito even used the
phrase in several of his rulings. It may have created the expectation
that at the conclusion of the trial, trumpets would blare, curtains
would part, and "the truth" would be revealed. Many viewers were
disappointed, because the verdict did not match their vision of "the
truth." That disappointment even led some to conclude that the "system" failed in the Simpson trial, that its mission to find "the truth"
was not accomplished.

I don't put quotation marks around "the truth" to ridicule or
denigrate it. I regard the pursuit of truth as one of the ultimate purposes of life itself. I certainly seek the truth in the library, at the
dinner table, in the classroom, and in the chapel, as well as in the
courtroom. I strive to keep truth at the core of my relationships
with my family and friends, my students, and my professional colleagues.

Quite frequently, we encounter competing visions of the truth,
asserted with equal passion by partisans of equal sincerity. The
competing visions of "the truth" in the case of *People v. O.J. Simpson* were polar opposites. On June 21, 1994, Marcia Clark explained

193

the charges she had filed against O.J. Simpson. She said, "It was premeditated murder. It was done with premeditation and deliberation. Mr. Simpson is charged alone because he is the sole murderer." That became the prosecution's vision of "the truth." On June 13, 1994, within minutes after stepping off an airplane from Chicago, where he had first been told of his former wife's murder, O.J. Simpson voluntarily sat down with investigating detectives at police headquarters, in the absence of his attorney, and gave them a complete, twenty-page statement. He answered every question they asked, and his answers were unequivocal: He had absolutely nothing to do with the murders of his former wife and Ronald Goldman. On June 17, 1994, in a note he wrote before he got into Al Cowlings's white bronco and went for his famous ride, O.J. Simpson declared, "I had nothing to do with Nicole's murder." When he was arraigned in Superior Court on July 22, 1994, O.J. Simpson proclaimed he was "absolutely, 100 percent not guilty." That's precisely what he told every lawyer representing him, and throughout the sixteen-month ordeal of his trial, he never wavered in his steadfast claim of innocence. That was the defense's vision of "the truth."

The adversary system requires both the prosecution and the defense to pursue their vision of the truth relentlessly, with every tool of persuasion the law allows. Neither vision is favored, although the defense vision must prevail if the prosecution does not meet its burden of proof. Regardless of how convinced an advocate may be that his or her "vision" of the truth coincides with objective reality, it must remain a "vision" until the jury has spoken.

Our pursuit of truth in a court of law must occasionally be tempered, to respect the boundaries that civilized society has erected so we can live peaceably with one another. We are not entitled to unreasonably invade the privacy of others, even when we're convinced such a mission will lead us to "the truth." Respect for the autonomy of others requires that we concede their right to remain silent, even when we're sure that their words would illuminate our search for "the truth."

Thus, when we speak of a trial as a search for "the truth," we must recognize that the "search" is subject to restraints that may ultimately affect the outcome. There are places we can't look. There are things we pretend not to see. Does that mean the outcome is no longer "the truth"? One could say so, but we would then concede our premise is false. A trial would *not* be a search for the truth, but a search for a verdict, which may or may not reflect the truth. One could also say a trial may be a "search" for the truth, but we don't always succeed in finding it. We tolerate a high margin of error to accommodate other goals. This, too, is misleading. A result in conformity with our goals should not be labeled an "error." It may be best to say that "the truth" has a unique meaning in the context of a trial. A trial is a contest between two visions of "the truth." Actually, neither vision may coincide with what we would call objective truth. Neither vision will be ordained as "the truth" until the trial is over. At the conclusion of the trial, the jury is empowered to choose between the competing visions. The choice it makes defines "the truth." But that choice defines "the truth" for a very limited purpose. In a criminal trial, that purpose is to limit the power of the state to punish an individual, by depriving him of his life or liberty. In a civil trial, the purpose is simply to transfer money from one pocket to another. Conceivably, the same events can produce two "truths" that appear inconsistent. The state cannot punish an individual, because he has been found not guilty, but the victim can recover a judgment requiring the same individual to pay damages, because he has been found liable. That doesn't mean either conclusion was wrong or erroneous. It simply reflects the differing levels of certainty we demand before a verdict can be rendered. Because we value liberty more than property, we require a higher threshold of certainty in a criminal case. The defendant must be proven guilty *beyond a reasonable doubt*. Where only money is at stake, proof by a preponderance of the evidence is sufficient.

When we look at a trial from this perspective, it may be more accurate to say that a trial is a search for certainty, rather than a search for "the truth." Certainty can be quantified, while "truth" cannot. "Truth" is absolute. Even absolute certainty does not define truth. Truth should never be confused with certitude. The fact

that a belief or conviction is universally shared does not make it
the truth. At one time, nearly every person on earth believed that
the sun revolved around the earth. That belief was confirmed by
their own eyes. They observed the sun rising and setting each day.
The "trial of the century" of the seventeenth century was the heresy
trial of Galileo Galilei, for teaching that the earth revolved around
the sun. He was convicted. While his conviction of heresy vindicated
conventional wisdom, it certainly didn't vindicate "the truth."

The verdict of a jury does not define historical "truth" either.
The American "trial of the century" of the nineteenth century was
the 1893 trial of Lizzie Borden for the murder of her parents in Fall
River, Massachusetts. Parallels to the Simpson case abound. The
badly lacerated bodies of two victims were found in pools of blood.
Police suspicion immediately focused on the defendant, in what
was later criticized as a "rush to judgment." The defendant announced a reward for the capture of the real culprit. The trial became a media circus. Reporters sensationalized every leak and
rumor. The evidentiary rulings of the court were publicly criticized,
including the suppression of an alleged confession to a spiritual
counselor overheard by a police officer. The defense argued the defendant was physically incapable of committing such a brutal
crime, and suggested the prosecution's failure to produce a weapon
or bloody clothing was persuasive proof of innocence. The defendant never testified on her own behalf. The jury deliberated less
than one hour before returning a verdict of not guilty. Pundits and
commentators roundly criticized the verdict. The public divided
along gender lines: men generally condemned the verdict, women
defended it.

Despite her acquittal, Lizzie Borden was treated as a pariah, a
social outcast. She was taunted for thirty-four years with the rhyme
every school child learned:

> Lizzie Borden took an ax;
> Gave her mother forty whacks;
> When she saw what she had done;
> She gave her father forty-one.

Is "truth" reflected in the verdict or the nursery rhyme? Many contemporary historians have concluded Lizzie Borden was guilty. Others suggest she was covering up for her sister. The "truth" may never be known, but the verdict of the jury did not end the quest of historians to find "the truth."

If we conceive of a trial as a contest between two competing visions of "the truth," should it not be an equal contest, in which each side has the same opportunity to challenge the credibility of the other side's evidence? The strength of the evidence should be the ultimate criterion of success. Here again, just as we distinguish between civil and criminal trials in quantifying the level of certainty required for a verdict, we recognize an essential difference in the constraints we impose on the adversaries. In a criminal case, one of the adversaries is the state. The individual, regardless of how wealthy or powerful he may be, can never match the resources or the power of the state itself. The Simpson case was no exception. O.J. Simpson depleted his personal wealth but didn't come close to "outspending" the Los Angeles Police Department, the Los Angeles County District Attorney's office, the state of California, and the Federal Bureau of Investigation.

In a criminal trial, this disparity between the adversaries demands that we give the accused an advantage to start with. That advantage is called the "presumption of innocence." Literally, that means we've tilted the contest toward the vision of "the truth" asserted by the defendant: that he is not guilty. We put the burden of proof on the state to convince the jury of its vision of "the truth." The defendant does not have to offer any evidence at all. If the state falls short in meeting its burden, the defendant walks free.

There are many good reasons for this allocation of the burden of proof, but the most fundamental reason is that we distrust the awesome power of the state. Is that distrust obsolete? In a democracy, the state is no longer an autocratic king, but our elected representatives. The lawyers who represent the state are honest, decent people who accept lower salaries in order to serve the public. Why should their vision of "the truth" be subjected to any greater

burden than the vision of "the truth" presented by the paid advocates of an accused criminal?

That question was answered resoundingly two centuries ago,
when we adopted a "Bill of Rights" as the first ten amendments to
our Constitution. Those who actually created our form of democratic government were most vigilant in recognizing the need to
limit its power over the individual. The ensuing two centuries can
hardly be cited as evidence that we no longer need to be vigilant,
that we can now "trust" those who hold power. As Justice Louis
Brandeis warned, "experience should teach us to be most on our
guard to protect liberty when the Government's purposes are be-
neficent. Men born to freedom are naturally alert to repel invasion
of their liberty by evil-minded rulers. The greatest dangers to liberty lurk in insidious encroachment by men of zeal, well-meaning
but without understanding." He could have been talking about Detective Mark Fuhrman.

Thus, the adversaries who present the contrasting visions of
"the truth" in a criminal trial are not playing on a level field. The
Constitution has tilted the field to favor the accused. The rules of
evidence, however, apply with equal force to both sides. Not all of
these rules serve the goal of finding "the truth," though. There are
some places we choose not to look, even when we are seeking "the
truth."

The privilege against self-incrimination, for example, prohibits
the state from compelling any person to testify and give evidence
that may tend to incriminate himself. Both sides made use of that
privilege in the Simpson case. Detective Mark Fuhrman was allowed to invoke the privilege to avoid cross-examination that might
have incriminated him of the crime of perjury. O.J. Simpson himself invoked the privilege by not taking the witness stand on his
own behalf.

Privileges for communications between lawyer and client, and
between clergyman and penitent keep out evidence of statements
that may further our search for "the truth." We are unwilling to
sacrifice the sanctity of these relationships, even to serve the cause
of "truth." Both sides in the Simpson case asserted such privileges.

The prosecution foreclosed access to the personnel records of Detective Mark Fuhrman based on a claim of governmental privilege. O.J. Simpson foreclosed access to his conversations with Reverend Roosevelt Grier based on a claim of the clergyman-penitent privilege.

The rule against hearsay evidence prevents either side from presenting out-of-court statements that have not been subjected to cross-examination. That rule prevented O.J. Simpson from offering the statements he made when interviewed by police the day after the murders occurred. That rule also prevented the prosecution from offering statements by Nicole Brown Simpson, expressing her fear of O.J. Simpson.

It can fairly be said that *both* sides "obstructed" the search for "the truth" by the tactical use of rules of evidence to keep relevant evidence out of the trial. Both sides also made decisions not to offer admissible evidence, based on a tactical judgment it might hurt their case more than it would help.

The bottom line, of course, is that the goal of both of the adversaries in a trial is *not* to find "the truth," but to increase the likelihood that their side's *vision* of the truth will prevail.

Occasionally, prosecutors claim the mantle of "truth" for themselves alone, saying they are obligated to reject a case if they are not convinced of its truth, while defense lawyers can take up the cause of the guilty with impunity. Marcia Clark even attempted to bolster her case in final argument by presenting this claim to the jury. If a prosecutor's belief in the guilt of the accused could itself be offered as evidence of guilt, the presumption of innocence would disappear. In reality, the personal beliefs of the lawyers on either side are irrelevant to the jury's task. And the lawyers on both sides are driven by the same goal in presenting their evidence in the most persuasive posture possible, and attacking and undermining the evidence of their opponent. That goal is to "win" their case—to have their vision of "the truth" prevail.

The question so frequently asked of defense lawyers is largely an academic one. "How can you defend someone who you know is guilty?" I've never had to "defend" a client I knew was guilty in the sense of disputing the degree of guilt he admitted. I've represented clients who admitted their guilt of a lesser crime, and I've represented clients who pled guilty and sought a lenient sentence. But I've never denied the guilt of a client I "knew" was guilty, because I never assumed the role of judging their guilt or innocence. It is true that defense lawyers are obligated to give the same vigorous defense to a client they believe is guilty as to one they believe innocent. But their "belief" is just as irrelevant as the "belief" of the prosecution. Both defense lawyers and prosecutors are subject to one ethical constraint, however. Neither can knowingly participate in the presentation of perjured testimony. If a defense lawyer "knows" his client is guilty, presumably because his client has told him so, he cannot permit that client to take the witness stand and deny his guilt. Just as a prosecutor cannot permit a police officer to lie about the grounds he had to seize evidence, if he "knows" the officer is lying.

Having been both a prosecutor and a defense lawyer, I was never troubled by the obligation to be a vigorous advocate on either side. I have always regarded the obligation of vigorous advocacy on *both* sides to be an essential prerequisite to the success of the adversary system. My greatest disappointments as a prosecutor were not the cases I lost, but the cases that were easier to win because the defense lawyer was incompetent. For me, the case of *People v. O.J. Simpson* was a defense lawyer's dream, because the resources were available to do everything right. The advocates on both sides performed at a consistent level of excellence and with great vigor. Both sides believed in their vision of "the truth," but neither that belief nor the vigor of their advocacy could substitute for credible evidence. An advocate cannot say to a jury, give me the verdict because I strived more mightily, or fought more valiantly.

Ultimately, the ascertainment of "the truth" is left to the jury. Twelve ordinary citizens stand between the power of the state and the liberty of the individual. Thomas Jefferson described the jury as "the only anchor ever yet imagined by man, by which a government can be held to the principles of its constitution." Yet Justice Oliver Wendell Holmes, Jr., confided, "I confess that in my experience I have not found juries specially inspired for the discovery of truth."

Justice Holmes went on to reaffirm his faith in juries, not because they unerringly discerned "the truth," but because they kept the administration of justice "in accord with the wishes and feelings of the community." What on earth do the "wishes and feelings of the community" have to do with searching for "the truth"?

Once again, we discover that when we speak of a trial as a search for "the truth," we can understand "the truth" only in the context of the limited purpose for which the trial is conducted. The jury's function is to serve as the conscience of the community as they choose betweeen two competing visions of "the truth." We value diversity on a jury because we recognize jurors will bring their life experiences with them when they go into the jury room. Those life experiences should reflect the full spectrum of the experience of the community. As we sort out the "truths" of our own lives, we don't all reach the same conclusions. We all wear tinted lenses and view the reality we experience from different perspectives. None of us will assess the credibility of a witness in precisely the same way, or give the same evidence equal weight. And what we accept as "truth" will be tempered by the importance we attach to competing values.

An appeal to the jury to consider their role as the conscience of the community as they choose between competing visions of "the truth" is *not* an appeal for jury nullification, asking the jury to disregard the law in the pursuit of their own conception of justice. To the contrary, it is completely consistent with the highest aspirations of our jury system that judgments should reflect our democratic and deliberative ideals.

Some may find in these words confirmation of their deepest concerns about our adversary system of justice. They will read what I say as another lawyer's game. I have perverted the concept of "truth" itself. Rather than objective conformity with reality, I have distorted the meaning of truth, and turned it into the "prize" awarded to the winning player in a chess game. I should be arraigned with all the lawyers condemned by Jonathan Swift, for "proving by words multiplied for the purpose that white is black, and black is white, according as they are paid."

I take the charge seriously, and plead justification. With a clear conscience, I've spent most of my career as a teacher training law students to realize that things are not always as they appear; that "white" may really be gray, and "black" may really be gray. And when things are "gray," they can go either way. But that is not to deny the existence of objective truth, or to suggest that the pursuit of objective truth is not one of life's highest goals. My defense is that truth can be defined only in the context of its purpose. The purpose of a criminal trial, in which the state seeks to deprive an individual of his life or liberty, can best be served by an adversary system in which two competing visions of "the truth" are contested. That contest must conform to rules which recognize that "the truth" is not the only value we cherish. And the ultimate resolution of the contest must reflect the life experience of the community, as well as its conscience.

The only plausible alternative denies our humanity. A clever spoof recently crossed my desk, bearing the letterhead of "The Solomon Project" of NYULAW Artificial Intelligence Research. It announced the perfection of a computer program to resolve legal disputes. Promising to serve "swift and blind" justice, with "minimum cost," the system weighs evidence and assesses credibility "using advanced polygraph equipment, sodium pentothal and newer technologies that guarantee the accuracy and truth of all input." It then accesses all existing law and renders a final judgment, not subject to further review. Even if the perfection of such a system were plausible, I would not choose to live under it. At that point, the pursuit of truth would be replaced by "truth" itself. We would be at the point imagined by Justice Oliver Wendell Holmes, Jr., in 1900:

> It was of this that Malebranche was thinking when he said that, if God held in one hand truth, and in the other the pursuit of truth, he would say: "Lord, the truth is for thee alone; give me the pursuit."

We keep searching for the truth, and it is the quest itself that defines our sense of justice, not the conclusion. The final lesson from the trial of *People v. O.J. Simpson* should be that a trial is a human endeavor. It is a "search for the truth" only in the sense that other human endeavors are a search for the truth. The "truth" is defined by the limited purpose which the endeavor serves. A trial is a highly structured contest between adversaries with competing visions of "the truth." There will be a winner and a loser, and there will be a cost to be paid. But to say, as some have said, that "truth" was a victim in the trial of *People v. O.J. Simpson* is itself a lie. It assumes the truth was "revealed" before it was pursued. The search for the truth defines the end of the adversary process, not its beginning.

SIXTEEN

A TRIAL OF
THE CENTURY

A s I noted at the outset of this book, my research has uncovered at least thirty-two trials since 1900 that have been called a "trial of the century." In reading contemporary accounts as well as subsequent histories of many of these trials, I was struck by how frequently the same elements recur.

The defense lawyers rarely emerge with their reputations intact. Frequently, they end up as defendants themselves in subsequent proceedings. Clarence Darrow was accused of bribing jurors after defending the McNamara brothers in the 1911 bombing of the *Los Angeles Times.* Vincent Hallinan and James MacInnis went to jail for contempt of court after their defense of Union leader Harry Bridges, accused of concealing membership in the Communist Party on his application for citizenship in 1949. In most "trials of the century," the defense lawyers were castigated by the press as obstructionists and charlatans, whose only conceivable motive for doing what they were doing had to be money. The public attitude toward criminal defense lawyers generally ranges between ambivalence and disgust, because the vital role defense lawyers play in protecting constitutional rights is not widely understood.

We were told the California state bar received lots of complaints about the conduct of the defense lawyers as the Simpson trial progressed. The state bar rarely intervenes in an ongoing trial, but at the conclusion of the trial they announced that the complaints would be "investigated." I remembered that twenty years ago, the state bar asked me to lead an "investigation" of lawyers who allegedly solicited clients in the wake of a huge DC-10 aircrash near Paris. It gave me a bit of a chill to hear that my own conduct as a lawyer would be "investigated." But defense lawyers must learn to live with such chills as a frequent companion. With the possible exception of the press conference blasting Judge Ito after his ruling on the admissibility of the Fuhrman tapes, I feel no regrets or ethical concerns about any step we took throughout the duration of the entire trial, and would not have done anything any different because of the threat of a state bar investigation.

One of my personal heroes has always been the late Edward Bennett Williams, who defended Senator Joseph McCarthy, alleged racketeer Frank Costello, union leader Jimmy Hoffa, and many other famous "villains" of the era in which I grew up. My biggest thrill as a student at Georgetown Law School was to argue (and win) a Moot Court case in which Edward Bennett Williams sat as a judge. His dignity, wit, and eloquence provided a powerful role model. When I graduated from law school, I proudly presented my father with a copy of *One Man's Freedom*, a wonderful book written by Edward Bennett Williams in 1962. I inscribed the book with a vow, to devote my own career in law to the ideals espoused by Williams in that book. In it, he documented that the history of civil liberties in America has been written in its criminal courtrooms, and that whenever the government infringes on individual rights, it begins with "the weak and friendless, the scorned and degraded, or the nonconformist and the unorthodox." Even with youthful stars in my eyes, I realized that this litany was not always a perfect match with the list of clients Edward Bennett Williams represented. But nearly all of his clients were scorned and publicly reviled as villains. And Edward Bennett Williams was frequently scorned and reviled along with his clients.

When I was staying with my parents during the trial of *People v. O.J. Simpson*, I came across the copy of *One Man's Freedom* I had presented to my father thirty years before. It was on the top shelf in his workshop. As I reread Williams's account of what it was like to be publicly identified as "Jimmy Hoffa's lawyer" or "Senator Joe McCarthy's lawyer," I recalled the feeling I experienced the first time I walked through an airport and heard one passerby whisper to another, "That's one of O.J.'s lawyers." I felt proud. As the "national shunning" movement continues to demonize O.J. Simpson despite his acquittal, and turn him into a social pariah, I'm certain the shunning will rub off on his lawyers. I can testify that some of it already has. But I still feel proud. As Edward Bennett Williams put it, "for the trial lawyer, the unpopular cause is often a post of honor."

In one posttrial interview, I was asked if there was anyone I would not defend. I probably didn't give the same answer Edward Bennett Williams would have given. I clumsily explained that a lawyer should not defend a client if he cannot defend with vigor, and I would have difficulty working up the necessary vigor to defend a purveyor of hate, to uphold the rights of an admitted klansman or Nazi to promulgate their venom. While I admire the ACLU for stepping up to the line in Skokie, Illinois, and defending, at great cost, the First Amendment rights of Nazis to march through a predominantly Jewish community, it would not be a task I personally could perform with vigor. I was taken aback by the interviewer's next question. "You mean you would not defend marchers, but you will defend slashing someone's throat with a knife?" I was surprised by the question because I never even conceived of what I was doing in the Simpson case as defending the *act* of murder. I was defending the liberty of a person who was *accused* of the crime of murder, not the crime itself. I would not defend the *act* of murder any more than I would defend words of hate. No one has a "right" to kill, and while we recognize a right to utter words of hate, I would not choose to defend that right. In the public mind, this distinction is too subtle, and criminal defense lawyers regularly become the objects of the same public scorn directed at their clients.

Previous "trials of the century" confirm that prosecutors fare better with the public. They are the "good guys" in the white hats, and often their performance in a "trial of the century" is a prelude to bigger and better things, whether they win or not. Owen Roberts rode directly to the U.S. Supreme Court in the wake of his role as chief prosecutor in the "trial of the century" of 1926, the prosecution of Edward Doheny and former Interior Secretary Albert Fall for the Teapot Dome oil scandal. The prosecutor of Lizzie Borden, William H. Moody, also ended up on the U.S. Supreme Court. Tom Dewey won a conviction of Lucky Luciano in the "trial of the century" of 1936, then went on to win the governorship of New York and two nominations to be President of the United States. Hiram Johnson took over the 1908 prosecution of San Francisco mayor Abe Ruef for taking bribes, after the chief prosecutor was shot through the head by a disaffected juror he had thrown off the case with a peremptory challenge. After the trial, Johnson launched a political career that dominated California for a quarter of a century, as governor and U.S. senator.

Both Marcia Clark and Chris Darden emerged from the Simpson trial as popular celebrities, if reported book advances are any indication. Frequently, such celebrity is resented by fellow prosecutors, who must slog on as underpaid civil servants grinding out the thousands of cases that never achieve public notice. Many prosecutors harbor ambitions to seek political office or appointment to the bench. I'm sure both of these options are now within reach for both Marcia and Chris.

Those who have presided as judges in "trials of the century" have often been the victims of what we might call the *"schlimazel* syndrome." *Schlimazel* is a Yiddish word describing an unlucky person. Most often, the bad luck of a *schlimazel* has rubbed off from a *schlemiel,* who attracts misfortune like a magnet.

The judges who have seen their judicial careers come to ignominious conclusions after a "trial of the century" include Chicago Judge John Caverly, who was persuaded by Clarence Darrow to sentence Loeb and Leopold to life imprisonment instead of death in 1924, and Judge Julius Hoffman, also of Chicago, who presided with great vitriole over the "trial of the century" of 1969, the trial of the "Chicago Seven."

Judges ordinarily begin a trial on a precarious pedestal, and when they make even a slight mistake, it is seized upon by the media as a crashing tumble. Judge John Raulston, who presided over the "trial of the century" of 1925, the Scopes evolution trial in Dayton, Tennessee, was greatly embarrassed when his investigation of who leaked one of his rulings to the press in advance led to the conclusion that the source of the leak was the judge himself.

The press has little sympathy for judges who seek to curry their favor. Judge Webster Thayer, who presided over the trial of Sacco and Vanzetti in Massachusetts in 1921, was himself a former newspaper reporter, a fact which he believed entitled him to favorable reviews by the press. At one point during the trial, he approached a lunching gaggle of reporters and announced, "I think I am entitled to have printed in the newspapers a statement that this trial is being fairly and impartially conducted." Instead, the correspondents reported that he called the defense lawyers "damn fools" and the defendants "anarchistic bastards." Although a later inquiry concluded the judge's bias was "harmless," Judge Thayer's reputation was ruined.

Occasionally, a judge parlays the spotlight of a widely publicized trial into career advancement. Judge Kenesaw Mountain Landis accomplished that in the 1920s. He rose to prominence presiding over World War I espionage trials, then became the Commissioner of Baseball. As Heywood Broun wrote, the career of Judge Landis typifies the heights to which dramatic talent may carry a man in America, if only he has the foresight not to go on the stage.

At the time the Simpson trial began, Judge Ito was destined for a long judicial career, with elevation to the appellate bench almost certain. He has now been brushed with the taint of controversy. "Controversy" is not an asset for a judicial career. The judicial quality that seems to gain widest admiration and quickest elevation today is the ability to keep your head down.

The most remarkable aspect of every "trial of the century" so far, however, has been the insight it provides into the tenor of the times in which it occurred. It is as though each of these trials was responding to some public appetite or civic need of the era in which it took place. The disorder and lawlessness of the depression era turned the trials of the Scottsboro boys, Bruno Hauptmann, and Lucky Luciano into national spectacles. The concern for national security and the paranoia of the cold war era were fed by the trials of Alger Hiss, Harry Bridges, and Julius and Ethel Rosenberg. The national angst over Vietnam was served by the trials of the Chicago Seven and Daniel Ellsberg. Our national preoccupation with terrorism and a revolutionary "counterculture" gave us the Manson case and the trial of Patty Hearst. From the perspective of the tenor of our times, it comes as no surprise that the case of *People v. O.J. Simpson* became a flash point for some of the most divisive issues that now confront America. A flash point, however, provides momentary illumination. It does not provide solutions.

The "tenor" of our times is characterized by self-doubting and pouting. We live in an era of declining attention spans and increasing stubbornness. We see our sense of cohesion disintegrating, as we create new boundaries to confine those we distrust. The gap between our "haves" and "have-nots" grows wider, and we respond by building higher walls between them. We shout and snarl at each other over the airwaves, but seldom listen to each other. We want our leaders to fail, and we facilitate their failure by personally demeaning them. We have an insatiable appetite for gossip and slander.

In these respects, the trial of *People v. O.J. Simpson* reflected the tenor of our times quite accurately. The trial was frequently called a "circus," and that characterization, too, is accurate. The word "circus" comes from the circular ampitheaters in which Roman gladiators battled, and the crowds rendered their verdicts with thumbs up or down. Other "trials of the century" were also ridiculed as "circuses." But there are valuable lessons to be learned, even at a circus.

The lessons a circus teaches are frequently exaggerated. The high wire seems higher than it really is. The dancing elephants don't really keep time to the music. We need to keep the lessons of the trial in perspective. It was one of 7,000 trials conducted in California in 1995. The arrest of O.J. Simpson after the Bronco chase was one of the 500,000 felony arrests in California in 1994. Nicole

Brown Simpson and Ronald Goldman were two of the 20,000 homi
cide victims in the United States in 1994. But there are lessons here
for everyone.

We learned that the pursuit of the "truth" is the pursuit of a
vision. Actually, two visions are pursued with equal vigor by two
adversaries. Which vision will be accepted is determined at the
conclusion of the trial, not its beginning. Neither side has a lock
on "the truth."

Our own vision of the truth, we saw, will be colored by the lens
through which we perceive it. We all wear tinted lenses, and we all
see "the truth" from different perspectives, shaped by our differing
life experiences. Ultimately, that is the only way a jury can see it,
so we want to be sure that the jury accurately reflects the diversity
of life experience in the community.

We learned that the tactics and strategies employed by both adversaries in a criminal trial are designed to advance their vision of
the truth. An adversary "wins" when his or her vision of the truth
prevails. Some of the rules are designed to protect values that we
cherish just as much as "the truth," such as privacy and autonomy.
There are places we don't look, and things we pretend not to see.

We learned that the system gives some advantages to one side
that it doesn't give to the other. The defendant is presumed innocent. The prosecutor can utilize a secret grand jury to gather evidence for trial. In recent years, "reform" initiatives have shifted
more and more advantages to the prosecution, including a "reciprocal discovery" law giving prosecutors access to defense evidence.
But a defendant still has a privilege against self-incrimination and
can refuse to take the witness stand at his own trial.

We learned that cops lie, especially when they conclude it is
necessary to avoid the rules that limit their power to engage in
searches. Some cops lie because they think convicting "criminals"
is an end that justifies any means. Some cops lie because they hate
black people.

We learned that the quality of justice one receives is strongly
affected by how much money he has available to defend himself.

Access to experts and the ability to insist on a speedy trial are powerful advantages not always available to indigent defendants.

We learned that information from "informed sources" may not always be reliable, and that rules seeking to silence lawyers may not always benefit the public. As the line between the legitimate press and the tabloids gets more blurry, we saw that bad journalism drives out the good.

We learned that tools like questionnaires, *voir dire* questioning, and jury consultants help lawyers and judges get past racial and ethnic stereotypes in selecting juries. Both sides have an equal opportunity to shape the jury that hears the case. Prosecutors, however, can stack the deck by moving the trial to a different location, or by seeking the death penalty.

We learned that cameras in court may broadcast a picture that is skewed by the presence of the camera itself. While there may be cases that will not be adversely affected by the presence of a television camera, a "trial of the century" most certainly will. The behavior of the lawyers, the witnesses, and even the judge will be affected by the exposure. Nonetheless, there will be benefits too, such as the discovery of additional relevant evidence.

We learned that spousal abuse is a problem in America that deserves serious attention. But rules of evidence that require a similarity to the charged offense before prior incidents may be put before a jury protect a fundamental right to be tried for the charged offense, rather than for one's general character or past bad acts.

We learned that even a "mountain" of DNA evidence can collapse if the collection and preservation of samples are compromised, contaminated, and corrupted. Evidence will be trusted by a jury only to the extent they trust the messengers who bring it to court.

We learned that racism is alive and well in America, and so is denial. Jurors cannot be "shielded" from evidence that a witness is a racist when that evidence relates directly to the credibility of that witness.

We learned that no one, black, white, or any other color, can be convicted of a crime in America unless his guilt is proven beyond a reasonable doubt. An acquittal based on reasonable doubt is a victory for every American. The fact that black Americans celebrate that victory when a black man is acquitted should not be perceived by white Americans as a gesture of defiance. White America may not wish to join the celebration, but to disparage it as motivated by revenge or hatefulness betrays a deep misunderstanding. Misunderstandings such as this reveal the deep racial divide that still separates Americans.

Hopefully, we also learned that a "trial of the century" is not a fair portrayal of our system of justice at work. It is an aberrent event that should not be used to justify systemic change or "reform." It can teach us lessons about ourselves and each other, but the strengths and weaknesses it exposes in our system of justice will frequently be exaggerated and exceptional.

We still have time for one or two more "trials of the century" before the turn of the millennium. Let us hope that some of the lessons from this trial of the century will be remembered for the next one.

ENDNOTES

Lessons *from the* Trial

ENDNOTES

CHAPTER 1: LOOKING FOR LESSONS

Page 1   *"The proposals include"* See, e.g., Judge Harold J. Rothwax, *Guilty: The Collapse of Criminal Justice* (Random House, 1996). If Judge Rothwax listened to all of the testimony in the O.J. Simpson trial, he must have neglected his other duties as a sitting judge. If he did not, he has little credibility in trashing the Simpson jury and pronouncing his own verdict. While Judge Ito may have been a victim of the *"schlimazel* syndrome"* (see Chapter 16, *inf.*), Judge Rothwax seems to have been afflicted with the *"schlemiel* syndrome."*

Page 2   *"another famous advocate"* For an account of Queen Caroline's case and Lord Brougham's advocacy, see Rt. Hon. Lord Denning, *Landmarks in the Law* (Butterworths, London, 1984), pp. 177–84.

Page 5   *"One such case"* Gera-Lind Kolarik, "DNA, Changed Testimony Gain Acquittal," *ABA Journal*, Vol. 82, January 1996, pp. 34–35.

Page 6   *"A law school commencement address"* Yale Kamisar, "A Call for Reform of Historical Proportions," *Los Angeles Daily Journal*, October 17, 1995, p. 4; Gerald F. Uelmen, "William Howard Taft, Jury Basher," *Los Angeles Daily Journal*, November 6, 1995, p. 4.

CHAPTER 2: THE DISAPPEARING KNIFE

Page 12 *"Professor Monroe Freedman of Hofstra" The Seventh Annual Judicial Conference of the United States Court of Appeals for the Federal Circuit,* 128 F.R.D. 409, 437 (1989) (quoting Monroe H. Freedman, who was present at the conference).

Page 13 *"If I did not disturb or alter the evidence"* See *People v. Meredith,* 29 Cal. 3d 682, 175 Cal. Rptr. 612 (1981) (an observation by defense counsel or his investigator, which is the product of a privileged communication, may not be admitted unless the defense by altering or removing physical evidence has precluded the prosecution from making that same observation).

Page 15 *"in a 1970 Florida case" Williams v. Florida,* 399 U.S. 78, 90 S. Ct. 1893 (1970).

Page 15 *"in the first decision applying the new reciprocal discovery law" Izazaga v. Superior Court,* 54 Cal. 3d 356, 377, 285 Cal. Rptr. 231 (1991).

Page 16 *"At the outset of the trial"* Jeffrey Toobin, "Ito and the Truth School" *New Yorker,* pp. 42–48, March 27, 1995.

CHAPTER 3: THE GRAND JURY

Page 19 *"to declare in 1978" Hawkins v. Superior Court,* 22 Cal. 3d 584, 150 Cal. Rptr. 435 (1978).

Page 22 *"It was the 1966 decision" Sheppard v. Maxwell,* 384 U.S. 333, 86 S. Ct. 1507 (1966).

Page 24 *"was also from a historic case" In re Ellsberg,* 446 F.2d 954 (1st Cir. 1971).

CHAPTER 4: TAKING THE FOURTH

Page 29 *"by the U.S. Supreme Court in 1914" Weeks v. United States,* 232 U.S. 383, 34 S. Ct. 341 (1914).

Page 30 *"in one of the most controversial rulings" Mapp v. Ohio,* 367 U.S. 643, 81 S. Ct. 1684 (1961).

Page 30 *"which adopted the exclusionary rule in 1956" People v. Cahan,* 44 Cal. 2d 434, 282 P.2d 905 (1955).

Page 31 *"and the case went all the way" Katz v. United States,* 389 U.S. 347, 352, 88 S. Ct. 507 (1967).

Page 32 *"the immortal words William Pitt thundered"* Thomas M. Cooley, *A Treatise on the Constitutional Limitations,* 365 n.4

(5th ed., 1883). Remarks attributed to William Pitt, Earl of Chatham.

Page 37 *"As one California appellate court put it"* People v. Dickson, 144 Cal. App. 3d 1046, 1063, 192 Cal. Rptr. 897 (1983).

Page 39 *"One of the classic studies"* Effect of *Mapp v. Ohio* on Police Search-and-Seizure Practices in Narcotics Cases, 4 Columbia Journal of Law and Social Problems. 87, 94 tbl. II (1968).

Page 46 *"The words of Justice Louis Brandeis"* Olmstead v. United States, 277 U.S. 438, 485, 48 S. Ct. 564 (1928) (Brandeis, J., dissenting).

CHAPTER 5: THE DREAM TEAM

Page 50 *"client-centered lawyering"* David A. Binder et al., *Lawyers as Counselors: A Client Centered Approach* 16 (1991). In a client-centered approach, the client actively participates in identifying his or her problems, formulating potential solutions, and making decisions. This approach emphasizes the value and importance of clients taking the role of primary decision maker as the attorney assesses the likely legal and nonlegal consequences of the course of action proposed. The attorney may recommend which course of action the client should take, but ultimately only the client can decide how willing he or she is to run the risks and bear the potential costs of adopting a particular course of action.

Page 51 *"Linder wrote in the* L.A. Times*"* Charles L. Lindner, "A Matter of Justice; Preparing the Defense; Assembling a Team and Devising a Strategy to Defend Simpson," *Los Angeles Times,* June 26, 1994, M1.

Page 54 *"had just published a column of my own"* Gerald F. Uelmen, "Point of View: The Afterwit of Alan Dershowitz," *California Criminal Defense Practice Reporter,* April 1994, p. 127. ("Afterwit" comes from the words of Richard Hooker, *Laws of Ecclesiastical Polity* (1600); "The afterwit of later days hath found out another more exquisite distinction."

Page 55 *"essays under the same title"* Alan M. Dershowitz, *The Abuse Excuse* (Little, Brown, 1994), p. 28.

Page 55 *"on their cover portrait"* Time, June 27, 1994.

Page 55 *"an especially ugly 'hit piece'"* Evan Thomas, "Day and Night," *Newsweek,* August 29, 1994, 42.

Page 64 *"he identified the lesson"* Erwin Chemerinsky, "High-

Priced Defense May Make All the Difference," *Times-Picayune*, July 6, 1994, A3.

CHAPTER 6: LEAKS AND GAGS

Page 66 *"a case from Las Vegas, Nevada"* Gentile v. State Bar of Nevada, 501 U.S. 1030, 111 S. Ct. 2720 (1991).

Page 67 *"At the press conference"* Id., Opening remarks of Dominic Gentile at a press conference on February 5, 1988.

Page 67 *"he violated a rule"* Nev. Sup. Ct. R. 177.

Page 70 *"he authored an article"* Robert Shapiro, "Secrets of a Celebrity Lawyer: How O.J.'s Chief Strategist Works the Press," *Columbia Journalism Review*, Vol. 33, No. 3, p. 25 (September 1, 1994). (Reprinted and adapted from *The Champion Magazine*, January/February 1993).

Page 70 *"one of the broadest shield laws"* Cal. Evid. Code § 1070 (West, 1995).

Page 71 *"The courts have carved out an exception"* Delaney v. Superior Court, 50 Cal. 3d 785, 268 Cal. 87 Rptr. 753 (1990).

Page 75 *"to take effect in California on October 1, 1995"* California Rules of Professional Conduct, Rule 5-120 (Effective October 1, 1995).

CHAPTER 7: PICKING A JURY

Page 85 *"One manual I consulted"* George W. Shadoan, ed., *Law and Tactics in Federal Criminal Cases* (Coiner Publications, 1964), pp. 265–66.

Page 85 *"a trend-setting decision in 1978"* People v. Wheeler, 22 Cal. 3d 258, 148 Cal. Rptr. 890 (1978).

Page 85 *"adopted a similar rule in 1986"* Batson v. Kentucky, 476 U.S. 79, 106 S. Ct. 1712 (1986).

Page 86 *"it is not difficult for a prosecutor"* The U.S. Supreme Court made it even easier in *Purkett v. Elem*,—U.S.—, 115 S. Ct. 1769 (1995), ruling that the prosecutor's explanation for a peremptory challenge need not even be "plausible."

Page 86 *"The Supreme Court of Virginia accepted that"* James v. Commonwealth, 247 Va. 459, 442 S.E.2d 396 (1994).

Page 89 *"In a recent Louisiana Supreme Court decision"* State v. Jones, 474 So.2d 919 (La. Sup. Ct. 1985).

Page 89   *"Another case from North Carolina" State v. Scales,* 113 S.E.2d 124 114 N.C.App. 735 (N.C.Ct.App. 1994).

CHAPTER 8: CAMERAS IN COURT

Page 97   *"His name was Mark Twain,"* Edgar M. Branch, ed., *Clemens of the Call* (University of California Press, 1969), p. 219.

Page 97   *"Now he argues that the cameras"* Court TV, *Facts and Opinions About Cameras in Courtrooms* (July 1995).

Page 100   *"Rather than a flat prohibition"* Cal. R. of Ct. 980 (1996). Rule 980 applies to all California courts where photographing, recording, or broadcasting in the courtroom is requested.

CHAPTER 9: DOMESTIC DISCORD

Page 106   *"One recent study revealed"* L.L. Lockhart, "A Reexamination of the Effects of Race and Social Class on the Incidence of Marital Violence: A Search for More Differences," 49 *J. Marriage and Family* 603, 606 (1987).

Page 106   *"That's a ratio of .0006 to 1"* Estimates of the the number of "batterings" each year come from the National Clearinghouse for Defense of Battered Women. *Developments in the Law: Legal Responses to Domestic Violence,* 106 *Harv. L. Rev.* 1498, 1574 (1993). Homicide rates are compiled by the FBI Uniform Crime Reports, 1992.

Page 108   *"The only authority cited"* Judge Ito cited *People v. Zack,* 184 Cal. App. 3d 409, 229 Cal. Rptr. 317 (Calif. Ct. App. 1986).

Page 111   *"That instruction provides:"* Cal. Jury Instructions-Criminal 2.50 (West Supp. 1995).

Page 113   *"The California Evidence Code addresses"* Cal. Evid. Code § 1107 (admissibility of expert testimony regarding the battered women's syndrome in criminal cases).

CHAPTER 10: THE MOUNTAIN OF EVIDENCE

Page 117   *"the case of* Frye v. United States" *Frye v. United States,* 293 F. 1013, 54 App. D.C. 46 (D.C. Cir. 1923).

Page 117   *"the case of* People v. Kelly" *People v. Kelly,* 17 Cal. 3d 24, 130 Cal. Rptr. 144 (1976).

Page 117   *"the California Supreme Court considered"* *People v. Leahy,* 8 Cal. 4th 587, 34 Cal. Rptr. 2d 663 (1994).

Page 117 *"join the federal courts"* See *Daubert v. Merrell Dow Pharmaceuticals,*—U.S.—, 113 S. Ct. 2786 (1993) (rejecting the *Frye* test and holding general acceptance in the scientific community is not a necessary precondition to the admissibility of scientific evidence, but rather it is a factor to consider along with other factors such as: if the evidence has been tested, subjected to peer review, published, and its error rate).

CHAPTER 11: THE FUHRMAN TAPES

Page 128 *"The ethical constraints"* ABA Model Rule of Professional Conduct 3.3 (1996); Cal. Rule of Professional Conduct 5-200 (1996).

Page 128 *"perjured testimony"* In addition to the prosecutor's ethical obligations concerning the knowing use of perjured testimony, a conviction based on such testimony will be reversed as a violation of the defendant's due process rights. *Mooney v. Holohan,* 294 U.S. 103, 55 S. Ct. 340 (1935).

Page 128 *"the 1963 case of* Brady v. Maryland*"* *Brady v. Maryland,* 373 U.S. 83, 83 S. Ct. 1194 (1963).

Page 129 *"several Supreme Court decisions since* Brady*"* *Giglio v. United States,* 405 U.S. 150, 92 S. Ct. 763 (1972); *Kyles v. Whitley,*—U.S.—, 115 S. Ct. 1555 (1995).

Page 130 *"in the case of* Pitchess v. Superior Court*"* *Pitchess v. Superior Court,* 11 Cal. 3d 531, 113 Cal. Rptr. 897 (1974).

Page 130 *"into the California Evidence Code"* Cal. Evid. Code §§ 1043, 1045.

Page 133 *"The California courts had long since resolved"* In re Anthony P.,* 167 Cal. App. 3d 502 (Cal. Ct. App. 1985).

Page 148 *"the disqualification statute"* Cal. Code of Civ. Pro. § 170.1 (West Supp. 1996) (available to both civil litigants and criminal defendants).

CHAPTER 12: THE SOUND OF SILENCE

Page 156 *"in the landmark case of* Griffin v. California*"* *Griffin v. California,* 380 U.S. 609, 85 S. Ct. 1229 (1965).

Page 156 *"has since been applied even to a suspect"* Doyle v. Ohio,* 426 U.S. 610, 96 S. Ct. 2240 (1976).

Page 156 *"the U.S. Supreme Court went a step further"* Carter v.

Kentucky, 450 U.S. 288, 101 S. Ct. 1112 (1981); Cal. Jury Instructions-Criminal 2.60 (1988).

Page 157 *"by the ethical rule"* ABA Model Rule of Professional Conduct 3.3 (1996); Cal. Rule of Professional Conduct 5-200 (1996).

Page 160 *"in a famous case handled by F. Lee Bailey"* United States v. Hearst, 563 F.2d 1331 (9th Cir. 1977).

Page 160 *"one division of the California Court of Appeal"* People v. Garner, 207 Cal. App. 3d 935, 255 Cal. Rptr. 257 (1989).

Page 162 *"under a grant of use immunity"* United States v. Mandujano, 425 U.S. 564, 96 S. Ct. 1768 (1976).

Page 164 *"a very broad statutory privilege"* Cal. Evid. Code § 1032 (West 1995).

CHAPTER 13: IF IT DOESN'T FIT

Page 167 *"This instruction informs the jury"* Cal. Jury Instructions-Criminal 2.01.

Page 170 *"The most serious objection was that"* ABA Model Rule of Professional Conduct 3.4 (1996); Cal. Rule of Professional Conduct 5-200 (1996).

Page 170 *"to pursue its own version of justice"* See United States v. Dougherty, 473 F.2d 1113, 1140 (D.C. Cir. 1972) (Bazelon J., dissenting) (defining jury nullification as a "mechanism that permits a jury, as community conscience, to disregard the strict requirements of law where it finds that those requirements cannot justly be applied in a particular case").

Page 172 *"In 1991, the Supreme Court of Pennsylvania"* Commonwealth v. Chambers, 528 Pa. 558, 559 A.2d 630 (1991).

Page 172 *"If Clarence Darrow were defending"* Gerald F. Uelmen, "The Nincompoops Aren't in the Jury Box," *Los Angeles Times,* November 19, 1991, p. 7.

Page 172 *"Justice Robert Gardner put it"* People v. Long, 38 Cal. App. 3d 680, 113 Cal. Rptr. 530 (1974).

Page 173 *"In the 1907 trial of labor leader Bill Haywood"* Arthur Weinberg, ed., *Attorney for the Damned* (Simon and Schuster, 1957), p. 451, quoting Clarence Darrow's closing argument in the Haywood trial: "Why, gentlemen, if Harry Orchard were George Washington, who had come into a court of justice with his great name behind him, and if he was impeached and contradicted by as many as Harry Orchard has been, George Washington would go out of it disgraced and counted the Ananias of the age."

Page 173 "*a CALJIC instruction of ancient vintage*" Cal. Jury Instructions-Criminal 2.21.2 (1988).

Page 173 "*the California Supreme Court handed down a decision*" *People v. Gionis*, 9 Cal. 4th 1196, 40 Cal. Rptr. 2d 456 (1995).

Page 174 "*an intriguing title caught my eye*" James Joseph Duane, "What Message Are We Sending to Criminal Jurors When We Ask Them to 'Send a Message' with Their Verdict?," 22 *Am. J. of Crim. Law* 565 (1995).

Page 175 "*the 1906 trial of Harry Thaw*" Paul R. Baker, *Stanny, The Gilded Life of Stanford White* (Free Press, 1989). Provides an excellent account of the Thaw trial.

CHAPTER 14: WALKING AWAY

Page 180 "*Certainly nothing the jurors said*" Amanda Cooley, Carrie Dess, and Marsha Rubin-Jackson, *Madam Foreman: A Rush to Judgment?* (Dove Books, 1995).

Page 180 "*the* Wall Street Journal *ran a lead story*" Benjamin A. Holden et al., "Color Blinded? Race Seems to Play an Increasing Role in Many Jury Verdicts," *The Wall Street Journal,* October 4, 1995, A1.

Page 181 "*In commenting upon the first Rodney King verdict*" Gerald F. Uelmen, "Need for Civilian Police Review Revisited," *Los Angeles Daily Journal,* May 15, 1992, p. 4.

Page 182 "*Even my esteemed co-counsel*" Alan M. Dershowitz, *The Abuse Excuse* (Little, Brown, 1994), p. 28.

Page 184 "*In one classic Massachusetts study*" Reid Hastie, Steven D. Penrod, and Nancy Pennington, *Inside the Jury* (Harvard University Press, 1983), pp. 88, 90.

Page 185 "*Writing in the* Washington Post" Paul Butler, "O.J. Reckoning: Rage for a New Justice," *Washington Post,* October 8, 1995, C1.

Page 186 "*in the 1987 case of* McCleskey v. Kemp" *McCleskey v. Kemp,* 481 U.S. 279, 107 S. Ct. 1756 (1987).

Page 188 "*carefully assembled and analyzed by the Federal Sentencing Commission*" Federal Sentencing Commission, *Executive Summary of Special Report on Cocaine and Federal Sentencing Policy,* February 28, 1995.

Page 190 "*Professor Paul Butler makes a compelling argument*" Paul Butler, "Racially Based Jury Nullification: Black Power in the Criminal Justice System," *Yale Law Journal,* Vol. 105, p. 677 (Dec. 1995).

Page 191   *"The conviction was set aside"* Ex parte Brandley, 781 S.W.2d 886 (Tx. Cr. App. 1989).

CHAPTER 15: SEARCHING FOR THE TRUTH

Page 196   *"the 1893 trial of Lizzie Borden"* See *13 Classics of the Courtroom: Highlights from The Commonwealth of Massachusetts v. Lizzie Borden* (Profess. Educ. Group, 1988) (partial transcript of case including closing argument for the defense); Edmund Pearson, *The Trial of Lizzie Borden* (Notable Trials Library, Gryphon Editions, 1989); Frank Spiering, *Lizzie* (Random House, 1984).

Page 198   *"As Justice Louis Brandeis warned"* Olmstead v. United States, 277 U.S. 438, 479, 48 S. Ct. 564 (1928) (Brandeis, J., dissenting).

Page 200   *"Thomas Jefferson described the jury"* Thomas Jefferson, *The Writings of Thomas Jefferson* 3:71 (H.A. Washington, ed., 1861). The quote is from a letter to Thomas Paine dated April 11, 1789.

Page 200   *"Yet Justice Oliver Wendell Holmes, Jr., confided"* Oliver W. Holmes, "Law in Science and Science in Law," in *The Holmes Reader* 85, 96 (Julius J. Marke, ed., 2d ed., Oceana, 1964) (1899).

Page 202   *"proving by words multiplied"* Jonathan Swift, *Gulliver's Travels,* Pt. III, Chap. 21.

Page 202   *"We would be at the point imagined"* Oliver W. Holmes, Speech at a Dinner Given to Chief Justice Holmes by the Bar Association of Boston, in *The Holmes Reader* 74, 75 (Julius J. Marke, ed., 2d ed., Oceana, 1964) (1913).

CHAPTER 16: A TRIAL OF THE CENTURY

Page 205   *"One Man's Freedom"* Edward Bennett Williams, *One Man's Freedom* (Atheneum, 1962).

Page 206   *"While I admire the ACLU"* National Socialist Party of America v. Village Of Skokie, 432 U.S. 43, 97 S. Ct. 2205 (1977).

ABOUT THE AUTHOR

Gerald F. Uelmen is a professor and former dean at Santa Clara University School of Law. He is the author of two collections of legal humor, co-author of the two-volume study *Drug Abuse and the Law,* and recipient of the Ross Essay Prize from the American Bar Association. He has represented a variety of high-profile clients, ranging from Daniel Ellsburg to Christian Brando.